Praise for *Mango Rash*

"In the turbulent 1960s Pokerwinski and her family move to American Samoa just as the author is between girlhood and womanhood, and just as the territory is balanced between Samoan and American cultures. Part travelogue, part family drama, part coming-of-age story, Pokerwinski deftly explores our fascination with teenage angst and exotic locations. Here, in loving, lush, and particular detail, is a welcoming yet troubled paradise for the reader to explore. As the Samoans would say, *Mango Rash* is *matagofie* – beautiful."
~ **Sue William Silverman**, author of *The Pat Boone Fan Club: My Life as a White Anglo-Saxon Jew*

***

"*Mango Rash* is a beautifully written coming-of-age story, where friendship and humour travel the same sun bleached pathways as loss and tragedy, through the heart and mind of young teenager Nancy, whose loving portrayal of tropical Samoa and its people will stay with you long after you turn the last frangipani-scented page."
~ **Lene Fogelberg**, author of *The Wall Street Journal* bestselling memoir *Beautiful Affliction*

* * *

"Nan Sanders Pokerwinski tells her memories of her year in Samoa fifty-some years ago with a light narrative touch, soft humor, and a poet's eye for detail— 'the ocean's brackish bouquet.' She has a novelist's skill for making her characters real and individual. Her memoir is a travelogue not just to Samoa but also into a young girl's mind as she toys with the edges of adulthood, with Margaret Mead as her travel guide. Yes, this is young Nancy Sanders'—late of Stillwater, Oklahoma—coming of age in Samoa.
~ **John Enright**, author of the Detective Apelu Soifua *Jungle Beat Mystery* series

* * *

NAN SANDERS POKERWINSKI

mango
rash

Coming of Age in the Land
of Frangipani and Fanta

Behler™
PUBLICATIONS
USA

Behler Publications

Mango Rash
A Behler Publications Book

Copyright (c) 2020 by Nan Sanders Pokerwinski
Cover design by Yvonne Parks - www.pearcreative.ca
Map by Brenda Huckins Bonter

Some names have been changed to protect their privacy.

Library of Congress Cataloging-in-Publication Data

Names: Pokerwinski, Nan Sanders, author.
Title: Mango Rash : Coming of Age in the Land of Frangipani and Fanta :
    (a memoir) / by Nan Sanders Pokerwinski.
Identifiers: LCCN 2019019625 (print) | LCCN 2019980448 (ebook) | ISBN
    9781941887066 (paperback) | ISBN 1941887066 (paperback) | ISBN
    9781941887073 (ebook) | ISBN 1941887074 (ebook)
Subjects: LCSH: Pokerwinski, Nan Sanders--Childhood and youth. |
    Americans--American Samoa--Biography. | Teenage girls--American
    Samoa--Biography. | Coming of age--American Samoa. | American
    Samoa--Description and travel.
Classification: LCC DU819.A1 P64 2020 (print) | LCC DU819.A1 (ebook) |
    DDC 996.1/3 [B]--dc23
LC record available at https://lccn.loc.gov/2019019625
LC ebook record available at https://lccn.loc.gov/2019980448

FIRST PRINTING

ISBN 13: 9781941887066
e-book ISBN 9781941887073

Published by Behler Publications, LLC, USA
www.behlerpublications.com
Manufactured in the United States of America

Sources of Samoan proverbs
Brown, Rev. George (1914) "Proverbs, Phrases, and Similes of the Samoans." Report of the Fourteenth Meeting of the Australasian Association for the Advancement of Science., edited by T. S. Hall. Sydney, Australia.

Schultz, E. (1950) "Proverbial Expressions of the Samoans." Translated into English by Brother Herman. The Journal of the Polynesian Society, Volume 59 (2): 112-134. Auckland, New Zealand.

Morton, Julia F. (2013). **Fruits of Warm Climates**. Echo Point Books & Media
Reprinted by Permission of University of Miami.

Sutter, Frederic Koehler (1984) *Amerika Samoa: An Anthropological Photo Essay*. Honolulu, Hawai'i. University of Hawai'i Press.
Reprinted by Permission of University of Hawai'i Press

Calkins, Fay G. (1962) *My Samoan Chief*. Honolulu, Hawai'i. University of Hawai'i Press.
Reprinted by Permission of University of Hawai'i Press

Table of Contents

To Neva and Harold,
who dreamed
and dared
and encouraged me to do the same

Author's Note

As I was writing the story that would become this book, I kept asking myself, Is this my story to tell? I'm not Samoan. I lived in American Samoa for less than a year. What right do I have to identify myself with that place and its culture?

The answer came down to this: Something about that place, that culture, and the experiences I had during those eleven months of my adolescence affected me so deeply that decades later the memories are still steeped in emotion. Those memories, and the story of how they came to matter so much, are indeed mine to share.

Memories, of course, are notoriously shadowy, slippery things, and writing about events that happened more than fifty years ago is tricky. When possible, I have sought to corroborate my memories with letters, diary entries, photographs, personal communications, historical information, and other resources. It was reassuring that, while these sources filled in some blanks, they did not contradict my recollections.

I have used terminology and place names that were in use at the time. Between 1962 and 1997, the nation now known as the Independent State of Samoa was called Western Samoa, so that is the name I use for it here. In addition, hurricane-like storms are typically called cyclones in the South Pacific, but in American Samoa in 1966, everyone called the terrible storm a hurricane.

Conversations have been reconstructed as accurately as possible, though sometimes edited to be more concise. I have tried to be faithful to the chronology of events, but have compressed or expanded time as necessary for narrative flow.

Some names and identifying details have been changed, either for privacy or to avoid confusion when more than one person had the same first name. No characters are composites.

In short, I have done my best to tell this story in a way that is both truthful and artful. Others who lived through the same times may remember or interpret the experiences differently. They have their own stories. Mine is simply one *palagi* girl's perspective on coming of age in Samoa.

—Nan Sanders Pokerwinski

Tutuila, American Samoa

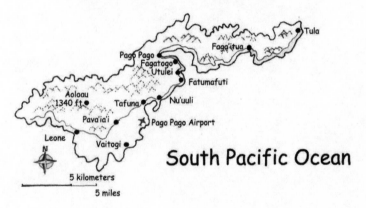

Tula

Fagaʻitua

Pago Pago
Fagatogo
Utulei
Fatumafuti

Aoloau
1340 ft

Tafuna

Nuʻuuli

Pavaʻiaʻi

Pago Pago Airport

Leone

N

Vaitogi

South Pacific Ocean

5 kilometers

5 miles

PROLOGUE

This old album I hold on my lap—its cover worn along the edges like well-traveled luggage, its gilt embossing faded to a dull vein—overflows with snapshots. Each one preserves a moment attached to a memory. As I turn the pages, it's as if I'm trawling for pearls, lustrous shells, souvenirs of my time in Samoa. At first, the moments I retrieve are slithery as *palolo*—wriggling sea worms that slide from a fisherman's grasp and scatter on the sand. Slowly, slowly, more substantial memories surface, and with them, sensations: the scents of frangipani and coconut oil and smoke from cooking fires, the tattoo of sticks on wooden drums, the scratch of bare feet on pandanus mats. The aching awareness of impermanence.

It's all here in this album, and for me, in this one photograph. Here I am, a barefoot teenager in a tank top and a *lavalava*—a length of hibiscus-printed fabric wrapped around my waist. I stand beside a black boulder that's nearly as tall as I am, and at my feet there's a blur of rushing water—the edge of a waterfall. Behind me, vines with leaves as big as my face flash in a patch of sun and vanish into darkened jungle.

I am on the brink, poised between child and woman, between where I've been and where I'm bound, between all those moments that flowed toward this one and those that cascaded downhill afterward. Yet my face registers neither apprehension nor exhilaration, only absolute comfort. In this one moment, I am where I'm meant to be, at home in my sarong, my suntanned skin, my surroundings. I have yet to learn about *ma'i Samoa*, Samoan sickness, but already I have been imbued with the healing Samoan spirit of *malosi*.

Chapter 1 — The Samoan Way

I saw that island first when it was neither night nor morning. The moon was to the west, setting but still broad and bright . . . The land breeze blew in our faces and smellt strong of wild lime and vanilla . . . Here was a fresh experience; even the tongue would be quite strange to me; and the look of these woods and mountains, and the rare smell of them, renewed my blood.
— *Robert Louis Stevenson, "The Beach of Falesā"*

*S*o here we are, finally, *in Pago Pago — palm trees, surf-washed beaches, perfumy air, the whole bit — and all I can think about is getting out of these clothes. Sweat is pouring from parts of my body I never thought would perspire, and the atmosphere is too saturated with its own moisture to soak up any of mine. A flutter of breeze, feeble as a butterfly, stirs the air. It's nothing but a tease, utterly incapable of cooling.*

This get-up that seemed so stylish when we set out on our journey — the perfect travel ensemble for a girl of sixteen, my mother assured me — was fine in Oklahoma City and Los Angeles and other points along the way. But here in Samoa, my outfit, so absurdly wrong for both climate and culture, only reminds me how out of place I am.

It was 5:30 a.m. on a September Sunday in 1965 when our Pan Am flight from Honolulu touched down at Pago Pago International Airport. As the jet taxied in from a runway that jutted into the Pacific, I squinted through the window, eager for my first glimpse of the island where my parents and I had come to live, hopeful that this pin dot on the map, six thousand miles from home, would be the paradise I'd envisioned, the setting for my transformation from flatlander to islander, from small-town girl to woman of the world.

The sky was still too dark to reveal much beyond the tarmac, the backdrop of mountains just a shadowy hulk, like a heap of rumpled bedding in a dim room at dawn. I could make out a low-slung, modern building with lava-rock walls and a roof that looked like thatch but was covered with wood shingles instead of palm fronds. It had to be the terminal, yet why did it look so deserted? The flight had been full—planes from Hawaii came only once a week—and most of the passengers surely expected friends or family members to meet them. Where were they? And wasn't someone supposed to meet *us*?

As the plane rolled toward the building, another structure came into view. Oval-shaped and about the size of a large living room, it had no walls, just a high, rounded roof—this one made from real palm thatch and supported around its perimeter by poles that rested on a raised platform. I recognized its type from photos I'd been studying since I'd learned we were moving to Samoa: a Samoan *fale*, the traditional building style used for houses and meeting halls. But in the pictures I'd studied, *fales* were small and spare. This one was jam-packed with people— really *big* people. Some sat cross-legged, others slept on woven mats.

How . . . primitive. A shudder wormed under my skin and wriggled to the top of my spine. *Have they been crammed in there together all night, when there's a perfectly lovely, up-to-date building sitting empty just steps away? Is this how people live here?*

I glanced at my parents—my mother beside me, my father across the aisle, both staring into the semi-darkness. My mother, sensing my gaze, patted my hand without looking away from the window and smiled, a bit tight-lipped. Was she trying to reassure me or herself? Either way, it was going to take more than an absent-minded pat.

When the plane came to rest and the engines stopped whining, the people in the *fale* rolled up their mats and moved toward the chain-link fence that bordered the airfield. Barefoot or wearing rubber flip-flops, they strolled toward the plane as if they were taking a morning walk down a beach, not bustling toward an airport gate. Taking . . . their . . . time.

A flight attendant swung open a door near the cockpit, and I followed my parents down the crowded aisle, my sky-blue Pan Am flight bag bumping against my hip and excitement thrumming my anxiety into submission. Our adventure was beginning—our *adventure*—and after living all my years in Stillwater, Oklahoma, where excitement amounted to incessantly circling the parking lots of Main Street's three drive-in hamburger joints, I was more than ready for a taste of something exotic. I'd always thought of myself as an adventurer, even if I'd never had a true adventure. I had adventure *potential*. I was sure of it.

As I stepped onto the metal stairway that was wheeled up to the cabin door, I felt Samoa before I saw it. The air was so dense with warmth and moisture, it weighed on my skin. Even my hair felt heavy, and I suffocated in the travel outfit I couldn't wait to shed: a one-piece dress with dotted red bodice and straight, pinstriped skirt; a matching pinstriped jacket; sheer pantyhose; and red calfskin pumps with two-inch heels. My parents, too, looked more like they were on their way to church than about to set foot on a South Sea island. My father's suit was charcoal, my mother's pearl gray. As we snaked through a sea of floral prints to claim our baggage, did we look as ridiculous as I felt?

No one seemed to notice, or care. When we'd stopped off for a few days in Honolulu on the way down, smiling girls in ti-leaf skirts had draped leis around our necks, and a photographer had snapped pictures we felt compelled to buy. Here, no flowers or flashbulbs or ukulele players greeted us.

Should I smile? Try to make eye contact? Say hello? Does anyone even understand English? All I heard was babble that didn't sound like words to me—strings of vowels punctuated with hiccups. Even the voices sounded foreign: loud, nasal, and abrupt.

At the far end of the baggage claim, a slight, ruddy-faced man in a flowered Hawaiian shirt stood out in the crowd of sturdy, bronze Samoans. When he spotted us and hurried over, I wanted to throw my arms around him—and believe me, I was not one to dole out hugs to strangers.

My father looked relieved, too. The sharp-edged expression he'd worn since we'd stepped off the plane softened into the Good-to-see-you face he wore in public back home, where he knew everyone, and everyone knew him. Big ol' smile filling the space between chin and ears, eyes tipped up at the corners like he was already thinking of a joke to share. He could relax a little now because the man headed toward us was a peer—not just another small, light-skinned person like us, but another *doctor* like my dad.

"Dr. Donaldson?" my father said.

Please, I prayed, *don't let him say, "I presume."*

Dr. Donaldson shook my father's hand and made a little bow toward my mother and me. "Welcome to Samoa," he said. He pronounced it *SAH-mow-uh,* as we'd been told the Samoans did. "Let's see if we can find your luggage. We'll drop it off at your apartment and then I'll take you on a tour of the island." His words were friendly, but there was something distant, wistful, about his delivery. As he spoke, his eyes scanned the sky above our heads as if he were watching for flocks of birds and preparing to fly away with them. His ethereality made his first name—Manley—seem like a lifelong joke at his expense. But never mind that, or his peculiarities. We'd arrived, we had a ride to town, and soon we'd see our new home.

By the time we collected our bags and loaded them into the blue government-issue Jeep, the sun had risen, but gray veils like vaporous cobwebs still hung over trees and gathered in low places, and a campfire-ish pungency scented the air. Smoke from underground ovens, Dr. Donaldson explained. In the villages,

Samoan men and women were preparing the Sunday meal of roast pork and *palusami* — coconut cream baked in taro leaves. My stomach mumbled a reminder that I hadn't eaten on the overnight flight from Honolulu. I had a distinct craving for fried chicken and mashed potatoes, our usual Sunday fare.

Dr. Donaldson pointed out some of the sights as he drove us along the fifty-five-square-mile island's one main road: here a coconut plantation, there the island's tallest mountain, a two-thousand-foot peak with jagged contours padded in dense vegetation. On either side of the sunlit road, the forest deepened and darkened with an intensity that gave me the willies. On family vacations I'd ridden in spooked silence through densely wooded Appalachian hillsides and stood, Lilliputian, in California's sequoia groves, but I'd experienced nothing as darkly alluring as this jungle and its impenetrable blackness. With the growing realization that I was half a world away from anything familiar, I slid closer to my mother in the Jeep's back seat.

We passed through a village where half a dozen *fales* sat in a semi-circle around a common green, and I picked up a scent that reminded me of flowers I'd seen everywhere in Honolulu. They looked like little stars carved from wax — five creamy petals with a smear of butter yellow in the center — and their fragrance melted in the air like the scent of gardenia or jasmine. What did my dad call them? Frangopango? Frangipani? That was it, frangipani; the entire village smelled of frangipani. My breathing slowed, and I dissolved into my seat.

My mother tapped my arm and tilted her head toward the village. "Nancy, look!"

I turned to see a small boy in what I would learn was a *lavalava*, chasing a scrawny dog, then stopping just short of the road to wave and smile as we passed. *Finally, a friendly gesture.* I grinned and waggled my hand like a doofus.

In the next village, the houses were all square, with sturdy walls and tin roofs, and some sat atop concrete pillars that hoisted them a full story off the ground. Better in hurricanes, Dr. Donaldson told us.

"Oh?" The lines between my mother's eyebrows deepened, and her voice came out like a sliver, barely piercing the thick air. *Hurricanes.*

Behind one house, a man bathed at an outdoor faucet. He held his *lavalava* around his body like a shower curtain, deftly maneuvering it from back to front and side to side with one hand as he washed himself with the other. Across the road from the village, boardwalks led from a narrow strip of sand into the ocean, and at the end of each pier-like walkway sat a privy. I tried to remember if indoor plumbing had been mentioned in the description of our quarters in Utulei.

"Do they still use those?" My mother nodded toward the outhouses.

"Afraid so." Dr. Donaldson turned his head toward my mother but gazed beyond her shoulder. "We're trying to phase them out and introduce flush toilets, but . . . "

He shrugged.

"*Fa'a Samoa.*"

Fa'a Samoa: The Samoan way.

Stretches of deep forest alternated with bright villages and views of the Pacific. Placid at the horizon, the ocean turned energetic near the shore, flexing and relaxing, glinting and glowing like a muscular showoff. Each time we passed from sun to shade, I shivered, though the air remained balmy. I twiddled the silver ring I wore, stroking its smooth sides, twisting it around my finger and pressing its angular designs into my skin to make x-shaped impressions, soothing myself with the familiar feel of the metal.

At last, the Jeep rounded the final bend. "Here we are," Dr. Donaldson said. "The Utulei apartments. You're in I-7."

Ahead was a cluster of new-looking, two-story buildings with corrugated metal roofs and cinder block walls at each end.

Each unit had a wide front porch overhung by a second-story balcony, and the buildings all faced a central courtyard, where a few American-looking families sat talking and laughing at picnic tables. Now *this* was starting to look civilized.

"Very nice," my father said, but his eyes darted across the road, where a row of squat, white houses faced a bay, offering views of green peaks on the other side. Penicillin Row — the houses usually offered to doctors. No vacancies there right now, but we were on a waiting list.

As we neared our apartment building, I noticed that the walls running between the cinder block ends weren't walls at all, but panels of screening.

Oh great, a see-through house. Isn't that the dream of every self-conscious sixteen-year-old? We might as well be living in a thatched hut.

Once inside, I saw that the screens were outfitted with wooden louvers that could be closed for privacy. A smile — albeit a tiny one — took hold of my lips, and I looked around to see what else our new home had to offer. The floors were covered wall-to-wall with woven mats that smelled like dried grass and scritched beneath our dress-up shoes. Very South Pacific-y. That should make my dad happy — my dad, the romantic whose Rodgers and Hammerstein-fueled fantasies had landed us here.

A galley kitchen separated the living room and dining room, which were furnished with rattan tables, chairs, and a sofa. I had nothing against rattan, but with the cinder block-and-jalousie walls, the overall effect was a bit like a cheap Florida motel — the kind we'd been forced to stay in while vacationing, on days when we'd spent too much time beachcombing and waited too long to start looking for the night's lodging. Not exactly the airy beach house I'd imagined. Then again, better than a *fale* stuffed with four-hundred-pound Samoans.

Dr. Donaldson said he'd give us some time to "get situated." He'd return in an hour or so to pick us up for the island tour. "I'm sure you'll want to freshen up" — he smiled vaguely as his eyes drifted across our dress-up clothes and fixated on a point on the wall just beyond where we stood — "and change."

I took a few more minutes to investigate the first floor, then dragged my suitcase up the staircase, past the — *yes, thank you* — bathroom, to have a look at the three bedrooms. I claimed the middle one, a narrow, nondescript box with tan vinyl floor tile, a plain dresser against one wall, and a twin bed against the opposite wall. Heaving my suitcase onto the bare mattress, I pictured my bedroom back in Stillwater: the wide bed with its Martha Washington woven spread, the coffee-colored wall-to-wall carpeting, the double doors that opened into an adjacent room my parents had converted to a sitting room for me after my older brother moved out and married. In that private suite, I entertained friends and, when alone, engaged in secret rites of diary-keeping and tracking on graph paper the ups and downs of my attitudes toward various interests, romantic and diversionary.

My new room in Utulei was maybe a quarter the size of the space I had at home and more suited to a novitiate than to a girl whose idea of deprivation was giving up her Princess phone. The room's one redeeming feature was a door that led onto the balcony, from which — by squeezing myself into one corner and craning my neck — I could glimpse the bay and inhale its bouquet: essence of ocean creature steeped with seaweed in a salty broth, a scent that gave me a vacation-y feeling.

I began unpacking the few clothes I'd brought to wear until the rest of our belongings arrived by ship in a month or two. I tucked white cotton underwear, denim shorts, and my aqua-and-lime striped two-piece swimsuit into dresser drawers and hung print dresses and blouses in the closet.

As I lined up my sneakers and sandals, I noticed a light bulb in a wire cage about eight inches above the closet floor. We'd been warned against bringing leather shoes; they'd mildew in the humidity. But just in case we were foolish enough to ignore the advice—which we were—the constantly burning light bulbs in our closets were supposed to help keep our shoes dry. The wire cage was there to prevent anything from resting against the hot bulb and catching fire.

We'd gotten other warnings as well, like about the geckos—tiny lizards with translucent skin and suction-cup toes. They weren't dangerous, but they were everywhere.

"They'll even get on your toothbrush, so check before you put it in your mouth," Dr. Donaldson had cautioned. I'd already encountered one when I'd taken a tumbler from the kitchen cabinet and—just as I was about to fill it with water—noticed a cricket-sized gecko attached to the inside wall of the glass, staring at me with its head cocked like a curious puppy. I set the glass back on the shelf. I could do without a drink.

Even grosser were the ants—black specks like marching coffee grounds that were attracted to body secretions and, we'd been told, would chew holes in your underwear if you left it lying around overnight.

As I puttered around the bedroom, I left the shutters open, hoping that immersing myself in the sounds and smells of my new environment would make this strange place seem more like the Shangri-La I'd imagined. I'd signed on for palm trees and surf, not moldy shoes, creepy lizards, and panty-eating ants.

But hey, I was in *Samoa*. I'd come here of my own accord—no whining or pouting when my father came up with the crazy notion of uprooting us and moving us from Middle America to the middle of the South Pacific. After all, being a teenager in Stillwater, Okla-boring-homa hadn't been all that hot; this *had* to be better, fungus, fauna, and all.

Still, I wished I'd packed a few knickknacks that would make the room feel like the haven I needed it to be. Then I remembered the one thing I had brought that would connect me with the life I'd left behind. Swaddled in tissue paper and stashed in a pocket inside my suitcase was a small, brass picture frame decorated with flower-like clusters of imitation pearls. I unwrapped it and gazed at the black-and-white photograph behind the glass.

Danny. My romantic fixation for the past twenty months and twenty-four days. Was it really possible I wouldn't see him for two years? Two years times three-hundred-sixty-five days. Seven-hundred-and-thirty days. That was longer than we'd known each other. That was forever. Picture-Danny beamed back at me like he didn't know the meaning of the word.

I set the framed photo on the dresser and sank onto the bed. Six thousand miles hadn't seemed so terribly far when, sitting on my bed in Stillwater, I'd considered the journey ahead. Fifty round-trips between Stillwater and Oklahoma City. Two Florida vacations. But now I understood that miles were not the only measure of distance. I was very, very far from home.

Overcome by heat and overwhelmed by surroundings, I closed the shutters, the slats clacking like some primitive musical instrument.

The clothes are coming off. I unbutton my jacket, tug my dress over my head, kick off my pumps, and peel my sticky pantyhose down like I'm skinning overripe fruit. Standing in my underwear, I feel the moisture in the air merge with the sweat on my skin. I could use a shower, I'm thinking, and as that thought enters my mind, I remember the man bathing in the open with only a lavalava between my eyes and his nakedness. Could I ever do that? I don't mean just the skillful whipping around of the sarong, but the comfort with lathering up al fresco. Could I do that? And could I drift off to sleep on the crushed coral floor of a fale, shoulder to shoulder with my kin, and rise to breakfast on boiled taro? And after sleeping and rising and breakfasting and bathing day after day in a village where my every move is exposed, who would I be? Would I be the same girl who'd left Danny and Stillwater behind, or would I be changed in some essential way?

I glanced at the room's one regular window—a vertical pane that ran alongside one of the screened panels—and wondered if anyone in the apartments across the courtyard could see into my room. Before I could give that possibility much thought, something else caught my eye. Nailed across the bottom of the window was a square of painted plywood with something scratched into its surface. I moved closer. The scratch marks were names, like you'd carve on a park bench or the top of an old school desk when no one was looking: PETA, MAIKA, TIVA, BELINDA + MEIF, BARB + ISIDORE.

I knew who had carved those names, brazenly defacing *my* room. It was Barb, the American girl whose family had lived in apartment I-7 before us. All I knew about her was her name and that she had recently graduated from Samoana High School and returned to the States to live with a friend while her parents continued working in Samoa. Still, staring at the graffiti she left behind, I pictured her whole life. I saw her dressed in colorful island prints, smiling, surrounded by the friends whose names circled hers on the plywood square. I imagined her dancing with brown-eyed Isidore, laden with flower leis and shell jewelry from her island beau. And then, flushed from the dance, laughing as he popped a piece of mango into her open mouth.

I saw it all, and I envied what I saw. Somehow, in this alien world, Barb had found her *fa'a Samoa*. Maybe, just maybe, so would I.

The garments of my former life, so tight and stifling, are heaped upon the floor. I kick them aside on my way to the closet and survey the selection hanging there. My hand reaches for a splashy, red-and-orange print, then hesitates and settles on a simple, flowered shift in muted shades of blue and green. I slip into the dress and slide my feet into sandals.

I'm an island girl now, I tell myself. As if transformation were as easy as changing my clothes.

Chapter 2—Island Girls

Sa matou tu'u la'au mai nei.
(On our journey we have enjoyed much hospitality.)
— Samoan proverb

The girl sitting across the table from me tipped her head and narrowed her eyes. "So, what do you think of Samoa?"

My parents and I had spent the afternoon touring the island with Dr. Donaldson, driving through countless villages of *fales* and tin-roofed shacks, taking in palm trees and lava-rimmed ocean vistas, along with occasional incongruities like the boxy building that housed a new TV station. This last stop, at the home of another American doctor's family on Centipede Row — a cluster of Navy-era quarters with an impressive view of the harbor — was supposed to make us feel welcome. So far, it hadn't.

For one thing, the pressure was on for us to make a good impression. The family we were visiting was that of my father's new boss, Dr. Puckett, medical director of the Hospital of American Samoa, where my dad was to practice obstetrics and gynecology for the next two years. And Valerie, the girl opposite me at the kitchen table, wasn't exactly putting me at ease. The oldest of the Pucketts' four children, she was younger than me by a couple of years, but the way she interrogated me right off the bat made me feel like a schoolchild searching for the right answer to please an exacting teacher. Older, worldlier girls had made me feel that way, but never someone younger. There was nothing tentative or deferential in Valerie's voice or manner, and because I was always tentative and deferential in such situations, her self-assurance rattled me.

"What do I think of Samoa? Oh, it's beautiful. And I—"

"Did you drive in the States?"

"Sure. I got my license last February, when I turned sixteen, and—"

"Well, you can't drive here. You have to be eighteen."

She fiddled with a spoon that lay on a placemat woven from pandanus leaves. I noticed a wart on her right index finger. She saw me looking at it and slid her hands into her lap. I kept my hands concealed, too, so she wouldn't see me twirling my ring.

"How do you get your hair straight like that?" Valerie asked.

I tried to answer economically, doubting she'd let me finish a sentence without interrupting again. "Orange juice cans. The big ones. Roll my hair on them. And I use this gel stuff, Dippity-do."

"Hm." She said it in a way that sounded more like an indictment than an expression of interest. "Good luck finding your Dippity-do down here." She raised her left hand—the wartless one—and twisted a strand of hair around one finger. Her hair had the color and sheen of polished cherry wood, but it lacked direction, pouffing out in some places and lying flat in others. Just above one eyebrow it curled upward, like a misplaced false eyelash.

Groping for conversation starters, I pointed to the lapel pin she wore on the collar of her sleeveless blouse. It was shaped like an artist's palette, with dabs of paint enameled around its edge and the words "Art Club" emblazoned across its center.

"Cool pin," I said. "You were in an art club?"

Valerie fingered the pin and smirked. "Yeah, last year. But down here, I've been telling people I got it from my boyfriend in the States, Arthur Club." She exhaled a barely audible chuckle.

"You have not! Has anyone fallen for it?"

"Couple people. Can you believe that?"

I laughed out loud, cheered by a thread of connection. Leaning across the placemat, I asked, "So do you really have a boyfriend back home?"

"Nah. You?"

"Yeah. Well, sorta. There's this guy, Danny. We've been going together for a while. Actually, he moved to Alabama before I moved down here, but we write to each other all the time, and he says he'll wait for me." I smiled at the thought of Danny's picture on my dresser.

"Wait for what?" Valerie, fiddling with the spoon again, shot me her slant-eyed look.

"Till we can be together again. I mean, we might date other people for now, but when I'm back in the States, we'll get together and get married someday." Arms crossed, I leaned back in my chair as my mind filled with images of candlelight satin, alençon lace, and peau de soie slippers—specifics I'd absorbed from reading wedding write-ups in the *Stillwater News Press*.

The *whap* of Valerie's spoon slamming against the table jolted me out of my reverie, but her next words jarred me more.

"That's bullshit."

Good God, is everyone from Michigan as blunt as this girl? That's where the Pucketts were from: Kalamazoo. Where *we* came from, people were not so direct, especially not in our family. Even at the dinner table, we weren't supposed to ask straight out to have something passed. The proper etiquette, according to my father, was to ask the person seated nearest the dish you wanted if *they* would like some of whatever was in it: "Would you care for potatoes, Mrs. Wilks?" And if Mrs. Wilks didn't catch on and simply said, "No, thank you," instead of the correct response: "No, but may I pass you some?" you were out of luck.

"Want a Fanta?" Valerie asked. I looked around to see if there was something I was supposed to pass.

"A what?"

"Fanta. We don't get Coke or Pepsi down here. Just Fanta. The orange isn't too bad. If you like fluorescent beverages." Valerie's lips eased into a half-smile, but her eyes were still like slits in a mask.

"Okay, one fluorescent Fanta, please." I mirrored her expression, allowing the corners of my mouth to rise only so far. "You wouldn't happen to have any Day-Glo Cheetos to go with that, would you?"

Valerie's half smile broadened into a bona fide grin, evidence that the test was over and I'd made the grade. My smile expanded, too, not in a copycat way, but reflecting real pleasure. I was still making up my mind whether I liked this girl, but I liked that she now seemed to like me.

Valerie pushed out of her chair, went to the refrigerator, took out a bottle of orange soda and set it on the table with two glasses, making no attempt to hide the warty finger.

"There you go. Would you like a napkin?"

So she does have manners. I reached for the bottle and poured us each a glass. "No, but thanks for asking."

"Just trying to be the perfect hostess, you know." With a theatrical flounce, Valerie flipped her head away, then looked back over one shoulder and showed a cheesy smile. "Mother says I have a flair for entertaining." She burst out laughing, buckling at the waist and gripping the refrigerator door handle as if too weak to support herself.

I was laughing, too. "Oh, you have, you have. A real flair."

I was still smiling and thinking about Valerie as Dr. Donaldson drove us back to apartment I-7. Just before our turnoff, another girl caught my attention. A Samoan girl about my age, the first I'd seen up close, ambled along the path that ran beside the road. She walked like those people at the airport, like she was going somewhere but didn't care when she got there. Her broad feet were bare, yet she didn't flinch as coral gravel crunched beneath them. She wore a red-and-white *lavalava* tucked around her hips and a white blouse buttoned all the way up to its Peter Pan collar. Her hair—black, thick, wavy, and coarse as sisal—was plaited into a single braid that hung to her waist. It looked like a cable that could hold up a bridge. Her features, too, were indelicate: wide, flat nose; full lips; narrow eyes under heavy, black eyebrows. Nothing like the pretty Polynesian girls I'd seen in cruise ship ads or the smiling hula girls in Honolulu.

As I watched her on the footpath, I tried to imagine us being friends, cozying up in my room, listening to Beatles records, leafing through teen magazines, and whispering about our boyfriends. But the picture wouldn't come into focus. Whatever American-style modernization was going on in Samoa, it didn't seem to have affected this girl. For all I knew, she had no idea who the Beatles were; I doubted she'd ever had a boyfriend, and she clearly wasn't keeping up on the latest styles. I was also fairly certain she would not find humor in the garish hues of soft drinks and snack foods.

I tried, but I couldn't see myself making friends with a Samoan girl, not this one or any other. That girl from Kalamazoo, though, maybe.

Chapter 3 — Sadie Thompson and Orange Samoa

When he came on deck the next morning they were close to land. He looked at it with greedy eyes. There was a thin strip of silver beach rising quickly to hills covered to the top with luxuriant vegetation. The coconut trees, thick and green, came nearly to the water's edge, and among them you saw the grass houses of the Samoans . . .
— W. Somerset Maugham, "Rain"

Happy talk, keep talkin' happy talk,
Talk about things you'd like to do.
You got to have a dream,
If you don't have a dream,
How you gonna have a dream come true?
— "Happy Talk," South Pacific, Richard Rodgers and Oscar
  Hammerstein

Whizzing coconut milk and chunks of coconut meat in a blender, my father improvised a sauce for the fish he was about to bake. Beside him in the narrow galley, my mother sliced papayas and wedges of lime to squeeze over the fruit, her knife rapping in counterpoint to the blender's steady whir. In this domestic task, as in everything else, my parents worked as a unit, moving around each other in a *pas de deux* as graceful as the steps they'd perfected in their ballroom dancing class.

Our first few days on the island, we'd been invited out for meals, joining fellow expats for lunch in the Rainmaker Hotel's bayside restaurant and dining at other doctors' homes (where my mother, who'd left the fine china in Oklahoma, was chagrined to discover the other wives had brought theirs along). Now we were settling into a routine of shopping and cooking for ourselves.

"I went to BP's today—" my father announced over the kitchen racket. The way his voice rose at the end of the sentence, I could tell there was more to come, and knowing how long he could ramble, I sat down at the table.

"—and that's why we're having fish instead of beans." He switched off the blender and lifted its lid.

"What do you mean?" I asked, knowing he was pausing for my question. I always took the bait, always listened to his stories, always laughed when he got to the punch line. I was the unofficial guardian of my father's feelings, a role I'd assumed more by instinct than by choice. My whole life I had sensed vulnerability beneath his mirth, a sinkhole in his psyche. Listening and laughing were the ways I tried to buffer him from disappointment and sadness. Years later I'd wonder why I, more than my mother, felt so compelled to validate and protect the man at the center of both our lives, but at sixteen I acted automatically on the impulse without examining it.

When he didn't respond, I prodded: "BP's—that's the place with the good candy, right?" I hoped he'd remembered to buy me a Caramello bar.

"That's the one."

There were no real supermarkets on the island, so we shopped at the open-air market and made the rounds of the various general stores in search of whatever we needed. It didn't take long to learn which stores to hit for certain items: Jessop's had its own bakery with a machine that sliced bread just right for sandwiches; Kneubuhl's carried New Zealand beef and real milk that came frozen and had to be thawed but still tasted better than powdered; Haleck's stocked an assortment of canned goods, along with bolts of bright fabric on shelves behind the cash register; BP's offered Cadbury chocolate. Though Samoan merchants tried to accommodate the tastes of the growing number of Americans, some of our favorite foods had been hard to track down.

"I really wanted to cook up a pot of pinto beans—a taste of home, you know?" my father said.

I sure did. Soupy brown beans with cornbread baked crispy in a bacon-greased skillet were staples on our table back in Stillwater. The mere mention of the dish evoked the meaty, pleasingly dirty flavor of the beans.

"And?" I urged him on.

"I looked all around the store and didn't find any, so I went up and asked the Samoan lady behind the counter, 'Do you have any beans?' And she said, 'Beeeeens? We have beeeeens. What kind of beeeeens you want?' "

He paused to pour the coconut sauce over a slab of fresh wahoo, a local, tuna-like fish. My father's hands, accustomed to sewing up lacerations and palpating for lumps, were just as adept at kitchen chores. He picked up a spatula and smoothed the sauce across the flesh, covering every bare spot as if frosting a cake.

"'Pinto beans,' I told her, and she said, 'Pinto beeeeens? I don't know what you mean pinto beeeeens. We have clothes beeeeens and straight beeeeens. No pinto beeeeens.' "

I laughed. Not a fake laugh to make my father feel good, but one that burbled up on its own when I got the joke: In spoken Samoan—or English spoken with a Samoan accent—"b" and "p" are virtually interchangeable.

My father continued: "I said, 'No, *beans, beans,*' but there was no way I could make her understand that I wanted beans, not peeeens. So I asked for wahoo." He opened the oven door and slid the pan of frosted fish onto the rack.

I laughed again. "Oh, well, Daddy. Fish is fine."

"Yes, but I really wanted beans."

He made a clownish, frowny face that I knew was only mock sadness. Conditioned as I was to respond to any hint of dismay, I cracked, "Clothes beeeeens or straight beeeeens?"

My father rolled his eyes. He smiled, and the pebble of anxiety that was rattling around my rib cage disintegrated. Whenever he launched into one of his tales about some everyday frustration—whether related with humor or sputtered out in anger—I worried he'd get so riled up and red-faced in the telling, he'd pop an artery and fall over dead. In these anecdotes, he was always engaged in a reasonable quest—back in Oklahoma it was usually something like correcting an error on his Sears bill or changing a procedure at his medical office—but he invariably met resistance from some stubborn or thick-headed functionary. One day it was a store clerk, the next day his office nurse, a strong-willed woman named Beulah who ignored his complaints and kept showing up for work when he fired her, which he did at least once a year.

Why, with his low threshold for frustration, had he brought us to a place where simply buying a bag of beans could be a trial?

He'd never really explained his attraction for Samoa. There were vague, dreamy references to Somerset Maugham and Rodgers and Hammerstein, so I supposed his South Pacific fantasies has been brewing for some time, fed by Hollywood movies and books read years before. One of the characters in Maugham's short story, "Rain," was a physician on his way to spend a year on a nearby island when he and his shipmates became stranded in Pago Pago. Maybe Maugham's Dr. McPhail was my father's inspiration. But the doctor in the story befriended the prostitute Sadie Thompson, something I couldn't picture my father doing. I'd heard him make derogatory remarks about women who wore tight dresses and grew their hair long. "Sexpots!" he'd say, hissing the word so it sounded more distasteful than provocative. Shopping at Haleck's general store—the current incarnation of the old boarding house where

"Rain" was set — was probably as close as my father ever would come to reliving the adventures of the fictitious physician. So what had possessed him, at fifty-two — a man with a thriving medical practice, every material comfort he'd ever hoped for, and two young grandsons he and my mother adored — to decide to set off for Samoa?

All I knew was that one night at dinner, he'd nonchalantly made the announcement.

"I saw an ad in the back of a medical journal," he said.

"Um-hm." Expecting one of his rambling anecdotes, I barely looked up from my mashed potatoes.

"They were looking for doctors to work in American Samoa. You know, down in the South Pacific? The government's got a big modernization campaign underway down there. They're hiring American teachers, doctors, you name it."

"Hmmm." I fed him the prompt I knew he expected, but I was more engrossed in chasing a pea around my plate than in following his narrative.

"I was just curious, so I wrote to find out more. That was, oh, about a month ago, and I'd forgotten about it until I got a letter back yesterday." The pitch of his voice crept upward, the way it did as he neared a punch line.

"The letter said I was hired, and could I be there by September?"

My fork was halfway to my mouth. I laid it back on the plate, potatoes, peas and all, and turned to look at my mother. Was she hearing this for the first time, too? Her expression offered no clues. She just raised her eyebrows, as if my father had said, "Let's drive to Dallas for the weekend," instead of "Let's completely uproot ourselves and go off to a place we know next to nothing about, out in the middle of nowhere."

"Samoa?" I said. "September?" That was only a few months away. School would be starting then — my junior year. I was just getting my bearings in high school, stumbling down the hallway of adolescence, jostled by new sensations, emotions, physical changes, and now I was supposed to start all over in a new place? And not just a new place but an *island* a kajllion miles from anything remotely resembling civilization? I started to protest, but stopped short before any words came out. *He did say Samoa, didn't he? This can't be happening.*

It was uncanny. My father couldn't have known—almost no one knew—but I'd been having my own South Pacific fantasies. And they were set, of all places, in Samoa. The whole thing had started the previous summer, when Danny and I were daydreaming about our futures together. We'd been dating for most of the year, I was wearing his simulated garnet ring on a snaky chain around my neck, and we were talking about getting married someday. But he was Catholic, and I was Baptist, and we were already getting grief from his priest and my pastor about being together.

"We'll just have to run away to an island somewhere," Danny said one afternoon as we sat on the family room sofa flipping through magazines.

"Okay. Where?"

He turned a couple of pages and started to laugh.

"What?"

He pointed to an ad on the magazine page. A dark-skinned woman with long, black hair held a can of fruit juice. "Orange Samoa," the label read.

"How about Samoa?"

"Samoa it is." I curled my fingers around his, still resting on the magazine ad.

For the rest of that summer, Samoa was our secret obsession. We doodled drawings of grass shacks on scraps of paper, and I pasted them in my scrapbook, alongside the Orange Samoa ad. I ordered a tiny silver palm tree from a catalog and hung it from my charm bracelet between the flattened, Lord's Prayer-inscribed penny and the St. Christopher medal Danny had given me.

But before we had a chance to run off to the South Seas, Danny moved to Alabama. His father had been transferred, and one August morning his whole family — mother, father, and all five kids — squeezed into their Ford Fairlane and drove away as I watched from the front yard, tearful and tortured with the anguish of first authentic heartbreak. I kept the ring, and Danny and I tried to keep up the fantasy in letters we wrote to each other on narrow-ruled notebook paper nearly every day.

By the following spring, though, when my father broke the news about moving to Samoa, my tropical daydreams were drifting in other directions, like the Kon Tiki blown off course en route to Puka Puka. A ticket to Samoa — or anywhere beyond the Oklahoma state line — had come to symbolize passage to a life that surely was more stimulating than the one I was living. High school was less than I'd hoped for. Not awful. Just not what *American Bandstand*, *Seventeen* magazine, and Annette Funicello had led me to expect. I had friends, I got invited to parties, I belonged to Tri Chi, a social club for girls my age, but the best that Stillwater, Oklahoma had to offer seemed not quite good enough — like settling for Tangee lipstick when you really wanted Revlon.

Tri Chi was fun enough, and there *was* something to be said for being part of a clique. In winter we wore identical Tri Chi sweatshirts; in summer, oversized Tri Chi T-shirts that doubled as sleepwear. We exchanged Tri Chi charms for our Tri Chi bracelets and hung Tri Chi pendants from silver neck chains. I even had a silver ring custom made with a trio of Xs — three Greek letter Chi's — carved into its surface, and I wore it day and night. Oh yeah, we Tri Chis were branded with belonging twenty-four/seven. But outside of weekly meetings and occasional rummage sales, we had no discernible purpose. Our principal activity was piling into our cars and driving up and down a one-mile stretch of Main Street, bracketed by the Sonic Drive-In on the south and Griff's Burger Bar on the north, while honking our horns at each other and at girls from the rival club, the TOGs.

Be-BEEEE-beep. *Hi TRI Chi!*

Be-b'bee-BEEEEP. *T-O-G TOG!*

All night long, up and down, up and down.

Be-BEEEE-beep.

Be-b'bee-BEEEEP.

Be-BEEEE-beep.

Honking like flocks of cacophonous birds staking out territories and announcing our status. Pulling into the Sonic for lime Dr. Peppers and tater tots—little bullets of potato, deep-fried to a crisp. Wiping the grease from our lips, checking our reflections in our rearview mirrors as we reapplied our frosted pink lipsticks, and backing out of our parking spaces to drive the circuit again.

Some nights, the Sonic was the only place in the world I wanted to be. But sometimes, sitting in the parking lot, I'd stare past the rows of souped-up '57 Chevys and family sedans borrowed for the night, stare into the distance, where Main Street turned into Highway 177, and imagine myself really going somewhere instead of around in circles.

My dreams of escape, in some strange way, were in sync with my father's island fantasies. But my mother? What were *her* dreams?

Years before, when she was the shoeless girl playing with kittens on a ramshackle porch that made her family's farmhouse look like it was missing some teeth, had she stared at the treeless horizon and wondered what lay beyond? Had she spun out intricate webs of dreams that she stuffed back inside when she married and my father's ambitions took precedence? If she had, she never told me, but hints of the life she'd envisioned for herself sometimes surfaced in her hopes for me, like settlers' abandoned belongings exposed when the wind sweeps away the prairie dust. Over time, my mother's agenda fused with my own, blurring the line between expectation and aspiration.

"Do you know what this means?" she'd say when I brought home A's on my French tests. "You've got an ear for language. You can be a translator. Work for the U.N. Travel around the world." And when the Tri Chis elected me publicity chairman, my mother didn't see it as an affirmation of my popularity; it was the first step in a career as a journalist and foreign correspondent.

There was also this to factor into any consideration of my mother's motivations: cancer. Double mastectomy and cobalt treatments two years before; everything apparently fine now, but who knew for how long? Though it didn't occur to me at the time, relatives' remarks would later make me wonder if my mother's illness had precipitated our move to Samoa. Remembering my father's exasperation at well-meaning friends who urged my mother to try crackpot cures or visit faith healers, I wondered if perhaps we packed up and moved six thousand miles just to escape the meddling. Or, if rather than running away from something, my parents were running toward dreams while they still had time to catch them.

Whatever the reasons, that night at the dinner table when my father broke the news that might have fractured some other family, he got no arguments from his wife and daughter.

It might not always be so. But *this* night, in apartment I-7, we could all agree on one thing: The fish was delicious. And so was the Cadbury chocolate we had for dessert.

Chapter 4 — Fiafia

Fa'atoetoe le muli o le ola.
(Keep the remainder of the basket for others.)
— Samoan proverb

From the balcony outside my bedroom, I scanned the courtyard of our apartment complex. A woman in a housecoat was setting out food for her cats. In front of another building, a little girl with blond curls clambered up a jungle gym.

After spending most of my life in a sprawling split-level on a double lot with mimosa trees and arborvitae shielding us from neighbors, this new communality — sharing an outdoor space smaller than a basketball court with half a dozen or so other families — was taking some getting used to. At first, I felt exposed and self-conscious every time I went outside, like I'd forgotten to button my blouse. But some aspects of out-in-the-open life were growing on me: I could perch unnoticed on my balcony and watch the goings-on for as long as I wanted, and if anything interesting happened, I could come down from my loft and join in.

Once in a while the other teenagers in the complex — the Baker sisters in the apartment directly across from ours and a burly Texas boy named Barry in the building by the jungle gym — wandered out, looking like they wanted company. As I watched the housecoat lady and the climbing girl, Barry moseyed over to sit atop a picnic table next to the playground equipment. I liked Barry; his drawl reminded me of home, and he was easy to talk to, partly because of his laid-back manner, but also because he was clearly off-limits. He had a girlfriend, Bev, who lived out by the airport in Tafuna, and they were serious with a capital S.

By the time I reached the picnic table, the little girl was there, too, telling Barry a rambling story in a five-year-old's singsong style.

"You know last Sunday? We went to this *fiafia*? It was wa-a-a-a-y out on the other end of the island? And they had so much food! I ate so much I popped my *puletasi*!"

I shot Barry a look. He laughed at my expression.

"A *fiafia* is a feast," he explained. "A big celebration. It means, 'happy.' "

"I know that," I said. "The feast part, at least. I'm supposed to go to one with my parents tomorrow. But *what* did she pop?"

Barry laughed again, eyes merry behind Clark Kent glasses. "Her *puletasi*? Oh, that's the kind of dress Samoan ladies wear. Gigi was wearing one last Sunday, right Gigi?"

The little girl nodded, ringlets bouncing like soft springs around her face.

"Oh," I said in a voice smaller than Gigi's. "Thank goodness."

I'd always prided myself on *knowing*. Knowing the right answers when the teacher called on me. Knowing how to spell *antidisestablishmentarianism* and *sphygmomanometer*. Knowing what people were talking about, even when I wasn't supposed to. I'd grown up around adults—my only sibling was already a teenager when I was born—and eavesdropping on their conversations, I'd learned to pay attention to context and tone. I'd gotten pretty good at figuring out what was being discussed, even if I didn't understand all the words. But that was in my old life; here in Samoa, I was as good as clueless. Here, I knew less than a five-year-old. I was desperate to learn.

From the moment we set foot in the mountain village of Aoloau, I knew this *fiafia* would be unlike any picnic back home.

The first tip-off: the men with heavily tattooed thighs flashing beneath their red *lavalavas* as they sweated over underground ovens. And then those centerpieces. I had to look twice to believe what I was seeing. Banana leaves were spread like a table runner down the middle of long, woven mats laid end to end to form a sort of banquet table flat on the ground, and artfully arranged on the leaves were fruits cut into flower shapes, along with the Samoan equivalent of party favors: glistening slabs of raw pork for guests to take home in palm baskets or offer back to the hosts.

The occasion for this ceremonial feast was the dedication of a new school, and many of the Americans on the island were invited to the day-long event—the new school was, after all, the product of the U.S.-funded improvement program. The villagers were feeding us in return for satisfying their hunger for American know-how and prosperity. My parents and I had driven up from Utulei with Dr. Donaldson that morning—our sixth day on the island—arriving in time to watch the tattooed men tending the *umus* where whole pigs and leaf-wrapped packets of *palusami* roasted. When I saw Valerie standing with her family, hand on outthrust hip in a stance that broadcast disaffection, I hopped out of the Jeep and crossed the wide lawn to join her and pick up where our kitchen conversation had left off.

"I hope they get that food done soon—I'm starved," I said.

"Tough luck." Valerie shifted her weight and switched hips. "The grown-ups eat first; the kids get anything that's left over. That's *fa'a Samoa*—you know, the Samoan way. We can't even sit with our parents."

"Wish I'd known. I would've have brought candy bars."

"Maybe Toni can sneak us something." Valerie looked past me toward the village green; I followed her gaze and saw a girl about our age approaching.

I hadn't met Toni yet, but I remembered Valerie mentioning her when she gave me the rundown on all the other American kids on the island. Toni's dad was principal of the Aoloau school, and their family lived in the village instead of in government housing at Tafuna or Utulei with most of the other Americans.

Watching Toni, I felt the same tug of awe and envy I'd felt when I found Barb's graffiti in my bedroom. Her hair—the tawny color of dried pandanus leaves and perfectly straight— hung to the middle of her back, and she had tucked a red hibiscus blossom behind one ear. She wore a *puletasi*—a hip-length tunic over an ankle-grazing wrap-around skirt—and her smile threw off sparkles. She looked like she smiled a lot, maybe because her overbite made it hard not to, but maybe also because she had a lot to smile about.

Toni, who came from Iowa, seemed completely at ease in her *puletasi*, in her mountain village where people lived in wide-open houses and cooked in the ground and spoke a language that made no sense to me. At least her family lived in a Western-style house—the kind that had walls and sat high on concrete pillars. Even so, she couldn't enjoy much privacy, could she? *Does she shower outside like the Samoans do? Do they all watch when she shaves her legs?*

The worm of discomfort inched up my spine again, the same one that made me shudder at the sight of all those Samoans crowded into the *fale* at the airport. The togetherness of village life was unimaginable to me; sharing an apartment courtyard in Utulei was a big enough adjustment. And yet— something about this place, with its clusters of cozy huts, its shrubs flaunting blossoms as big as saucers, its *umus* huffing out aromas of roasting pork and coconut cream—something about the place took hold of me and generated an inner warmth intense enough to shrivel the worm.

I'd experienced a similar feeling on the drive from Utulei to Aoloau that morning. As we rounded one bend, the sight of the ocean straight ahead dazzled me: the waves broke at an angle, and the sunstruck aqua water glowed like backlit bottle glass.

With a froth of whitecaps, that patch of sea reminded me of a marble I'd found when I was a kid, clear turquoise with swirling veins of white. As the memory whirlpooled with my new surroundings, I was buffeted by a sensation I'd known only in the throes of infatuation.

It was the feeling I'd had the night Danny and I first touched. After days—maybe weeks—of exchanging looks and chaste, exploratory notes in algebra class, we'd finally made physical contact at a classmate's party. We knew next to nothing about each other, but we knew *something* that made us want to know more. Danny arrived on his Cushman motor scooter, a rattle-trap assemblage of metal that in my mind was as enticingly wicked as any Harley. I remember the darkened den, the Beach Boys on the stereo, and Danny—a skinny kid who'd just moved to town from Cupertino, California—appearing in the doorway and crossing the room to take my hand and move with me in that awkward, swaying hug that passes for dancing when you're fourteen. His skin smelled of plain soap and gasoline, a combination that excited me more than the scents of citrus, wood, and old leather other boys splashed on themselves from bottles. I wanted to breathe him in with every breath until my last.

But Danny was a boy; boys were supposed to make girls feel that way. Now I was being romanced by—what exactly? I did not *know*.

The shouts sounded angry and defiant: "*Ku-sa-fa! Ku-sa-fa!*"

I wheeled around; Valerie didn't even glance toward the noise.

"Relax. It's just Rex," she said. "He does this whenever we go to a *fiafia*. He thinks he's a Talking Chief."

Valerie's five-year-old brother, bare-chested and wearing a pint-sized *lavalava*, stood at the head of the table-like mats, in the place where Samoan dignitaries would sit during the feast. He shook his fist and scowled and shouted long strings of words in what sounded like perfect Samoan.

"How'd he learn the language so fast?" I asked. I'd been struggling to memorize vocabulary lists from the *Teach Yourself Samoan* book I'd picked up at the London Missionary Society bookstore in Fagatogo. I'd learned a little about pronunciation — that "g" sounded like "ng," so Pago Pago was *PAHNG-oh PAHNG-oh*, and Fagatogo was *fahng-uh-TOHNG-oh* — but not much more. Now another five-year-old was reminding me how much I didn't know.

"That's not Samoan." Valerie's folded arms rose and fell with her chest as she heaved a sigh. "He just makes up words that sound like Samoan. *Ku-sa-fa* is his favorite. In case you hadn't noticed."

I looked around to see if anyone else was paying attention to Rex; no one was, and that was good. On the way to Aoloau, Dr. Donaldson had impressed upon us the importance of adhering to Samoan protocol, and I worried that Rex's antics might offend our hosts. The name *fiafia* sounds carefree all right, but traditional Samoan feasts — and the kava ceremonies that precede them — are highly structured events with formalities that must be followed to the letter.

Only the ranking village chiefs — the *matais* — and certain other officials and honored guests are permitted to participate in the kava ceremony, and they follow a complicated series of sacred steps and speak in a language style that no one else understands, Dr. Donaldson had told us. Most of the oration is done by the High Talking Chief, the *matai's* designated mouthpiece. It was this respected elder that Rex was impersonating.

As the adults gathered around the mats, Toni ushered us to one side of the clearing and told us we could watch from there; then she went off to help the other village women and girls prepare and serve the feast. I marveled at her ease in playing hostess, at how she understood all the rules and seamlessly shifted from American teenager to village maiden, laughing and joking with the Samoan girls.

I watched my mother, in her striped pink shirtwaist, lower herself to the ground as gracefully as if she dined this way every day. She crossed her legs in front of her — sitting any other way at a *fiafia* would insult the hosts — and tucked her skirt over her knees. She, too, seemed guided by some instinct that I lacked.

Baffled by customs I didn't understand, hungry for delicacies I was forbidden to taste, I took my rightful place on the sidelines.

There was music — strums and plinkity-plinks of guitars and ukuleles and rat-a-tatting on something like a biscuit tin — and a dozen or so variously-aged women in matching *puletasis* came bounding out in a single-file line, moving in arm-pumping, *step-step-step-HOPs* that looked a lot like the Locomotion. Then the rhythm changed, the music softened, and the women began doing a sideways, toe-to-toe, heel-to-heel shuffle: the Samoan *sivasiva*. There in their midst, executing the steps like a born islander, was Toni.

Of course. She knows the dance, too.

After the music and dancing, a group of Samoan men wearing *lavalavas* and solemn faces made their way to a small *fale* near the feast area and sat in a semicircle. All were shirtless, and some had ceremonial fly whisks, which looked like horsetails attached to wooden handles, draped over their shoulders. When the men were seated, a young woman appeared from the crowd wearing an outfit that made me gape. Instead of a *puletasi*, she wore a finely-woven pandanus mat wrapped around her body. It looked softer and more pliable than the typical floor mats, but she still looked like she was rolled up in a rug. On her head was a mop of bleached, human hair from which sprouted half a dozen or so slender, red sticks, each about two feet long and decorated with tufts of white feathers and round mirrors as big as the one in my Cover Girl compact. With the wild mane and the sticks standing straight up like antennae, she resembled some phantasmagorical creature, equal parts lion, insect, and space alien.

"That's the *taupou*," Valerie informed me. "Village virgin. She's the only one allowed to make kava for the ceremony. It's some kind of purity thing."

I wondered how the villagers knew she was a virgin. I didn't even know for sure about my best friends back home. They all said they were, but that's what they *would* say. The subject hadn't come up with Valerie yet, but I was pretty sure she was—she was only fourteen, after all. Toni, too, most likely. She didn't strike me as the type to do anything bad. What about Barb, the girl I knew only from her bedroom graffiti but pictured as Toni's double, perennially cheerful and poised, throwing parties in apartment I-7 that the other kids raved about for months? Had she "gotten in trouble" with her Samoan boyfriend? Was that the real reason she'd gone back to the States? I hadn't gone far enough with Danny to get into that kind of mess, but I wondered if our probing and stroking were enough to disqualify a *taupou*.

The *taupou* took her place in the *fale*, in front of the semi-circle of men. Before her was a shallow, six-legged wooden bowl, big as a birdbath. After a couple of speeches that might as well have been in Rex's made-up language, the *taupou* washed her hands and sat with her spine straight as the posts that supported the *fale's* roof. She rested the palms of her hands on the bowl's rim and appeared to wait for a signal.

When the High Talking Chief gave the go-ahead, a choreographed ritual began. Using a wad of something that looked like a dish scrubber (shredded coconut fiber, I later learned), the *taupou* swished ground kava root around in the water-filled bowl, then held the dripping mass up high for all the chiefs to see. She wrung the liquid into the bowl, wiped the rim and, staring straight ahead, flung the fibrous sponge over her shoulder to an assistant kneeling behind her. The assistant caught it, swung it left and right, and handed it over the *taupou's* right shoulder into her waiting hand. Even under the scrutiny of the village elders and esteemed guests, the *taupou* never fumbled. She knew her stuff. The talking chief might be fluent in a secret language, but in this ceremony, the *taupou* held the vital knowledge.

The *taupou* and her helper repeated the sequence three times before getting a signal from another assistant that the kava was ready. Then the ceremony dragged as one assistant, following chanted instructions from another, distributed kava to the chiefs and high-ranking guests. He dipped the cup into the kava bowl and served the highest chief, holding the vessel in both hands and raising it to forehead level before handing it over. Then he backed away from the chief, refilled the same cup and served the next chief.

Just outside the ceremonial *fale*, Rex pantomimed the process but uttered nary a *ku-sa-fa*. Even he possessed some instinctive grasp of protocol.

"Are you bored?" Valerie said after half a dozen cups had been served. "I am. Let's go find Mike. He said he'd take us up the mountain."

Mike was Toni's younger brother, whose sheer, pale skin reminded me of a gecko's. Valerie and I found him sitting by one of the pilings that held his family's house high off the ground.

"Enough *fiafia*?" he asked.

We nodded without speaking, dull from hunger and tedium.

"Come on. There's a trail that goes up the mountain. We can see the ocean from there."

Mike led us to the edge of the village, where a narrow but well-worn path sliced through tangles of vines, clumps of banana trees, and masses of plants I'd never seen before. Single file, the three of us tramped up the path; the higher we climbed, the fainter the aromas from the underground ovens became and the less I thought about my hunger and the festivities we'd left behind. Watching fruit doves with iridescent green wings flutter through the forest, hearing their strange calls—a cross between a moo and a purr—and breathing in the moist air with its ever-present blend of floral fragrances, I found myself caring less and less about anything at all except what we might encounter around the next bend.

We were *exploring*—a word that gave me a soft thrill—just as I'd explored my neighborhood as a child. From the time I was old enough to leave our backyard on my own, I'd wandered the nearby woods, climbing up and down the banks of its muddy creek and imagining myself to be trekking in exotic places. Getting to know my surroundings—and myself—through the challenges I devised. Never mind that the creek was no wider than my twin bed, with banks barely higher than my head. When I scrambled up its sides I was scaling the Matterhorn like the boy in *Third Man on the Mountain*. When I tottered across the narrow drainage pipe that spanned the creek, placing one foot in front of the other and holding my arms out for balance, I was a tightrope walker traversing the Colorado River. In these fantasies, the unknown was more alluring than unsettling, and I was ever the plucky adventurer.

In all my imaginings, though, I never saw myself here on a mountain slope in Samoa. If I thought about the South Seas at all as a child, I probably pictured expanses of sand with clumps of palm trees—cartoon desert islands. Even when Danny and I daydreamed and drew pictures of our island hideaway, Samoa looked like a palm-studded pancake.

I never dreamed of the mountains, and if I had, I never would have dreamed such mountains as these. Upholstered in tufted green, like mounds of cut velvet cushions, they rose from the sea and were robed in mist like the *taupou* in her fine mat. What vital knowledge did *they* possess? Would they share it with an outsider like me?

As we neared the summit, Mike led us to a clearing where we could look out in all directions. Straight ahead, the ocean glinted as if sequined, and in every other direction were those mountains. Those mountains.

This place. This curious, velvety, luscious place. This begging-to-be explored place. This possibly unknowable place that might test my limits in ways I could not imagine. I was not—and might never be—prepared to embrace island life in its entirety. But I was, in my own awkward, swaying way, ready to make my own *fiafia* with this island.

Chapter 5 — Mango Rash

It is a matter of astonishment to many that the luscious mango, Mangifera indica L., one of the most celebrated of tropical fruits, is a member of the family Anacardiaceae — notorious for embracing a number of highly poisonous plants.
— Julia F. Morton, Fruits of Warm Climates

A thatch of sun-bleached hair caught my eye. Then a white T-shirt. The hair, the shirt, and the rest of the boy materialized from the shadowed edge of the tennis court, where Valerie had brought me to meet the tribe of teenagers who hung out there every night.

I'd seen that hair, that shirt, that boy, somewhere else. Or did I only think I had?

It came back to me like a recollected dream, fleeting images at first, and then the thread of context: from the back of Dr. Donaldson's Jeep, our first day on the island, I'd seen the T-shirt boy — blond hair combed straight back, surfer-style; jeans stretched taut — as he pulled into the parking lot of Nia Marie's general store on his motorcycle, switched off the engine and lit a cigarette. When my mother's head was turned, I'd glanced over my shoulder for a second look and felt that feeling — half-flutter, half-tingle, radiating south from my solar plexus — a sensation I associated with boys and activities my parents would not appreciate. The rest of that day, I'd watched for him on the road, but he'd disappeared, and I started thinking I'd imagined him, a phantom surrogate for the real boy I was missing. Now here he was again, real as could be, and Danny was the one who existed only in fantasy.

I felt the boy's eyes on me, but I didn't meet his gaze, pretending to be riveted on the scene unfolding around me. By day, the tennis court was nothing but a rectangle of pitted concrete surrounded by rusty chain-link fencing, but every evening, it was *the* place to make the scene and socialize, like the Sonic in Stillwater, sans carhops and tater tots.

Girls in Bermuda shorts and summer tops clustered together, alternately whispering and shrieking, glancing over their shoulders at the older boys, who hung back in the shadows, cigarettes dangling from their lips. A couple of younger kids, not yet in their teens, rode Stingray bikes in figure-eights, slicing through the crowd like swift fish through a reef. A Samoan boy shinnied up a palm tree and threw down coconuts; someone cleaved off the tops and passed around the unhusked nuts for drinking. Not exactly lime Dr. Pepper, but I'd give it a try.

The night had the feel of a midsummer evening in the small-town America of my childhood, where all the neighborhood kids drifted out of their houses after supper for a game of Kick the Can. Without cars or other signs of status, we weren't adolescents posing as adults; we were just a bunch of big kids who'd come out to play under streetlights and stars.

Except for that blond boy whose eyes were burning through me. I sensed his games were not so innocent.

"New girl, eh?" The boy was walking toward me now, regarding me evenly as he took a drag of his cigarette.

New girl. I liked the sound of that. Until now, I'd been so absorbed in my own reactions to this foreign place, it hadn't occurred to me that *I* would be considered a novelty, fascinating for the simple fact of my unfamiliarity. Living sixteen years in the same town where I was born, I'd never been the newcomer, but I'd often wondered what it would be like. Would other girls clamor to be my best friend? Would boys nudge each other when I walked by? Or would I just blend in with the kids nobody noticed? In my daydreams, I imagined I'd somehow become more likable, less flawed, in a new setting. That simply changing residences would erase my insecurities and transform me into the sort of girl I imagined Graffiti Barb to be.

Now here, with this boy, was my chance to find out if I *had* been reconfigured into a brand-new, better self. I'd had a trial run when Valerie introduced me to the other girls a few minutes earlier, but I wasn't sure how I'd come across; I was still trying to figure out what they thought of me—and what I thought of them.

There was Marnie from Alaska, whose hair—wavy in all the wrong places—was offset by brown eyes as appealing as the eyes of a little animal you wanted to cuddle. And Suzi, skinny, with a peeling sunburn, who came from Wisconsin ("America's Dairyland," she informed me in a sarcastic tone). And Joyce, a copiously freckled Californian who wore mismatched, oversized rings on all ten fingers, calling attention to the peculiar color of her hands and arms, like a nicotine stain run amok. My suspicion, later confirmed, was that she'd been experimenting with QT, a lotion that was supposed to turn your skin golden but produced a shade more like tangerine.

Like the places they came from, the girls' reactions to me were all over the map. Marnie played hostess, gliding over to greet Valerie and me as we crossed the street from Valerie's house, directly across from the tennis court.

"You like parties?" she asked straight off. I nodded; she smiled. "Good, you'll fit right in."

I'd fit right in? Graffiti Barb status just like that? Could it be so easy?

Suzi made me think not. With a smile that was more like a sneer, she'd made a snarky remark when we were introduced. I chalked her attitude up to immaturity and tried not to take it personally, but I knew from that moment we'd never be close.

Joyce fell somewhere between Marnie and Suzi on the congeniality scale: no caustic remarks or sneers, but not what you'd call chummy. Reserved, I guess you'd say. She asked about my silver ring: "What are the Xs for?"

"It's a club. Back home. They're Greek letters: Chi Chi Chi." I could've said more, but I didn't want my new acquaintances to think I was comparing them to friends I'd left behind. Even if I was. Anyway, we were interrupted when one of the older guys—not the T-shirt boy yet, but another—sauntered over, moving slower than I'd ever seen anyone move, swaying from side to side and rolling his head and shoulders with each step. Fluid, like a slow-motion scene in a movie. He looked Samoan, but he wore American-style pegged pants and Beatles-style ankle boots; his hair, a rusty shade much like Joyce's QT tan, rose straight from his forehead into an unruly pompadour of frizz. It made him look like a clown, but a hipster clown, with a goatee and sideburns. I stifled a giggle.

"Hey, girls, who's your new friend?" His words rolled out as slowly as he walked, and he slurred them as if his tongue was too big for his mouth.

"This is Nancy, Fibber," Marnie said. "The new doctor's daughter. From Oklahoma."

"Okla! Homa!" Fibber said it like it was a figure of speech, not the name of a place, and he laughed, a slow-motion ha-ha-ha, as if someone had told a joke. "Where's that? Is it close to California?"

"Not in any way," I said. "It's nowhere, really."

"Nowhere!" He laughed again. Then he called toward the shadows, "Hey, Dick, come meet this cool girl from Nowhere." That's when the boy in the white T-shirt appeared and made his move. That's when this girl from Nowhere lost her cool.

I stared at the ground, absorbed with the meanderings of a crack in the concrete, trying to figure out how my brand-new self would react to the T-shirt boy's overture. He was within inches of me now. I could smell the just-laundered whiteness of his T-shirt, the sea water baked into his hair, the duskiness of his cigarette.

"So, new girl from Nowhere, do you have a name?" he asked.

I was dumbstruck—not just in the figurative, flabbergasted way, but actually unable to make words come out of my mouth. I wasn't accustomed to boys coming on so strong; they were usually the ones acting sheepish and tongue-tied. But this motorcycle-cigarette-T-shirt boy was nearly a *man*, exuding maturity, experience, and something else I had no vocabulary to describe.

Your name, stupid, just tell him your name. What's so hard about that?

The night was warm, but I was more aware of its moisture, an enveloping vapor like breath on my skin.

"Hey, I know I don't look too good with this mango rash, but you could at least look at me." Dick crooked a finger under my chin and tried to tilt my face toward his.

I peeked up. "Mango rash? What's that?"

Dick pointed to his lips, ringed in red as if he'd painted on a clown mouth and tried to wipe it off with Kleenex. "See? This is what happens when you eat a green mango. Neat, eh? Don't ever try it. Burns like hell."

"She'll never kiss you now," Fibber said. "Ha-ha-ha."

In the distance, a motorbike whined through the progression of gears—first . . . second . . . third—the pitch rising with each shift. I absorbed the sound in a visceral way: inside me, clutch engaged, throttle revved. I met Dick's eyes with a gaze level as the Oklahoma panhandle.

"I guess there's a lot I'll have to learn about this place. And to answer your question, I'm Nancy, from Oklahoma, also known as Nowhere."

"Well, Nancy, let's get away from this crowd, eh?" Dick rested a hand on my shoulder and guided me to a crumbling curb. I sat down; he sat beside me, close enough for our knees and shoulders to touch. The tingle returned; it fizzed in my stomach and made my skin feel surprised.

"So, what's it like in Oklahoma? Pretty flat, eh?"

"Well, actually, no. Not where I'm from—it's more rolling, and—" Dick was looking at me like he wasn't really interested in the topography of my home state. He offered me a cigarette from a pack of Kents. I shook my head "no."

"Don't smoke, eh?" He pulled out a cigarette for himself, lit it and inhaled deep and long, watching me the whole time.

"Well . . . not really, no." I wished I did. Girls who smoked gave off a bored, too-cool-to-be-bothered-with-you vibe that contrasted distressingly with my eagerness to please. I'd tried smoking, but it made me feel seasick.

"So you're a good girl." Was he teasing or mocking me?

"Well . . . not always," I lied. Actually I was, in comparison. There were some things my parents didn't know about, mainly involving Danny and our tentative excursions into each other's erogeny, but for the most part I followed their rules. It just seemed easier than dealing with my father's anger—the quiet kind that stung as much as a slap.

I toyed with my ring, embedding its Xs deep into my palm. Dick grabbed my hand and pressed it against my thigh to keep it still.

"See, if you'd have a smoke you wouldn't be all fidgety like this." He raised my hand to get a closer look at the ring. "What are the Xs for?"

I almost launched into a discourse on Greek letters and high school social clubs, but I stopped myself. Narrowing my eyes in an imitation of Valerie's squint, sly and knowing, I said, "I can't tell you. It's secret."

Dick smiled in a way that also was sly and knowing; the mango rash exaggerated his expression. "So, the good girl has a shady side. Will you tell me if I guess it?"

"Maaaybeee." I gave him another angled look as I drew out the word, amazed at how easily coquettishness came to me now.

"I'm guessing it's kisses from your boyfriend back home. Am I warm?"

Another sly smile. A shrug.

"Well, hey, if there *is* a guy back home, forget him. I'm taking you to a dance Friday. Goat Island Club. I'll pick you up on my bike. You live in Barb's old apartment, right? Been to some bitchin' parties there."

I tensed up, flushed, my hand still in Dick's. I pictured Danny's face in the frame on my dresser, perpetually smiling, unsuspecting. When we'd discussed "dating other people," it had seemed so abstract, so unlikely. Now I couldn't remember exactly what we'd agreed to. Was it okay to go out, but not make out? Had we even made any rules?

"So? Pick you up at seven?" Dick stubbed out his cigarette on the concrete and flicked the butt into the darkness bordering the bright rectangle where the other girls flirted with the pack of Samoan and American boys who'd drifted over. Their laughter faded in and out like a party overheard through a wall.

My hand itched. Was mango rash contagious? How odd that something so juicy and inviting could cause such misery.

"So?" Dick asked again, his fingers pressing mine.

Answer him. Just tell him no. Or yes. No, definitely no. But maybe . . .

I shifted my weight away from him and felt my muscles strain. I shifted back and rested my shoulder against his. Oklahoma Nancy would not be waffling like this. She wouldn't have flirted with this boy in the first place, not when she already had a boyfriend. But Samoa Nancy? She'd come here open to new adventures; taking up with T-shirt boy could be the beginning of a big one.

Headlights from passing cars swept over us like a tide. I took comfort in knowing the Pontiac Tempest my parents had shipped over was still on a boat somewhere in the Pacific. There was no way my father could cruise by to spy on me tonight, as he often did when I was out with friends in Stillwater.

I looked at Dick. He was smiling as if he already knew my answer.

"Okay, sure," I said. "But not on the bike, okay? My dad won't let me."

"Wouldn't want to upset Daddy, would we?" That mocking tone again.

I slipped my hand out of Dick's, stood, brushed off the back of my shorts, and took a few steps toward the road. "I've got to get home," I said over my shoulder, "I'll see you Friday." A few more steps. I turned.

"Unless . . ."

Still sitting on the curb, Dick was smoking again, watching me with a half-smile.

I half-smiled back. "You *could* give me a ride home tonight—if you drop me off a little ways from the apartment."

We took off, Dick smoothly working the clutch and shifting gears: first . . . second . . . third . . . the engine humming more urgently as it neared each peak and then settling into a murmur. I didn't wrap my arms around Dick's waist—I hung on to the back of my seat with both hands—but our thighs touched. And just before the end of the ride, I leaned close, brushed my cheek against the white T-shirt, and committed its scent to memory.

Chapter 6 — Double Ugly

Tiki — a large carved talisman of humanoid form, common to the Polynesian cultures of the Pacific Ocean. These talismans often serve to mark the boundaries of sacred sites.
— Wikipedia

The way my father cradled the parcel, I thought he was carrying a baby. As he crossed the courtyard and neared our front porch, though, I realized the figure in his arms was not a child, but a carving — his latest find from the tourist *fale* in Fagatogo where villagers sold handmade wares.

He'd been making frequent forays to the new craft market — built to attract the swarms of tourists expected when the fancy hotel opened in a few months — as he and my mother attempted to improve our apartment's ambiance. The resources they had to work with — mats woven from pandanus tree leaves, bark cloth wall hangings, and crude carvings made from some kind of smooth, reddish wood — weren't quite what they were accustomed to. When they'd remodeled our house in Oklahoma, they'd traipsed around to specialty shops and showrooms, selecting damask, terrazzo, no-wax vinyl flooring, and Formica. No such stuff could be found here. Yet my parents, Dust Bowl and Depression veterans who knew a thing or two about sows' ears and silk purses, seemed exhilarated by the challenge of tapping their creativity more than their checkbook. Maybe the effort brought back memories of their first years together, when my father was a country schoolteacher. Before he went to med school and more than a decade before my birth, they'd lived in a one-room house in western Oklahoma. Dust as fine as baby powder blew in through a gap under the front door, but they'd prettied up the place as best they could. Even later, when my parents could afford to hire decorators and handymen, they'd spent evenings and weekends stitching draperies, upholstering chairs, and hanging pictures, most of which my father had drawn in pastels or painted with globs of oils. Now they were applying the same energy and imagination to decorating the Utulei apartment.

"What do you think?" My father lifted the brown paper that swaddled the new artifact, as if unveiling a Brancusi.

Until now, his additions to the apartment's decor had been tasteful in their own Pacific-primitive way—tapa cloth panels decorated with geometric designs, glass fishing floats encased in knotted nets, a miniature outrigger canoe like the *paopaos* we'd seen Samoans paddling in Pago Bay. But this new treasure, a totem-like tiki with two heads stacked one atop the other, was grotesque. The eyes were round shells of a cloudy green color that made the tiki look like it had glaucoma. Both heads wore grimaces—or were those smiles? Their oversized teeth were bared, but their eyes stared so vacantly it was hard to tell what emotion their faces meant to express.

"I call it 'Double Ugly,' " my father said, stationing the tiki by the front door.

My mother glanced up from the sofa, where she sat flipping through magazines and tearing out the most colorful pages. "Whatever possessed you to bring that thing home, Harold?" Her nose scrunched up like she'd caught a whiff of something vile.

My father patted the tiki's head. "He's got a kind of charm. You'll see, he'll grow on you. And if we keep him here by the door, he's bound to scare off anything really evil."

When Dick came to pick me up for the Goat Island Club dance that night, my parents were making beads. This was another of their decorating projects: a beaded curtain to hang in the pass-through between the kitchen and the narrow entry hall. Instead of buying beads, they were making them the way my mother had fashioned necklaces when she was a girl, cutting magazine pages into little triangles, rolling each scrap around a toothpick, applying glue to keep the bead rolled tight, and slipping the toothpick out to leave a hole through the middle. Night after night, my parents sat in the living room, snipping and rolling and gluing and tossing the beads into a bowl on the coffee table. Most nights I snipped and rolled and glued and tossed right along with them, enjoying the wordless intimacy, but this night I'd been too consumed with primping and pacing.

If I'd had my way I would've dashed out the door as soon as Dick arrived, but I knew I had to invite him in to meet my parents—to be scrutinized and sized up, that is. We took the two rattan easy chairs facing the sofa where my parents sat rolling and gluing. I perched on the edge of my seat; my eyes traveled around the room as if they might find conversation starters printed on the walls. Dick smiled over at me and sank back in his chair. Either he didn't grasp what was at stake here or he'd done this meet-the-parents thing often enough to be unfazed.

"What's that you're doing?" Dick craned his head toward the coffee table and squinted at the bowl of multicolored tubes.

"Making beads," my mother said. She showed him how to make one, but didn't invite him over to the couch to try it.

"Huh. Neat," Dick said and changed the subject to California, where he'd lived before coming to Samoa. My mother kept on rolling and gluing, looking up occasionally to nod or ask an innocuous question, but my father laid down his toothpick and triangles, rested his chin on his fist, and fixed his gaze on Dick.

"I understand your mother runs a boarding house," he said.

How'd he know that? I didn't even know it.

"Right. Atauloma—it's an old girls' school out on the west end. Mostly Air Force guys stay there now. Great bunch of guys." Dick put his arms behind his head and stretched out his legs.

I thought my father was heading for common ground, about to mention that he and my mother had run a boarding house when he was in med school, but he stiffened and his eyebrows arched. Was it something Dick said or his cocksure make-yourself-at-homeness? Was it the long hair? The cigarette pack in his pocket?

I made a show of checking my watch but knew without consulting the hour it was time to leave. Snatching my purse from the floor and rising from my chair in a single swoop, I dashed across the room, brusquely kissed my parents, spun around, and headed for the door, bumping the table in my haste and spilling the bowl of beads.

Dick lit a Kent as soon as we were out of sight. The smoke rose in a single stream toward a palm leaf silhouetted against a sky the color of deep water.

"I've never dated a girl whose father makes beads." Even in the semi-darkness I could see his smirk.

Our sneakers crunched in unison on the gravel path. I counted five steps before responding. "He's not like most fathers, okay? He's different."

"I'll say."

Another five steps. *Crunch-crunch-crunch-crunch-crunch.* I was weighing words, wanting to defend my father, but then not wanting to, as my affections shifted to the boy beside me. Then wanting to again but not knowing how, never before having felt the need. Back home, no one thought it odd that my father would rather plant tulips than play golf or putter in the garage. He didn't hunt or fish and couldn't talk sports, but if anyone thought less of him for it, they kept it to themselves. My mother's friends always told her how lucky she was to have a husband who liked shopping and decorating as much as she did; my friends admired his paintings and said they wished *their* dads baked cookies. Even Judy, whose pop was a college football coach nicknamed Moose, seemed to think my father was as charming and talented as I thought he was.

Walking next to Dick as we'd left the apartment, I'd felt that shiver in my midsection again, but now the sensation slid up into my throat and made it tickle and tighten. In the place where the tingle had been, a hollow chill crept in. This was my *daddy* that Dick was disrespecting, and I was my daddy's protector. I had to speak up for him—didn't I?

Dick took my hand. A fresh wave surged through my insides, erasing my angst like warm surf smoothing a beach. I liked the feeling. And I hated myself for liking it.

Even before the music started, everything seemed amplified—the noise, the lights, the colors of the girls' flowered dresses, the smell of the coconut oil Samoan boys used to tame their hair, a scent so assertively unctuous it could be nauseating. On the walk over, I'd imagined we were on our way to a grown-up nightclub, a dim, smoky place with multicolored lights over the bar and candles on the tables—or maybe those little lamps with beaded shades, like in *Casablanca*. But no. Goat Island Club, an expat hangout on the second floor of a warehouse near the cruise ship dock, was bright as a schoolroom. Empty metal folding chairs stood like wallflowers around the room's edges. Teenagers—about half of them Americans and half Samoans—gathered in clumps, talking and laughing loudly. Boys elbowed each other and feigned combative stances; girls fussed with each other's hair and yelled challenges at the boys: "Hey, Gus! You gonna dance with me tonight?" Unlike the barefoot girl I'd seen on the footpath my first day on the island, the Samoan girls in this crowd—with their straight skirts, sandals, beehives, and bobs—seemed more like my friends and me. I could envision doing typical girlfriend things with them.

All the tennis court crowd was there; Toni, too, from the *fiafia* village. She'd shed her *puletasi* and *fa'a Samoa* ways and now, in sleeveless shift and ponytail, looked every bit the all-American high school girl—except for her bare feet. She smiled with a sweetness that seemed sincere yet for some reason annoyed me. As Dick steered me past the group, Marnie and Valerie raised their eyebrows and nodded their "way-to-go" approval. Suzi pretended to be absorbed in conversation with Joyce, but her eyes shifted in our direction as we passed.

Dick bought me an orange Fanta, and we leaned against a wall watching as the band—a Samoan group called The Vampires—set up electric guitars, a drum set, microphones, and amps and began their sound check. *Electric guitars! Here on this dinky island in the middle of the ocean. This place has more promise than I thought.* The drummer's straight, black hair swooped Beatles-style over his brow; the bass guitar player wore a scowl and a towering frizz that made him look like a Samoan Bob Dylan. All the others sported hairstyles that were nothing like boys at home wore: cut close on the sides and long on top, combed back from their foreheads and slicked with oil that accentuated the waves. Their faces were handsome, but I couldn't get over the hairdos. I was glad for the beach-boy blond at my side.

The music surprised me as much as the club's mood. I knew most of the songs—"Wooly Bully," "House of the Rising Sun," "Mustang Sally"—but I'd never heard them played the way the Vampires played them, with notes held long and embellished with vibrato and wah-wah flourishes. The sound reminded me of Hawaiian music, but the beats and melodies were pure rock 'n' roll. In between the songs I knew, the Vampires played other tunes I'd never heard, slow instrumentals like yearning rendered as music. Had my ears ever been touched by anything more sublime?

From the very first note, the dance floor blurred with couples in motion—no timid wall-hugging like at dances in Stillwater, no pairs of girls twisting together out of desperation. Everyone danced, not just swaying, but gliding, dipping, *moving their hips.* Among the first to hit the dance floor, Toni pranced out with one of the well-oiled, wavy-haired boys, whose eyes, brown and gooey as bonbons, never wandered from her.

Dick guided me onto the floor and began to move with the same rhythmic fluidity as the other dancers. I swayed noncommittally in place for a few bars; then, involuntarily, my body mirrored Dick's, gliding and dipping when he glided and dipped, my hips moving in sync with his. As the evening passed, lights dimmed, and the crowd mellowed. With my eyes closed and my head against Dick's shoulder, Goat Island Club began to feel more like the place I'd pictured.

Then the dance ended, the lights came back on, and we hurried outside as if romance were a delicate artifact we had to protect from the glare. We stepped out into liquid air that carried the fragrance of unseen flowers; I started walking toward the road.

"No, this way." Dick pulled me toward the docks. I wasn't sure I should follow, but I did. We walked along a row of corrugated metal warehouses set back from the bay on an expanse of asphalt, then down a few steps to a walkway overhung with palm trees. It was the sidewalk that ran behind Centipede Row, the line of houses on our right, Pago Bay on our left. The bay was maybe a half-mile wide at this point, and we could see the lights of villages and Japanese fishing boats on the other side. Behind them, mountains rose like the sloping shoulders of proud, old men.

Until that moment, the most romantic place I'd been alone with a boy was Couch Park, a corridor of green that ran along Stillwater Creek, out by the county fairground. The water in the creek was brick red and opaque, but tall trees and a swinging bridge lent an air of enchantment on summer evenings. Now, in a tropical setting that required no imagination to feel dreamy, I strolled under palm trees in moonlight, hand in hand with a boy who until days ago had seemed half-fantasy.

"Let's sit here for a while." Dick pulled me toward a park bench that faced the bay. I peeked at my wristwatch, knowing my father would be checking his. Then I sat down beside Dick.

When he kissed me, I tasted cigarettes, a taste I'd thought I hated, but didn't any longer. Didn't hate at all.

I knew better than to ask, but I blurted out the question first thing the next morning: "What do you think of Dick?"

My father was making coffee. My mother, setting out cups, said nothing, as if lining up their bottoms with the saucers' indentations required her full attention. I, too, avoided eye contact.

"Dick?" my father said. "Oh, you mean Double Ugly?"

I shot him a look that shattered my pretense of nonchalance.

"That's what he looks like, you know," my father continued. "One of those tiki heads, with his slicked-back hair and pug nose."

It was only too true. Writing to my girlfriend Cindi a few days earlier, I'd described Dick as "all the Beach Boys put together, only better," but the fact was, he wasn't that good looking. His nose looked like it was permanently pressed against an invisible pane of glass, and his eyes, though blue, were small. Still. I *liked* him. We'd had fun the night before, we'd started something that felt good, and I wanted to keep feeling good, even if my father tried to spoil it. He always came up with some bogus criticism to diminish boys he didn't want me to date: "That boy's a compulsive liar," or "He'll never amount to anything."

All of that was just a smokescreen. The real problem was never truthfulness or ambition—or motorcycles or cigarettes or a mother who kept a boarding house full of flyboys. The problem was, boys like Dick wore their sexuality a little too close to the surface, and there was no way my father was going to let me rub up against the ugliness of that.

As if he—or the tiki guarding our door—could stop me.

Chapter 7 — Shifting Sands

Se'i fono le pa'a ma ona vae.
(Let the crab take counsel with its legs.)
— Samoan proverb interpreted as "Consider the implications before
you act."

The five girls clustered in my living room formed a mixed
bouquet of complexions, from Suzi's sunbaked pink to
Sylvia's mocha brown. But it was other characteristics —
hairstyle, mannerisms, wit, and likability — on which I rated
them as I surveyed the room, imagining the five as contestants in
a pageant for which the grand prize was — *ta-da!* — my friendship.
It was a prize I wasn't sure any of them actually coveted, but
friendship — and lunch — were all I had to offer.

My mother had said I could bring someone home for lunch
on this first day of classes at Samoana High. I think she meant
Valerie. But when the noon bell rang and I rushed out into the
hall to look for Val, I found her talking to the other four girls:
Suzi, Sylvia, Clydeth, and Wendy. There was no way I could
invite only Val and not the others — my Oklahoma manners
wouldn't allow any such thing — so I asked them all to come
along.

If my mother was perturbed when half a dozen schoolgirls
trooped into her tiny kitchen, *her* Oklahoma manners wouldn't
allow her to show it. She just smiled, opened an extra can of
wahoo, and set out the whole loaf of bread she'd bought at
Jessop's bakery that morning. We all made sandwiches and took
them into the living room, leaving — to my mother's silent

consternation, I'm sure—six separate trails of breadcrumbs on the pandanus matting.

As we ate, I mentally compared the girls to my best friends back home. I'd known most of my Stillwater cronies since grade school, and even the ones I hadn't known as long weren't from far away; they'd just gone to different elementary schools across town. Not only had we grown up together, we fully expected to go all the way through college together, right there in Stillwater, at the state university, whose Williamsburgish buildings our parents had been pointing out since we were toddlers. Here in Samoa, my classmates—mostly displaced Americans like me— hailed from different cities and states, with no common geography, no shared experiences or reference points, and no expectation that our lives ever would intersect again.

Lost in my thoughts and mental assessments, absently fingering my silver ring—that sterling symbol of Tri Chi sisterhood—I wasn't really following the conversation, but I tuned in when everyone laughed at Val's description of Mr. Siefried, a stork of a man who taught social studies. Whenever Val said something especially witty, Suzi repeated it, as if to claim some of the cleverness as her own, and each time Suzi parroted her, Val and I exchanged expressions of incredulity, arching our eyebrows and bugging out our eyes. With each such incident, Val moved up and Suzi moved down a notch or two on the likability scale.

Sitting between Suzi and Val on the sofa, Sylvia interjected non sequiturs, unaware she was getting off track.

"You should rat your hair," she commented in the middle of Val's side-splitting account of how Mr. Oster, the math teacher, had whacked a ruler on the desk of some Samoan boy who'd nodded off in class. Dark-eyed Sylvia, whose faint accent hinted at her Mexican heritage, was the same age as Val and Suzi, but acted younger. She wore an outfit she'd made: sleeveless shell and straight skirt, both baby-girl pink, with her hair teased into a bouffant style that dipped over one eye.

Sewing and doing hair—her own or that of anyone else who'd let her—were Sylvia's favorite pastimes, and she talked of little else. I gave her points for appearance and industry, but had no choice but to mark her down in the repartee category.

Clydeth, a diminutive Filipina with arms as slender and golden as bamboo shoots, perched on an ottoman with her ankles crossed, smiling but not saying much. On her, I reserved judgment, pending further observation.

Sunk into one of the rattan easy chairs in the corner, Wendy—a Californian whose father was principal of our section of the school—bantered with Val, tossing out quips, laughing at Val's retorts, and blurting confidences.

"Do you know how *mortifying* it is to have your *father* standing up making speeches in front of the whole *school*?" Wendy covered her reddening face with her hands and dropped her head. "I could *die*, for God's sake!"

This girl was so funny, so self-effacing, so all-in-all appealing I wasn't even jealous of her hair. Well—I was, but I didn't *hate* her for it. Chin length and lush, it behaved exactly the way I wanted mine to, curving under in back, slanting slightly forward at the jaw line, and swaying like the fringe on a flapper's hemline when she shook her head.

I decided on the spot I wanted her for a friend. No, not just a friend, a *comrade*. I envisioned a chummy triad—Wendy, Val, and me—spinning records in each other's bedrooms and laughing ourselves silly over everyday events. Would we grow as close as I felt to my dearest friends at home? And if we did, what would happen to *those* long-standing friendships? Was a heart like a hotel, with a no-vacancy sign that switched on when all the rooms were full, or could it expand to hold everyone I invited inside?

On the walk back to school, my lunch guests and I passed "The Turtle," and the sight of it reminded me I wasn't the only one trying to decide how much to cling to the past, the familiar, the constant, and how much to embrace the new, the exotic, the ever-changing. Samoan society was wrestling with the same issues, and the building nicknamed The Turtle (because its rounded roof resembled an oversized tortoise shell more than the thatched *fale* canopy it was modeled after) symbolized the ambivalence. Though the building was new and modern, its nickname signified deep connections to the past.

In Samoan legend, Turtle and her sidekick Shark are the animal forms of a human mother and daughter who long ago fled famine and cold-hearted relatives on another island and sought refuge in the seaside village of Vaitogi, on the island of Tutuila. Turtle and Shark swam up onto the beach, changed back into human form, and sought out the village chief, who welcomed them like kinfolk and made sure the villagers doled out the best food and nicest clothes they had to offer. In gratitude, Turtle and Shark told the chief they would return to the sea and live just below the Vaitogi cliff, coming to the surface to entertain spectators whenever the villagers chanted a particular incantation. For centuries, Turtle and Shark have kept their promise, performing as reliably as Yellowstone's geyser, but only in response to the age-old chant, never seduced by new-fangled music.

If you stood on Vaitogi's lava outcrops and listened to the ancestral chants—as my parents and I had done on a recent visit—you could easily imagine yourself in the same Samoa that Europeans first encountered in the 1700s, a Samoa where people passed unhurried days collecting coconuts, angling for neon-bright fish, weaving palm baskets, and dozing through the heat of midday. Vaitogi's Turtle was indeed the Turtle of the ancients: steadfast, unchanging, steeped in tradition, mystery, and magic.

But Utulei's Turtle—the one we passed on our way back to school—called to mind a very different Samoa. Officially known as Lee Auditorium, the building bore the name of the present governor, H. Rex Lee, an American with a penchant for bow ties and a mandate to upgrade Tutuila, the territory's main island.

The auditorium was just one of many monuments to change, all fashioned in the same, pseudo-Samoan architectural style. Just down the road, directly opposite the bluff from which the governor's imposing, white house looked down its nose, a luxury hotel was being built on a spit of land that jutted into the harbor. The hotel's main building and guest cottages looked like traditional *fales* from the outside, but the resemblance ended there. Unlike real *fales*, with their crushed coral floors and nonexistent walls, the hotel would have indoor plumbing, air conditioning, telephones, and even a swimming pool and poolside snack bar where—it was rumored—real American hamburgers, hot dogs, and milkshakes would be served. Hungry for a taste of home, we American kids couldn't wait for it to open. Neither could the islanders, hopeful that tourists now would flock to American Samoa, which never had been as popular as nearby Tahiti and Fiji. All of us attached individual dreams to each silvery shingle nailed in place and every grain of sand trucked in to create the swimming beach.

We were all just as enthralled with the Turtle, where crowds of Samoan and American kids gathered for dances, swaying, dipping, and gliding to live bands that played surf music and rock standards in the same *fa'a Samoa* style as the Vampires. The boys with whom I twisted and frugged at those dances were as paradoxical as the music. Fibber and friends spoke Samoan among themselves and preferred *palusami* to hamburgers, but wouldn't be caught dead in *lavalavas* and flip-flops. They wore tight pants and Beatle boots with pointed toes.

The changes all around us pulled me in different directions, too. While I'd come to Samoa hoping to experience something utterly unlike what I'd left behind, the island was becoming a microcosm of stateside life. I was drawn to both Samoas—the one of age-old customs and chants and magical beings, and the one with rock bands and sharp-dressing boys who sped around the island on motorbikes—and I couldn't shake the feeling that merely by being here, all of us outsiders were tipping the scale toward Americanization and away from a culture that had developed over millennia and might vanish in a generation.

Just beyond the Turtle lay the main campus of Samoana High School: a compound of mint green, two-story structures that faced a ball field. The school was as up to date as any my American classmates and I had left behind in the States, and like many of the newly-built schools dotting the island, it wasn't just a bunch of pretty buildings—it was part of a radical educational experiment. Distressed at the state of education in American Samoa when he took office, Governor Lee had made overhauling the school system his top priority. In the past, classes had been held when teachers felt like it, in one-room *fales* with no desks, blackboards, books, pencils, or paper. Instruction was supposed to be in English, yet most teachers hadn't been schooled past fifth grade, so their language skills were lacking.

Governor Lee came up with the idea of beaming top-notch, televised instruction to outlying villages, in addition to building new schools and hiring stateside teachers. In short order, the island had a transmitter atop Mount Alava and a three-channel television system. Now, Samoan students spent several hours a day watching TV.

Watching TV in school—now that was something I could get into, even if the programs were educational instead of my daytime favorites *Password* and *American Bandstand*. But not a chance. Such newfangled stuff was not for my lunch mates and me. We American kids—and some Samoans who'd passed the stringent entrance exam—attended conventional classes in a Navy-era building at the edge of the schoolyard, whose featureless façade hinted at the drudgery inside. Standard Academic Program was the official name. We called it SAP school.

The school's battleship gray stairway led up to double doors that opened into a small vestibule where a single row of lockers stood against the rear wall. As my companions and I entered, I saw Dick standing with his back to the door, fiddling with a lock. Val gave me one of her raised-eyebrow looks and headed down the hallway. I walked over and touched Dick's arm.

"Hey," he said. "I've been looking for you. Hold out your hand — I've got something to give you."

I caught a glimpse of something golden and metallic.

A ring? Already?

Not that I didn't know Dick was trying to lay claim to me. Since that night at the tennis court two weeks earlier, he'd been calling at least once a day, hanging out at our apartment, or showing up wherever I went, even at the most unexpected times and places — like over the past weekend, when my father took Val and me to the airport at 2 a.m. to pick up Val's dad, who was returning from a conference in Australia. There, in the throng of Samoans who entertained themselves with every arriving and departing flight, as if takeoffs and landings were a spectator sport, was Dick.

The attention — and the fervor of it — sharpened my every sensation: every bite of ripe mango a flaming sunset in my mouth, every guitar chord a strumming in some deep and jittery recess, every waft of frangipani-scented air, instant intoxication. But another boy was vying just as ardently for my affection. In the canvas bag of mail my father picked up at the post office every Sunday, I could count on finding five or six letters from Danny mixed in with the magazines and flower-imprinted envelopes from my girlfriends. There was every bit as much passion on those ruled pages as in Dick's persistence, and my affections ping-ponged like crazy. Whose court they landed in depended on little more than who had my attention at the moment; choosing between my two admirers seemed impossible.

But did I really have to? Couldn't I, like the Samoans, hold on to the past while embracing the new, at least for a while?

No no no. How could I even consider such a thing? Danny was my real boyfriend. Loyal, unwavering Danny.

Six-thousand-miles-away Danny.

On second thought, maybe I *could* consider such a thing. Dick was right here, right now, and a helluva a good kisser.

I quickly rehearsed in my mind what I'd say when Dick dropped the ring into my hand. *Does this mean what I think it means? Then, yes, of course, I'll go steady with you!*

Would we kiss right there in the vestibule or wait until after school when we found some privacy?

I held out my hand. *Steady, Nancy, steady.*

"Close your eyes."

A skitter crossed my chest as a small object fell onto my palm. I wrapped my fingers around the thing. The skittering stopped short. Something wasn't right. The object in my hand felt cool, like metal, but sharp-edged, not smooth. I opened my hand and eyes at the same time. On my palm lay a small, brass key, the kind that opens a padlock.

"Neat, eh?" Dick said. "We're locker mates. I signed us up."

"Yeah. Neat." I hoped my eyes didn't betray my expectation.

"Lemme see your schedule." Dick grabbed the folded paper I'd taken from my purse and scanned the list of classes. "We've got art and typing together. I'll save you a seat."

He turned and made for the staircase, leaving me staring at my hands, the paper, the key. Through the open double doors came a blast of rock music from a passing car; from a nearby classroom in the school's Samoan section, the drone of a televised lesson. As I absorbed the sounds of Samoa in transition, I thought about change and its consequences: how very easy it is to let the allure of the new destroy something precious.

Chapter 8 — Between Sea and Sky

O 'oe ole Penina ole Pasefika
(You are the Pearl of the Pacific)
— Line from "Amerika Samoa," American Samoa Territorial Anthem

The morning's rain had left puddles on the crushed coral path; my flip-flops sucked the ground with each step, flinging shrapnel of wet stones and pale mud against my calves, prickling and leaving splashes of white on my bare legs. The path paralleled the main road — arteriole and artery pulsing from the heart of Fagatogo's business district — and a perpetual parade of cars and trucks rolled by. Rusted-out Chevys, Fords, and Toyotas shipped over by American contract workers (like my dad) and left behind to decay in the salt air. I winced at the sight of all those junk heaps. *Typical American indifference.* Signs of it were everywhere on Tutuila, in spite of the current modernization campaign.

The Samoans crammed inside the passing vehicles whooped and giggled like they were on a carnival ride, and once in a while one leaned out the window and yelled, "*Palagi!*"

Palagi. Spoken softly, the word has a mellifluous lilt: *pah-LAHNG-ee.* Charming origins, too, I'd learned. The first Europeans to visit the islands arrived by ship, and when Samoans saw their sails on the horizon, they thought the ships had popped through the slit that separated sea and sky, so they called the white-skinned visitors *papalagi:* sky bursters. Over time, *papalagi* became *palagi*, a word that loses a lot of its magic when shouted from a car window.

Each time someone called out, "*Palagi!*", I dropped my head and stared at the ground, as if ducking could deflect the taunt. I wished I could unzip my incriminating skin and step out of it right there on the path, leaving a heap like dirty laundry and continuing on my way to Val's house wearing no trace of my ethnicity.

In a rhythm steady as my pulse, guitars and ukuleles strummed; voices twined over and under each other and looped around like patterns in the basketry on sale at the tourist *fale*. High above the harbor, suspended from cables that stretched from Solo Hill on one side of the bay to Mount Alava's peak on the other, a school bus-yellow tram swayed and showered hibiscus blossoms onto the cruise ship dock below. The flowers floated in the air like the tops of tiny red umbrellas and landed gentle as breath. Val and I, on our way to the wharf in search of amusement to take my mind off the Dick-*vs*-Daddy dilemma, soaked up the enchantment, even if it wasn't meant for us.

It was meant for the pale-skinned strangers streaming past us on the sidewalk, wearing Bermuda shorts and puzzled expressions. American tourists from the cruise ship *Mariposa* searching for exotic mementos to display in their family rooms.

"Get a load of that one." Val jerked a thumb toward a man whose paunch spilled over white shorts that stopped a few inches above his black knee socks.

We looked at each other and snickered. We might be undeniably *palagi*, but we, more than these day-trippers, belonged here.

At the dock, a dozen Samoan women in matching red-and-white floral print *puletasis* sat cross-legged on pandanus mats before a large, hand-lettered sign that read "TALOFA—WELCOME" and was decorated with drawings of a kava bowl and Samoan and American flags. The women wore their hair twisted into tall buns that sat atop their heads like pineapples. Some had flowers tucked behind their ears, some wore necklaces of shells or seeds; all had taken care to look their best for the American visitors. Even more care had gone into practicing the songs and dances they would perform, not just on this day, but every day a cruise ship slid into port with a grace that seemed improbable for its heft.

The women, as robustly graceful as those ships, sang and clapped their hands in rhythm as tourists streamed by, some pausing to listen, most hurrying on to explore the island in the short time their itineraries allowed. I slowed down, but Val tugged at my arm. We had our own itinerary.

The *Mariposa's* towering, golden stack, emblazoned with an enormous navy blue letter M, beckoned. The rest of the ship was white and crisp as a sailor's hat, dazzling in the heat that softened the asphalt beneath our flip-flops and wafted the scent of drying copra through the air, a smothering blanket of sweetness and musk. Clutching passes that allowed us all-day access, Val and I headed straight for the ship's gangplank.

"Want to have some fun?" The tilt of Val's eyes was playful, and the curl above her eyebrow, bobbing in the breeze, looked alive. In the background, musicians drummed on old biscuit tins — *tat-tat-tatta-tat-ta-ta-ta-ta-tat* — and a young woman in a long grass skirt shook her hips so furiously they blurred. Val raised her voice to compete with the din. "When we get on the boat, pretend we're Samoan. If anyone talks to us in English, act like you don't understand, and speak Samoan."

"But I don't know that much Samoan," I protested.

The clatter gave way to a soft melody, sung in harmony with ukulele accompaniment. Val adjusted her volume to match the music's.

"No one's gonna know what we're saying. Just recite the Samoan anthem — you know, that song that comes on just before TV goes off for the night."

A sunburned couple shuffled down the gangplank, stopped beside us, and held out a map. Overhead, the cable car dumped another load of floral parachutes. The couple paid no attention.

"Which way to Fagatogo?" the man asked, butchering the pronunciation.

Val squinted at the map, then wrinkled the space between her eyebrows, looking first at the couple, then at me. I shrugged.

"*Amerika Samoa*," I said. "*Lo'u atunu'u pele oe!*"

Val picked up the anthem's second line: "*Oute tiu i lou igoa, o 'oe o lo'u fa'amoemoe.*" With my delicate features and Val's fair skin and russet curls, we looked no more Polynesian than the tourist couple did, but we thought we were convincing enough to pass as *afakasi*—half-Samoan, half-*palagi*.

"Oh," said the sunburned woman. "We'll find someone else to ask."

I watched them walk away—headed toward Utulei, not Fagatogo—and had an impulse to run after them and point them in the right direction. Instead, I waved and called out "*Amerika Samoa!*" Then turning to Val: "Stupid *palagi* tourists!"

Bored and hungry after an hour or so of touring *Mariposa*, of jabbering in ersatz Samoan, and stuffing souvenir cocktail napkins, matchbooks, and swizzle sticks into our purses, Val and I debarked and walked across town to our favorite hangout, Tropic Isle snack bar. A one-room café with a couple of gas pumps out front and a screen door that banged, Tropic Isle was the only place in town that served hamburgers, and though they weren't like hamburgers back home—the buns were homemade and heavily coated with mayonnaise, and the patties were thin as poker chips—they were nonetheless hamburgers, and we were American teenagers craving American teenager food.

Inside the café, an electric fan droned and stirred air that smelled of frying meat and fresh-baked bread. Two unsmiling Samoan women with towering chignons like those of the women at the dock stood behind a Formica-topped counter.

"Yesssssss?" said one, her eyes sweeping over Val and me with an indifference too deliberate to be truly indifferent.

"Can we get two hamburgers, two donuts, and two red pops?" I used my meekest voice and clasped my hands at my waist like a penitent. Val, hand on cocked hip, displayed a cheekier attitude.

The woman raised her eyebrows, turned away, and said something in Samoan to the other woman. I took that as a yes. It was a more accommodating response than we often got when we shopped in Fagatogo's general stores, where clerks routinely ignored us while waiting on a dozen Samoan customers who came in after we did. I never knew whether to act even nicer to the contemptuous clerks and grudging waitresses or to return their haughtiness with a dose of my own, as Val did. Neither strategy changed the outcome, and with each rebuff I shrank a little more into myself.

Still, the hamburgers satisfied our need for grease. The donuts—fresh, yeasty, and sprinkled with granulated sugar that crunched between our teeth—provided the perfect counterpoint to the red pop's fizz. We sat at a table beside an open window, in a mild stupor from the sugar and the fan's hum, and swigged the last of our pop, licking lingering sugar grains from our fingers as breezes lapped our faces and riffled our hair. We would've lingered, too, but the women's glares discouraged that, so we went looking for other diversions.

At another dock near the new hotel, where Coast Guard and Navy ships tied up, we found Suzi with her sidekick Kathi—small, spunky, with brown eyes set like polished river stones in a heart-shaped face, and a paint splatter of freckles across her nose. With the two girls was Suzi's older brother Karl, who had the same sharp features as his sister—a face that looked like it was assembled from spare elbows—and a personality to match. He stood talking to a sailor from a ship that had docked the day before.

"So, what's there to do here—besides get drunk at Pago Bar?" the sailor asked. A tuft of sand-colored hair drifted onto his forehead, and he swept it back with fingers held stiff like the tines of a comb.

"Get drunk at the Kava Cup," said Karl. His upper lip twisted in a way that reminded me of Suzi's smirk, but Karl was signaling something other than sarcasm: a kind of knowing, *stick-with-me-buddy* semaphore.

Diesel fumes masked the pastel scents that usually surfed in on breezes from the bay, and mechanical clanks and whirrs from the nearby ships drowned out the voices of the singers at the cruise ship dock.

"What about girls? How do you meet local girls?" the sailor wanted to know. Did he not see the four of us standing there? Or were we not the sort of girls he was interested in meeting?

"Funny you should ask," Suzi said. For once her expression resembled a real smile more than a sneer. I knew her well enough by now to doubt its sincerity. "See that girl over there?" She pointed toward a Samoan teenager walking by. A slender girl. A pretty girl. A seaman's stereotype of Polynesian perfection, right down to the flower behind her ear: a red hibiscus like the ones that rained down on tourists from the cable car. "She saw you in town today and told us she thinks you're cute."

Kathi nodded with exaggerated zeal. "Yeah, she said she'd like to meet you."

"Really?" The sailor twisted his head to look at the girl, then turned back to Suzi and Kathi, grinning like the tiki at my apartment's front door. "What do I have to do?"

Suzi and Kathi traded sly looks, but the sailor, swiveling to steal another look at the girl, missed them. Val and I looked at each other, too, clueless, but curious what the other girls were up to. This might be good.

The Samoan girl was close enough now for us to see her look of friendly interest—eyes widened, lips a curvaceous arc. The shipboard clamor had died down, and the singers' voices reached our ears again. Another load of flowers drifted downward, as if the sky had burst and begun delivering not pallid strangers from an unknown land, but things of beauty straight from heaven.

"Just call out to her," Suzi told the sailor. Then turning to Karl, "What's that girl's name again?"

"Mimi," Karl said. His lips contorted again. "Just yell, 'Mimi!' "

Anthems aside, my Samoan wasn't very good, and the word wasn't in my *Teach Yourself Samoan* book, but I was pretty sure *mimi* was a Samoan vulgarity related to genitalia.

Wait!

I didn't care if Suzi and the others messed with the sailor, but that girl—

No! Stop!

Though I had the urge to yell those words instead of only thinking them, to turn things around and point us all in a different direction, I hesitated. These were my new friends, and I was trying as hard to fit in with the expat kids as to be accepted by the Samoans.

The sailor's lips moved, forming a word. I couldn't will mine to open. Another moment passed, barely long enough to shoot a helpless glance at Val.

"MIMI!" the sailor shouted. "Hey! Mimi! Come here!"

The girl's face changed. Her mouth twisted, but not in the self-satisfied way that Karl's and Suzi's did; her eyes shifted left and right and then fixated on the path as she hurried away.

I could not presume to know how she felt. Traveling that same path, I'd been yelled at, too, but "sky burster"—though it stung as much as the gravel my flip-flops flung against my calves—was no match for what that girl had just been called.

I was not the one who'd been disgraced, yet I felt my shame growing like some strangling tropical vine, and I wished I could disappear through a slit in the heavens. Now it was clear to me why the Tropic Isle ladies and their sisters in the shops of

Fagatogo weren't singing any welcome songs to my friends and me.

We might shed our stateside clothes, we might pick up the language and legends, we might dress in *puletasis* and tuck blossoms behind our ears. But before we'd ever really belong here, we'd have to learn to harmonize.

Chapter 9 — Taboo

Taboo — also spelled tabu, Tongan tabu, Maori tapu, the prohibition of an action or the use of an object based on ritualistic distinctions of them either as being sacred and consecrated or as being dangerous, unclean, and accursed . . . Taboos were most highly developed in the Polynesian societies of the South Pacific, but they have been present in virtually all cultures.
— *Encyclopedia Britannica*

Val had something to show me. She wouldn't say what it was.

"You'll have to come over to my house," she said on the phone one night, her voice low, conspiratorial, "when Mom's not home."

After school the next day, when our mothers were playing bridge with the other expat women, we headed straight to the Pucketts' house. Instead of ushering me to her room as usual, Val led me around to the back. Like all the houses on Centipede Row, the Pucketts' sat on concrete piers so high you could walk in a crouch beneath the structure. Val disappeared between two piers, her bouncing auburn curls like a headful of beckoning fingers.

"Would you mind telling me what we're doing down here?" I swatted cobwebs. "It's creepy."

"You'll see." Val reached into a space at the top of a post and pulled out a sheaf of onionskin stationery with typing on each page. She handed me the manuscript. "You gotta read this."

I scanned a few pages and saw words I'd never seen in print and a few I'd never even heard. I hoped the dim light would conceal the flush that bled across my cheeks and around the tops of my ears.

"Where'd you get this?"

Val smiled. Her eyes slanted wickedly in the semi-darkness. She told me that during a stopover in Hawaii on the way to Samoa, her family had met the family that had just moved out of the house the Pucketts were moving into. Their teenage son had told Val about the hidden book, a typed copy of a paperback another kid had swiped from his parents' bedroom.

The pages softened, almost melted, in my damp hands. "You haven't told anyone else, have you?"

Val's look could've withered a taro patch.

"Please. If I tell the other girls, it'll be all over the island. Mom will find out for sure."

That we did not want.

We both lived in fear of Mrs. Puckett's wrath. Sweeping imperiously around the island in floor-length muumuus that exaggerated, more than concealed, her broad hips and torpedo breasts, she was one scary woman. It wasn't just her size; it was her eyes, a look that made me think she knew things about me that my own mother didn't know, things I hadn't even done but might want to do. And her smile. It was the smile of a woman — a *woman* — who was absolutely sure of herself, afraid of nothing and no one. She should have been an inspiration, but with her bold pulchritude and sheer amplitude, Mrs. Puckett personified everything about womanhood that terrified me.

We huddled under the house, reading silently, the hush broken only by gasps at vivid passages. What astonished me was not just the language, but also the power of mere words on a page to elicit sensations — surges of warmth, throbs that ached, shivering twinges — in the strangest places.

Though the book's content was steamy, the writing was laughably bad, even by our sophomoric standards. We immediately appropriated the silliest lines for our own inside jokes.

I glanced at my watch. "Won't your mom be home soon?"

Val nodded. "Let's go downtown, if you have any money, that is."

"I think I have a few pennies in my purse," I said, borrowing a line from the book and setting her up to deliver the punch line.

Val leaned close and, in her best imitation of lechery, breathed, "Sweetheart, you've got a gold mine in your pants."

At home in Utulei, I had my own clandestine reading material. It wasn't smutty like Val's, and my parents probably wouldn't have grounded me if they'd found it. Still, I felt the need to keep it under wraps.

I'd developed a ritual for reading my special book. First, I changed into my *lavalava*, a midnight blue sarong with a border of white philodendron leaves and hibiscus blossoms. Next, I selected a record, slipped it from its jacket, and centered it on my stereo's turntable. My mood music wasn't the Beach Boys or any of the other albums I'd brought with me from Oklahoma. It was a compilation of Samoan songs I'd bought at South Pacific Traders.

From my stereo speakers, Samoan quartets and choruses sang about flowers and doves and chanted staccato incantations to summon sharks from the depths, all accompanied by guitar strums, ukulele riffs, hand claps, whoops, and clattering sticks on hollowed-out logs. Sometimes I skipped over boisterous tracks to play songs that made me feel pleasantly heavy-hearted, with lyrics about searching for love, finding love, and losing it, only to search again. In some songs the object of desire was an elusive lover; others were songs of farewell written to Samoa itself, testaments to the islands' haunting sweetness and the anguish of leaving the homeland behind to travel overseas.

Once the atmosphere was right, I turned the music low, dug through my underwear drawer, and extracted my book: *Coming of Age in Samoa*, anthropologist Margaret Mead's classic study of "primitive" youth, based on her field work in the islands during the 1920s. I pored over its pages, absorbing as much as I could about the mores of Samoan society. Most fascinating were Mead's discussions of taboos: practices that were forbidden, not because they were indecent or immoral, but because they were too sacred for ordinary people to engage in, or in some cases simply because of practical considerations. Taboos weren't all about sex, as I'd always thought. Mead wrote about "taboo fish" that had to be relinquished to the village chief and a host of pregnancy taboos that forbade expectant mothers from sitting, dancing, gathering food, or eating alone.

She also wrote a lot about sex. About adolescents slipping away for clandestine, "under the palm trees" encounters, about stealthy elopements and formal courtships, and about *moetotolo* — sleep crawling — in which boys spurned by day crept into girls' *fales* at night to commit rape. Mead concluded that Americans might be better off adopting certain Samoan habits and attitudes — not the sexual assaults, but the practice of looking the other way when consenting young couples stole off to the coconut grove.

Referring to American adolescents, she wrote: "The present problem of the sex experimentation of young people would be greatly simplified if it were conceived of as experimentation instead of rebellion, if no Puritan self-accusations vexed their consciences."

When I read those words, listening to songs about love and longing, with frangipani-charged breezes stirring teenage desires, I had to agree. This anthropologist the Samoans called *Makelita* already had my respect for venturing off to the South Seas when she was only twenty three; now I idolized her even more for championing sexual freedom and chastising overly protective parents.

Sexual freedom and overprotective parents were still on my mind a few days later, when I noticed the woman sitting alone in a dingy café. The shape of her face, framed by hair that streamed and glowed like hot lava, reminded me of someone else. But who?

I'd seen the woman when I first entered the café with the gang of girls I'd come to think of as my tribe—a shifting pack that always included some combination of my schoolmates Val-the-cynic, Wendy-the-wit, snide Suzi, perky Kathi, not-a-mean-bone Marnie, and hair-obsessed Sylvia. It was Friday of the second week of classes, and already we'd established an after-school routine: wandering Fagatogo's cluster of shops, trying on cheap, plastic jewelry, browsing through the latest shipment of record albums from the States, and stopping for Fantas at a local eatery.

This afternoon, we'd just appropriated a table when Marnie nudged me and nodded toward the woman. "That's Dick's mother."

Of course. That same, flattened face my father had compared to the hideous tiki's head. I tried not to stare, but stole glances when the woman looked away. She wore bright colors that clashed with her hair, and she smoked a cigarette—not in the slow, stylish way my mother sometimes smoked after dinner, but sucking the smoke in and puffing it out the side of her mouth.

Oh God, wouldn't you know she smokes like a chimney — and has long hair. Red, too, probably dyed. I could imagine my father's reaction to this dame, who not only kept a boarding house full of single men, but also violated his standards of appearance and behavior acceptable for a lady. Never mind that Dick also had a father with a respectable Public Works Department job. In my father's eyes, I might as well be dating the son of Sadie Thompson.

I desperately hoped my parents hadn't yet encountered Dick's mother. Even if not, I had a feeling the omniscient Mrs. Puckett had given them a full rundown. I suspected that was how they knew I'd been sneaking rides on the back of Dick's motorcycle, a Honda like the one Elvis (another bad influence) rode in *Roustabout*.

No doubt Mrs. Puckett had reported on Dick's profanity, too. It wasn't that he used an impressive range of swear words. He just found a way to integrate a particularly earthy few into nearly every sentence. He carried this off with an attitude that projected not so much defiance as entitlement, as if impropriety were such an integral a part of his being, speaking any other way would be false. As if to underscore his identification with the obscene, he insisted on being called not "Richard," not "Rick," but "Dick." Marnie and I tried calling him "Richie" for several days, around the same time we talked him into letting us comb his hair into an eyebrow-grazing, Beach Boys style. At first he went along with both makeover attempts—loving the attention, no doubt—but before long he'd reverted to his swept-back hairstyle and to being, incontrovertibly, a Dick.

Evening came, and with it another routine: a stop at the tennis court to see who was out and about, then on to Suzi's house, which served the same social function as the tennis court but in a less public setting. The Jorgensen kids—Suzi, Karl, and their younger brother Nat—had connections to everyone in our school, thanks to the age range they spanned, and every demographic was represented at these nightly gatherings at "Jorg's pad." The older boys showed up on the pretense of visiting Karl, knowing all the girls would be there with Suzi, while Nat gave the preteen crowd an excuse for hanging around us teenagers, alternately spying and trying to fit in.

Whether or not Mr. and Mrs. Jorgensen were home, they seemed not to care what went on in the house, so beer, cigarettes, and loud music were the adjuncts to all sorts of fooling around. We girls styled each other's hair, spun records, and danced. The boys—Karl, Dick, a charmingly gangly boy named Eric, the Vampires' Beatle-haired drummer Pili, slow-mo Fibber, and several other Samoans and *palagis* from the tennis

court crowd — smoked, swigged their beers, and teased us. Once
in a while an amorous couple would sneak away to a screened-
in sleeping porch off the living room. Before long the rest of us
would hear shrieks and the clatter of feet and know that Nat had
slipped in unnoticed and dumped cold water on the lovers.

These evenings followed a pattern, in that the same cast of
characters showed up every night and engaged in predictable
behaviors. But the nights also carried the overarching sense that
unexpected things could happen. We were, after all, a bunch of
adolescent males and females with all the attendant impulsivity,
fickleness, and colossally poor judgment.

If even ordinary nights had an open-ended, expectant air,
this night held still greater promise. Suzi had invited the girls for
a sleepover, sure to devolve into an all-night party with boys,
beer, and exploits we'd whisper and giggle about later. Parental
restraints would be breached. Rules would be violated. Webs of
secrets — and alibis to conceal them — would be woven.

It wasn't my first experience with boys at a girls' slumber
party. There'd been times in Stillwater when guys showed up
after midnight, knocking on windows for brief rendezvous with
girls who seemed unfazed at being caught in their baby-doll PJs
and sponge-rollered hair. This night would be different. Boys,
my new boyfriend included, could conceivably stay the whole
night. They could *sleep* with us, and even if it was only literal
sleeping, we'd be crossing a line I'd never crossed. A line I was
certain my parents did not want me to cross.

Suzi slid a record onto the turntable and set the needle on
the first track.

*They say we're young, and we don't know, won't find out until
we grow*, Sonny Bono intoned. I glanced at Dick sprawled on the
sofa, jeans stretched across narrow hips. He was already looking
my way.

I swayed in time with the music, self-consciously at first,
but then with a growing boldness that set off sensations like
those I'd felt while reading Val's secret book. Suzi and Kathi

picked up the beat; one by one, the other girls joined in, and by the time Cher was belting out "Then He Kissed Me," we were all undulating like crazy in our flowered shifts, copying each other's moves and experimenting with new ones. Breezes slipped through the living room's screened walls to stroke our hair and play across our bare arms and legs. Smoke from the boys' cigarettes blended with the bay's fishy fragrance and the Evening in Paris cologne we girls had dabbed on our pulse points. I locked eyes with Dick—no more timid glances now. The sensations grew stronger.

Outside, couples strolled along the sidewalk that ran behind the houses, but inside we were so engaged in dancing and flirting and imagining the night ahead, we weren't aware of any other activity. When the screen door slammed open, we all started as if shots had been fired. Val's mother stood in the doorway, her figure filling the frame. She looked around the room, at Dick and the other boys scrambling to stash beer bottles behind sofa pillows, at the girls frozen mid-watusi.

"Valerie, you're coming home with me. Now."

Her voice was not loud; it didn't need to be. Her posture and mass carried enough gut-roiling authority. Val turned toward us and rolled her eyes. Her hair, normally a riot of exuberant unruliness, clumped in damp strands around her face. I shot her a *tough luck, kid* glance and pressed against the wall, impersonating a shadow. Across the room, Dick looked like he was trying not to laugh.

"You, too, Nancy," Val's mother said, menace beneath her controlled calm. "You know very well your parents wouldn't approve of this monkey business. You can spend the night with Val."

Now I was the target of the other girls' pitying looks and the boys' snickers. Without making eye contact with each other or anyone else, Val and I slunk out the door and down the sidewalk behind her mother, the two of us filled with shame more burning than we would have felt for any of the forbidden things we'd considered doing that night.

My parents said nothing about the slumber party when I came home from Val's the next day. But when Dick called that evening, my father appeared beside the phone the moment I hung up. The lips that angled up at the corners when he told one of his funny stories now leveled into a pair of tight lines. I knew that look. It made my stomach feel like a fist.

"I don't want you seeing that boy anymore," he said.

"Fine," I said. "It's not like we're really dating."

That was technically true. Dick and I kept company at every opportunity, but we usually met up somewhere instead of going there together. Since we didn't go on actual dates, I reasoned, we weren't actually dating.

"I mean I don't want you even talking to him. That boy's bad news, and his mother's a disgrace, living out there with all those men. I won't have you associating with people like that."

My fingernails dug into my palms as I pushed past my father and stumbled toward the door, nearly colliding with the tiki Double Ugly and muttering to myself. Who *could* live up to his standards?

Val showed sympathy with nods and murmurs when I burst into her room and spewed out the story.

"What're you going to do?"

"I don't know—throw myself off a cliff into the *sami*?" I used the Samoan word for "sea" because it sounded more dramatic.

"How about we go to the movies instead? They're showing *Zulu* at the Rec Hall." She pulled me up from the bed where I'd flopped and steered me out the door and down the path toward Fagatogo's business district.

Clamor and bright light engulfed us when we entered the community center's makeshift movie theater. But even with the commotion, I couldn't stop thinking about the conversation with my father.

Why can't he just look the other way, like Margaret Mead says?

Just before the lights dimmed, Dick slid into the empty seat beside me and draped an arm across the top of my shoulders. Without looking at him I blurted, "I have to talk to you." Then, in a voice stretched thin: "But I don't really know how to say what I have to tell you."

"Is it bad?"

"I think it is." My words felt like they were coming from a character in some crappy movie I'd been cast in against my will.

"Will I think so?" Dick leaned forward, turned toward me, and tried to position his face in front of mine. I kept my eyes fixed on the opening credits.

"Maybe. I don't know." I did know. I just hoped he wouldn't care enough to be wounded.

"Well, if it's something like I can't see you anymore, then it's very bad," Dick tried again to make eye contact.

I exhaled and turned to face him. "Yeah. That's what it is."

I waited for Dick to say something, do something — smash his fist into the back of the chair in front of him, swear, stand up and walk out. But he just slouched in his seat, arms crossed, head down, silent. Finally he reached for my hand. "Let's go."

He led me to the shadowy end of the building and leaned against the wall, a freshly lit cigarette glowing between his fingers. I stood close to him and replayed in my mind other shadowed scenes: that first night at the tennis court, the stroll down Centipede Row's palm-lined sidewalk after the dance at Goat Island Club. The atmosphere of this night was the same, but the feeling was stripped of sweetness.

I told him my parents had heard rumors about him, that my mother's bridge club friends had warned her he was "a troublemaker," and that she'd "better watch him." I had no idea what offenses Dick supposedly had committed; my parents refused to discuss the details, and I didn't know if that was because Dick's misdeeds were so heinous or because the rumors were so vague.

"I know about the rumors," Dick said, "but I haven't done anything bad here."

Before I thought to ask if that meant he'd done something bad elsewhere, he continued in a voice that had lost its swagger and sounded more like a whimper.

"I wanted you to go steady with me. I was going to ask you to take this." He took off his ring and held it out to me. It shone dully in the faint light.

Through the theater wall came the muted, pulsating rhythm of Zulus beating their spears against their shields, a sound that approximated the feeling in my chest. I shook my head.

"Go ahead, take it. You don't have to wear it. Just take it." His face looked even more compressed than usual.

"I can't." I felt bad saying it. Bad, as in one emotion like a blistering red coal and another like a burr. Hot, hot anger at my father for forcing me into this role; prickling guilt for not hurting as much as Dick had to be hurting. No one was rejecting *me*, no one was questioning *my* worth.

My eyes darted back and forth between Dick's crumpled face and the road, where I half expected to see my father appear at any minute, cruising by to check up on me. I chafed at his intrusions, longed to experience a world without restrictions, where I could be the bold adventurer of my childhood fantasies. But when it came right down to it, I wasn't brave enough to take a single defiant step, even if my cowardice meant crushing the feelings of someone I cared about.

"I've gotta get back inside," I said. "You should leave now." Dick reached for my hand. I backed away. "I mean it. Go."

For the next week, Dick followed me around between classes and after school, begging me in that pitiful voice to take the ring, asking what he could do to make my parents like him.

"What if I cut my hair?" he'd ask. "What if I quit smoking?"

I didn't know what to say. Changing his hairstyle and habits wouldn't sway my parents; it would only make him less himself. Whenever I thought of Dick now, I pictured him behind a sign like the one that stood at the entry to the governor's driveway. *UA SA*, it read: *FORBIDDEN*. There was no questioning its authority, no asking for explanations. My parents' edict, in my mind, was just as inflexible. But like an off-limits sign that tempts trespassers, my parents' prohibition made the forbidden more desirable, and the drama heightened my emotions. If I was infatuated before, I was love-crazed now. I wrote tormented entries in my diary and mooned over the picture hidden between its pages: a photo booth shot of Dick and a friend mugging with cigarettes dangling from their lips.

At the end of that week, Sylvia threw a party at her house on a hillside overlooking the village of Pava'ia'i, fifteen miles from my parents' eyes and Mrs. Puckett's meddling. Sylvia's parents treated their daughter and her friends far more leniently than Val's and mine did—her dad openly shared his beer with the guys, and her mom didn't rat us out to the other moms—so the atmosphere was relaxed and drenched in the smell of the chicken mole and homemade tortillas Mrs. Vallez was whipping up for us.

The other girls and I clustered around the stereo, ears close to speakers, and played one track of one album over and over. It wasn't Sonny and Cher this time, and the beat and lyrics weren't the source of our fascination. I'd discovered a place on the *Beach Boys Today!* album where one of the Beach Boys spoke a few words in a voice that sounded exactly like Dick's: high pitched, but with enough sandy grit to abrade any hint of femininity. My friends, bless them, indulged me as I wallowed in longing for the banned boy.

I tried not to notice as boys began arriving, but wavelets of anticipation swelled and flattened every time the door opened and someone other than Dick entered. Just as we were loading our plates with chicken, beans, and tortillas, a motorcycle hummed up the driveway. The engine clicked off. Dick walked in, blond hair bouncing in time with his step. He grabbed a fork from the table and playfully tried to snitch a bite of refried beans from my plate.

"Can I have some?" he asked in the Beach Boys voice. "Oh, that's right, you can't talk to me. Val, ask Nancy if I can have some of her beans." He was his irreverent self again, teasing and scoffing at adult censure. I couldn't help smiling, buoyed by his defiance and a similar attitude ballooning in me.

After dinner, there was dancing, drinking, smoking, kissing, and cuddling in dim corners—a scene that played out much as I'd imagined the night at Suzi's would. A Beach Boys album played on the stereo, but instead of straining to hear a snippet that sounded like the boy I'd fallen for, I slow danced with the boy himself as five other Californians harmonized:

Now here we are together,
This would have been worth waiting forever.
I always knew it'd feel this way.

Toward midnight, Dick and I slipped out to sit on the darkened hillside below the house. We kissed. We kissed some more. The kisses tasted of beer and cigarettes and inflamed youth, all now familiar to my tongue. The night air streamed around us like a blood-warm ocean; we floated in its currents. Kisses grew longer. Hands ignored posted warnings and rushed headlong into restricted areas.

In the midst of all that nicotine-tinged kissing and clutching, an uninvited image flashed into my mind: my father's disapproving face, hard-edged and contracted. A stab of guilt followed. Then a fleeting thought: *Is this really* wrong, *or just forbidden?*

Another face appeared and blotted out my father's scowl. It was the face of a woman, now sixty-something, I'd seen on television a year or so before. It was that feisty, freethinking anthropologist, *Makelita*. And she was smiling.

Chapter 10 — Anthropology

Said Tagaloa, "To each of you from above I now impart a will. Your faces they must shine, I so ordain. That they may Tagaloa entertain."
— Frederic Koehler Sutter, Amerika Samoa: An Anthropological Photo Essay

Makelita's face and the mountaintop make-out session were fresh in my memory the next afternoon when I curled up on my bed to record the previous evening's events in my ivory-and-gold leatherette Every Day Diary. With emerald green ink loaded into my cartridge pen, I meticulously printed the date in the designated space. Then, pen poised on page, I hesitated. I wanted to preserve every ardent moment for all time, but I sensed my parents, always on alert, might be tempted to peek at my private thoughts.

My parents. Their rules and expectations—borne of Baptist Bible study and middle-class propriety—were maddeningly confining to a girl all set to experience the world. I wanted to shake loose of their code of conduct, yet what would I substitute in its place? I knew of no guidebook telling a girl like me how to grow into the kind of woman I hoped to become. Fearless like Val's mom, but with a touch of my mother's restraint. Decent. Dignified. But *alive* and *free.*

I stared at my hands and twisted my Tri Chi ring, talisman and emblem of the girl I'd been before I came to Samoa. Back in Oklahoma, my moral compass received weekly adjustments at Baptist Training Union meetings, which I willingly attended, being more inclined toward righteousness at the time. Training Union was like Sunday school, except that instead of learning

Bible stories and verses, we discussed moral and ethical dilemmas—in the form of hypothetical scenarios—with our leader Evelyn, a college girl who was close to our ages and so much cooler than our parents. Though I'm sure the lessons were structured to lead us to Baptist-approved conclusions, the discussions at least made us think we were thinking for ourselves.

Those meetings with Evelyn gave me a sense of right and wrong that stuck with me, but with no Baptist church in Samoa, my principles no longer got weekly tune-ups. Lacking handbook or regular tutelage, I turned to my anthropologist idol, Margaret Mead. Not her book—it was forty years old and mostly about a culture to which I didn't belong—but her example. In the spirit of *Makelita*, I resolved to become a student of human behavior, specifically adult behavior, in hopes of finding some worth emulating.

I didn't have to wait long to begin my field work: my parents and I were invited to dinner at another doctor's home on Penicillin Row that evening.

"I'm sure Edith will be in fine form tonight," my father said as we walked from our apartment complex to the row of houses across the road.

My mother grimaced. "I just hope she doesn't corner me. You'll rescue me, won't you?"

"Oh, gawwwwd, yes, darling!" My father's voice rose a decibel, and his words came out slurred. I whipped around to see what was wrong; then he grinned and I realized he was impersonating the party hostess.

"I'm serious, Harold," my mother hissed. Then turning to me, "If Mrs. Finley gets me in a corner, and I give you a sign like this"—she tapped her cheekbone with her index finger—"come and tell me you're sick and need to go home."

So, deception is acceptable under certain circumstances. I made a mental note.

Before my father could knock on the front door, Dr. Finley, flushed and amiable, greeted us and escorted us into the living room. With canvas curtains pulled back to let breezes through the screens, the spacious room looked and felt like the living rooms in Suzi's and Val's houses, but the view, across the mouth of the bay to Mount Rainmaker's flocked-velvet slopes, was more Bali Ha'i-ish. Dr. Finley offered my parents a drink; they asked for old fashioneds (they were *that* kind of Baptists, and they danced and played cards, too), and our host headed for a small table that held a bacchanalian still life of liquor bottles, ice bucket, and tumblers.

Mrs. Finley, an angular woman whose exaggerated facial features looked like caricatures of themselves, lifted her glass, her reddened lips curving up at the corners like a panting dog's.

"Oh, A-r-r-r-r-r-nold!" Her husband's name came out like a whine. "Get me one, too, while you're up."

Dr. Finley took the glass, refilled it, and handed it back, all without looking at his wife. Then, serving my parents their cocktails, he put on the cordial face again, but his smile involved only his mouth. His eyes expressed something else—a flicker of apology? A plea for sympathy?

Subject appears conflicted, I noted. *Resentment is evident, but not outwardly displayed.*

Dr. Finley took a seat on the rattan couch—identical to ours—and made small talk about progress on the new hotel down the road.

"Oh gawwwd, A-r-r-r-r-r-nold," Mrs. Finley wailed. "I'm sick to death of hearing about that damn hotel. Who the hell's going to come to this godforsaken heap of lava for a hawl-i-daaay?" She laughed, a long bray, and—*clunk*—set her glass on the coffee table. Liquid sloshed over the rim and left a puddle that she made no attempt to wipe up. "I mean, am I right, or am I r-i-i-i-ght?"

I watched my parents, prepared to record their reactions. My mother, eyes lowered, swirled a swizzle stick around her drink. My father smiled with closed lips. "I guess time will tell, won't it, Edith?"

Committed as I was to my anthropological project, the conversation made me squirmy, and I wasn't the only one. The Finleys' daughter Paula, a year ahead of me in school, stood and reached for my hand. "Come on, I'll show you my room. We can listen to records." Her eyes had the same look as her father's.

Over the next few days I expanded my observations to Samoans I encountered on the footpath, in the schoolyard, on the open-air buses that ran from one end of the island to the other, and in the villages through which we passed. The men and women I met on the path carried woven palm baskets of bananas and breadfruit from the market in town and were friendlier than the shopkeepers and waitresses. They'd raise and lower their eyebrows in the classic Samoan eyebrow flash, an expression of acknowledgement, and sometimes hail me with "*Malō!*" —hello. I didn't know these people, knew nothing of their home lives, but in their broad-footed gaits and the regularity of their daily routines, I found a reassuring steadiness.

On Sunday drives, I saw women, generous in girth and gracious in bearing, ambling down the road in their white *puletasis*, matching parasols held decorously over their heads, on their way to the whitewashed churches that anchored every village. In town on weekdays, I watched bare-chested men in flowered *lavalavas* husking coconuts at the dock and briefcase-toting men in dark *lavalavas*, suit coats, and closed-toe, leather sandals coming and going from the *Fono*, the territorial legislature. In the schoolyard, pairs of Samoan girls my age, pigtailed and dressed in full-skirted cotton frocks, strolled hand-in-hand in an unselfconscious show of friendship. Just below the surface of all this everyday activity wriggled a playfulness that erupted with the slightest nudge into uninhibited laughter. On the bus, in the villages, outside the shops of Fagatogo, everywhere I went, I saw people of all ages teasing and swatting each other, shrieking and doubling over with hilarity.

No wonder *Makelita* was drawn to these people. They were magnificent.

In the Samoan creation myth, the Creator Tagaloa placed the Peopling Vine on a council ground and left it in the sun until masses of worms slithered from it. Tagaloa shredded the worms into strips he fashioned into a human head, face, body, arms, and legs. Then he added heart and spirit and produced four people who went on to populate the land. The longer I observed the Samoans around me, the more convinced I became that these people, who could behave gravely through a kava ceremony but would collapse into giggles over a runaway pig, who were fashioned from a wondrous multitude of earthly worms and furnished with heart and soul from the heavens, were among the Creator's finest works. Strong, decent, dignified, but *alive* and *free*, Samoans were everything I wanted to be.

My own people, the *palagi* expats, maybe not. Yet the irony was, my Samoan friends seemed to want to emulate *us*.

I gathered more anthropological data during a beach party at Tafuna Lagoon, a waist-deep, bathwater-warm inlet near the airport and the government housing where many *palagi* contract workers and their families lived. Wendy and I had spread our towels on the sand and stretched out to deepen our baby-oil-and-iodine-enhanced tans.

"Tafuna is a weird place, Nance," Wendy said, her voice sleepily sun-dazed. "I mean, here we are sunbathing by a lagoon straight out of National Geographic, but just around the bend are houses that look like they were airlifted out of some Bay Area housing tract. It's suburbia all over again." Her face screwed up as she gestured toward rows of identical one-story units.

"What's wrong with that?" I asked, not sure I'd ever seen or set foot in a suburb. "I think the houses out here are kind of neat." I pictured the interior of the one Wendy's family lived in, with its beamed ceilings and clean, contemporary lines.

"Okay. But perhaps you've noticed they're all alike?" Wendy said, sarcasm lifting her eyebrows.

"So? All the Utulei apartments are alike, but that doesn't bother me."

Samoan *fales* were all the same, too, and for good reason, according to legend. Long ago, Samoans built houses in different shapes, but each builder specialized in one design. This caused problems when someone wanted a particular style of house but the only builder who knew how to construct that type was busy. Unable to agree on a uniform shape, the builders appealed to Tagaloa, the Creator. He pointed to the dome of heaven extending down to the horizon and decreed that all houses be built in that shape. Hence, the round *fale* with its convex roof and poles reaching down to the ground.

So, if Tagaloa ordained it, homogeneous housing couldn't be all that bad. "Really, what's the big deal?" I asked.

Wendy pressed her lips together and waited for words to take shape. She peered through her glasses toward the tidy neighborhood in the distance and shook her head as if dislodging disturbing thoughts.

"Okay, it's not just how the houses look, it's what living in a place like this does to people. Some people. It's like the anonymity of the neighborhood makes them feel anonymous, too—like they can get away with things they wouldn't do if everybody knew what they were up to. But see, the thing is, everybody *does* know what they're up to, because this is a small community, and everybody talks about everybody else."

"I wish I knew what *you* were talking about," I said. I felt eclipsed by Wendy's worldliness. She moved as easily in adult circles as among peers and had an assortment of more mature friends—young wives, oddball bachelors, and other lonely neighbors—who confided in her.

"Let's just say—" Wendy paused and let her perfect pageboy swing forward to curtain her face. "—there's a reason they call these places *bedroom* communities."

"Ohhhh," I said. "Kinda like Peyton Place?" Now that I thought about it, there *had* been whisperings around school—something about "wife swapping" and "swingers" in that outwardly bland community out by the airport. Rumors about some of my classmates' parents, in fact.

I wondered what else lay beneath the surface and what drove people to do such things. Was it simply lust, or were they, like me, hooked on novelty and the thrill of the forbidden? And if we were alike in that way, in what other ways was I like these people?

It was something to think about. Despite my ideals of decency and dignity, I was more concerned these days with deception, sneaking around to see Dick and encrypting my diary entries in case my parents went snooping. I used a code my junior high friend Judy and I had devised to exchange notes about Mr. Banfield, the social studies teacher and wrestling coach, whose solid shoulders and gummy smile had us aflutter. The code wasn't exactly impenetrable—we just substituted Greek letters and a few made-up symbols for the Latin counterparts (κισσ for "kiss," for example)—but it was so tedious to decode we figured no one would bother trying. So when I wrote in my diary the day after Sylvia's party, I reported in ordinary English all the innocent stuff—who was there, what a good time we had—but then added: Δικ τολδ με ηε λο7εδ με ανδ I βελιε7ε τηατ, documenting that Dick had declared his love and I was convinced of his sincerity.

I was also engaged in another ruse, with my parents and the governor's teenage son Carlson as unwitting accomplices. Carlson was tinny-voiced and short—maybe five feet tall, maybe not quite—and reminded me of Mickey Rooney in those old movies where Mickey played the spunky little guy putting on backyard shows with Judy Garland. With Carlson's automatic yes-ma'am, no-sir, please-and-thank-you manners, the governor's son had the bearing of a kid who'd spent his childhood in the company of adults who expected him to act just like them. For that—and for being the governor's son, and for being anyone but Dick—my parents adored him. Consequently, any time Carlson invited me, alone or with friends, to go for a ride in his father's chauffeur-driven stretch limousine, my parents shooed me off with their blessings.

"Floor it, Tuke!" Carlson would order the driver, an impassive Samoan man, and we'd be off to Tafuna Lagoon or Larsen's Beach for an afternoon of swimming and sunning. Apparently it didn't occur to my parents that Dick, though never a passenger in the limo, would make his way to these beach parties, and that the strength of my resolve to keep distance between us ebbed and surged with the tides.

This very day, I'd ridden in the governor's car out to the lagoon, where Dick, Fibber, and some other kids waited. As I emerged from the limo with Carlson and crew, Dick leaned against a palm tree and watched me with a narrow look that was hard to categorize: equal parts aloof, appraising, amused, and amorous. His stance—weight shifted onto one slim hip, head cocked—conveyed the same mix of attitudes. We chatted awhile, flirty, teasing talk, then he splashed into the lagoon, and I stretched out with Wendy on the shore.

Now, as I lazed on the beach, my mind replayed the conversation with Wendy, the dinner at the Finleys', my other anthropological observations. *Palagis,* I concluded, were a blight on the island, a corrupting influence far worse than any long-haired, cigarette-smoking boy with a motorcycle. But did that excuse my deceptions?

Dick dropped onto the towel beside me and gave my arm a playful punch. Sand clung to his skin and scratched me when we touched.

"Hey, girl from Nowhere." His eyes disappeared into crinkles. "Let's get outta here and go Somewhere. Anywhere. I've got the bike."

It was late afternoon, and the Tafuna kids were drifting back to their look-alike homes. Carlson and the other kids from town gathered up towels, suntan lotion, and snacks as Tuke stood by.

I brushed grains of sand from Dick's arm and avoided his eyes. "You know I can't do that," I said. "I have to go back to town with Carlson."

Dick's face unfolded and hardened. "Can't do that," he mocked. "Can't do this. Can't go on the bike. Can't go out with me. Can't talk to me. What the hell can you do?"

A low, mechanical mutter signaled Tuke had started the limo. Car doors opened with a metallic complaint, and kids piled in amid gales of laughter. Glancing up, I saw Carlson motion for me to come on.

"I don't know." I stared at my hands and worried my Tri Chi ring. "I guess that's what I'm trying to figure out." I was living out one of those Baptist Training Union scenarios. I wished I had Evelyn to lead me through it.

"Well, when you *do* know, let *me* know." With that, Dick stood and brushed himself off. I looked up at him, but already he was walking away, a featureless silhouette backlit by tropical sun. Moments later, the bike whirred and Dick sped off, headed for somewhere I would not be going. Not today, at least.

Chapter 11 — Language Lessons

matagofie	beautiful
motu	island
gagana	language
mātua	parent
ita	anger

"Sunday, October 10, 1965. We're sending along a few of our better slides to show you some of the sights on the island."

My father spoke into the microphone of a portable tape recorder. A projector set up on the dining table beamed a bright square onto the cinder block wall. He clicked a button on the projector, and a scene of verdant peaks and shimmering water replaced the square of light.

"This view is what greeted us when we first arrived from the airport, at Utulei, near Pago Pago. This was taken from just off our front step, facing toward the bay and the mountains on the opposite side."

The projector's click punctuated the travelogue my father was recording to mail with the slides to relatives in the States, and as he continued his narration, I noticed the way he drew out his words in a voice languid as a stroll down the streets of a small town. He still used a schoolteacher's diction and grammar, combined with the measured delivery of a doctor accustomed to calming anxious patients.

"This is looking across the *malae*, or city square, in the main business district of Fagatogo, which is the downtown part of Pago Pago. Beyond the *malae* are Haleck's and Kneubuhl's and several other general merchandise stores. Also, the Pago Pago Angel Den bar is over there."

He stumbled over the word *malae* the first time, but pronounced it perfectly on the second try. It was the way he said "downtown," though, that made me take note. I remembered him telling me how his mother used to try to purge him and his siblings of their Oklahoma accents before visits to relatives in Iowa. She'd make them practice saying, "I'm going downtown to shop around" until they could pronounce *downtown* with only two syllables instead of four. Over the years, my grandmother's elocution lessons had worn off, and my father had slipped back into the cadence and twang of western Oklahoma. I hadn't noticed until now.

He paused and clicked the button on the projector, and another scene slid onto the wall. In the reflected light, I studied my father's face—the upturned nose, hazel eyes, and heavy eyebrows I'd inherited; the full, wide lips I wished I had. Except for a fan of lines at the outer corners of his eyes and silver streaks in his dark hair, he showed few signs of his fifty-two years. The laugh lines and graying temples made him more handsome, I thought. Distinguished, my mother said.

"This is the newly completed marketplace. Another part of the market has stainless steel bins for the fruits and vegetables, but we chose to get this view because the natives were sitting Samoan-fashion on the floor."

The *natives*? The word conjured up mental pictures of wild-eyed savages with bones in their hair, awaiting a meal of stewed missionary, not the fine men and women in the photo my father was describing.

The projector made a shuffling sound, and a new scene appeared.

"This is the view from our back door, looking up the mountain . . . and this is one of the many Samoan houses stacked on the mountain behind us. You can also see the rising smoke from one of their cooking fires, which is very common."

The house in the picture was neither a traditional *fale* nor a modern frame dwelling, but a mere wooden shack with chickens running around outside. In the mornings, when sunlight seeped over the mountains and the rooster crowed, I often saw an old, *lavalava*-clad man sitting in front of the house. A native, sitting Samoan fashion, my father would say. I assumed the man lived alone, except for the chickens, so I was stunned one day when, walking me home from school, Fibber — that hipster clown from the tennis court crowd — pointed to the shack and told me that was where he lived.

I tried to picture him getting dressed for parties in such a setting — shining his Beatle boots, styling his coppery pompadour — but the images were too incongruous. The knowledge that Fibber could look down on my apartment from his hillside home made me feel a special bond with him, though. And the feeling seemed to be mutual: he often stopped by our doorstep to chat and sometimes accepted my invitation to come inside and listen to records or do homework together. I'd been seeing less of Dick since the Tafuna beach party, and I welcomed the company. Fibber's from-the-neighborhood status carried some weight with my parents, too, who viewed him more like Barry, the benign Texan in our apartment complex, than the daughter-ravaging delinquent, Dick.

After a few solo visits, Fibber started bringing his cousin Peki, a boy with a whisper of mustache, a schoolgirl giggle, and a funny kind of appeal.

Ah, Peki . . .

The projector's click snapped me out of my island-boy daydreams and back to the slide show.

". . . and here's a view of the runway at Pago Pago International Airport, with the lagoon and the mountains in the distance. These pictures were made at the inauguration of a jet flight from New Zealand to Pago Pago. The natives in the foreground here are quite typically dressed."

That word again. *Natives.* It nettled me like sand in my swimsuit. And what was "typical" dress — *lavalavas* and *puletasis*, or the American-style clothes most of my Samoan schoolmates wore?

From the projector came a smell like melting plastic as the bulb heated each snippet of acetate in its cardboard jacket. Feeling warm myself, I escaped to the kitchen and opened the refrigerator's freezer compartment.

"I'm getting ice cream, Daddy, want some?" Ice cream was one of our father-daughter things. My mother occasionally indulged in a single scoop of vanilla, daintily spooned from a tulip-shaped dish when we had guests, but for my father and me, loading up crockery with tennis-ball sized servings of chocolate was a nightly ritual. I reached for the carton, already sensing the cool sweetness in my mouth.

"You're getting *what*?" Over the drone of the projector, my father's tone sounded surprisingly brittle.

"Ice cream. We have chocolate — want some?" The rime on the carton's surface melted beneath my hand.

"Don't say it that way." Frost in his voice like the blast from the open freezer. "It's ice *creeeam*, not *ice* cream."

My father's sudden preoccupation with pronunciation bewildered me. Surely there were other words we pronounced differently, but he'd never commented on them before, much less erupted in anger. How was my deviation from Okie drawl any different from his practiced "downtown"?

"*Ice* cream, ice *creeeam*, what's the difference?" I snapped.

In the projector's glow, I could see my father's complexion darken and his lips purse. Even the streaks in his hair looked more steely than silver.

"It's ice *creeeam*, ice *creeeam*. That's the way *we* say it. You've been spending too much time with that tennis court crowd, especially those West Coast beach bums you've taken up with, and now you're starting to sound like them. But you're not like them, do you hear me?"

So that was what this was about: not inflection, but identity. I was rejecting my "native" tongue, allying with another tribe, and it was too much for my father to bear.

Once, I would have given in and revised my pronunciation just to appease him. What were a couple of words, anyway? If I could keep him happy with a simple shift of emphasis, then why not? But this time, something was crystallizing in me, freezing solid and refusing to melt.

"Good grief, Daddy," I said before slamming the freezer door and stomping upstairs, "it's only *ice* cream."

My copy of *Teach Yourself Samoan*, a slender volume with a cornflower blue cloth cover, lay on my nightstand. I opened the book and read the foreword:

The purpose of this manual is to enable a student to acquire a working knowledge of the Samoan language without the personal tuition to be obtained in a classroom or from an individual teacher. It is believed that a careful study of the Lessons will equip him with all the knowledge required to read written Samoan as is likely to swim into his ken and, with practice, to carry on conversation with Samoans on all subjects he is likely to find it necessary to discuss.

I shook my head. I could hardly make sense of the author's English; how was I supposed to learn Samoan? For weeks I'd been memorizing vocabulary lists and poring over the book's lessons on nouns, definite articles, indefinite articles, and verb particles, but I still felt ill-equipped to carry on any but the most simple-minded conversation. I could ask "*Alu i fea?*" — "Where are you going?" — but not respond to the same question asked of me. Keeping up with an exchange between my Samoan friends was completely out of reach, and I felt left out even when they prefaced their lapses with a courtly, "Pardon me while I speak the Samoan language."

What's more, I wasn't sure the book's author — one C.C. Marsack, whom I pictured as a pasty, balding English ex-missionary — was such an expert. He admitted in the acknowledgements that his stenographer Taialofa not only transcribed his dictation but "from time to time by a frown of disapproval or a smile of amusement has compelled me to recast some of my Samoan phraseology." Better to learn the language straight from Taialofa or, failing that, someone else who grew up speaking Samoan.

Someone like Peki.

Ah, Peki . . .

He giggled and shrugged when I made the suggestion after school a few days later, but that evening he and Fibber showed up at my door.

"Time for Samoan school," Peki said. He ducked his head and looked away, embarrassed, before kicking off his flip-flops and coming inside.

Fibber and Peki were as different as sand and sky. Fibber was a flirt and a smooth talker; Peki was so shy he'd hide behind a porch post until I spied him and urged him out. Fibber wore stateside styles; Peki was all island boy in loose pants and baggy shirts. If he wore anything on his broad feet, it was flip-flops, never pointy boots. Fibber had a comical look about him with his tuft of orange-red hair; Peki was travel-poster handsome: mahogany-skinned with high cheekbones, a slender wedge of nose, and teeth like chips of white shell. He stood nearly six feet tall, and his coconut-oiled black hair—cut close on the sides and left long on top—added another two or three inches to his height.

Granted, Peki's looks weren't the kind that would've made me circle the Sonic a second time in Oklahoma. It was the era of the Beach Boys. The guys whose yearbook pictures I fantasized over were all blue-eyed, with long, straight hair worn in an eyebrow-sweeping style like Danny's. But Peki—dark-eyed, curly-haired Peki—had a charm that transcended haircuts. Maybe it was the way he laughed at everything, sometimes out of nervousness, but usually out of pure, uncomplicated mirth.

The three of us sat at the dining table where I'd been typing a paper for my English class. I put on my glasses to communicate the seriousness of my intent.

"OK," I said. "Let's start with some easy words."

Peki tapped his chest with his index finger. "*Tama.*"

"Boy?"

He nodded. "Good."

Then pointing at me, "*Teine.*"

"Girl!" I pushed up my glasses and ran two fingers through the ends of my hair to check for upstart waves.

Another nod.

My mother had set a plate of packaged cookies on the table when the boys arrived. Peki took one from the plate and bit it in half; crumbs fell from his fingers and littered the floor. Using his wide foot like a whisk broom, he swept the bits under his chair and glanced up to see if I'd noticed. I shook my finger in a mock-scolding gesture.

He laughed, a sheepish sniff, before swooping down to pick up the crumbs and deposit them on a napkin.

Across the table, Fibber doodled on a sheet of typing paper. He kept his free arm across the page so I couldn't see what he was drawing, and when I tried to peek he covered the whole thing with both hands.

"OK," I said to Peki. "I've got *tama* and *teine*, what's next?"

He laid his right hand over his heart as if pledging allegiance and clasped his left hand over the right.

"*Alofa.*" He dipped his head again and giggles spewed out like silvered bubbles from a surfacing pearl diver.

"I know that one. Love."

"*Alofa* Nasty?" Fibber said, and both boys cracked up, Fibber laughing his lazy ha-ha-ha and Peki covering his mouth in a vain attempt to suppress his high-pitched titters.

"What's the joke?" I had a feeling it was on me.

Peki stared at the table top and shook his head.

Fibber laid down his pencil. "We've never known any girls named Nancy, and when Peki first heard your name, he thought it was 'Nasty.' We've been calling you 'Nasty' behind your back."

"Oh, that's real nice, guys." I pretended to sulk, but secretly felt pleased they'd been talking about me, no matter what they called me.

"Not nice. Nasty," Peki said and expelled another stream of giggles.

Fibber pushed his drawing across the table. "Now you can look."

In the center of the full-page cartoon was a pot-bellied figure holding a spear and wearing nothing but a grass skirt, arm bands, and a hoop earring: the stereotypical "native" I'd pictured while listening to my father's travelogue. Flies swarmed around his oversized head, which was dominated by protruding lips the size of Frisbees. He stood on a curving path that led to a grass shack like the ones Danny and I used to draw. A crooked television antenna poked out of its roof, and a sign over the door read, "Nasty." The cartoon's caption: "Welcome to Samoa!"

It was a flippant sketch, and a skillful one, but it didn't make me laugh; it made me wonder. Did Fibber see himself that way? Did he think I did?

INTERLUDE—MEDICAL MARVELS

Oh, child of the moon
Keep far away
Disease and Death
— Samoan prayer to the deity Aloimasina, offered at the new moon

Oloā: *Sores. Very painful. The Samoans believe that they are caused by the bite of Nifoloa, a cannibal God who dwells at Falelima, Savai'i. Treated with medicine made from leaves of trees. Very common and afflicts young and old.*

Puela: *Ague and is usually associated with mumu or elephantiasis. Body is covered with many mats or clothing and hot water applied. Common.*

Toma: *Yaws. Very common amongst young children. Treatment is to scrape sores with a shell and cover with medicine made from leaves of trees.*

Mumu: *Elephantiasis. Most common in legs, feet, arms, breasts, scrotum. Young and old are afflicted with the disease which sometimes assumes astonishing proportions. Commences as a fever and is ultimately associated with gradual swelling of the part afflicted which swelling remains permanent.*

Treatment is by native medicines and rubbing with occasional puncture by sharp instrument.
— Te'o Tuvale, "The More Common Diseases from Which the Samoans Suffer" in An Account of Samoan History up to 1918

Wings beating in a blur, the mosquito hovered over my knee and homed in on a swath of exposed skin. I watched it land and mentally defied it to stab my flesh. It rested on my leg, then took off without even trying to bite.

No surprise there. Since coming to Samoa, I'd noticed mosquitoes left me alone, especially if I harnessed my powers of concentration to deter them. I was impervious—convinced of it—and that was a good thing. Here in Samoa, mosquitoes weren't just an annoyance that left you itchy and welt-spotted, they were bearers of disease. Filariasis. I'd never heard of it before coming to the islands, but now I saw evidence of it every day: men and women with legs that looked like they belonged on a brontosaurus—a late-stage manifestation of filariasis known as elephantiasis. So I willed mosquitoes away, and they obeyed.

My superstitious behavior might have seemed wacky back in Oklahoma, but not here. Every day, my father came home from the hospital with tales of ailing men and women whose symptoms had no medical explanation but who'd taken sick after being cursed by enemies. He marveled at "incurable" diseases that vanished when patients abandoned Western medicine and put their faith in traditional Samoan healers.

I marveled at this new way of looking at sickness, health, and the span between the two. In the traditional Samoan view, health and well-being depended upon balance among the social, natural, and supernatural aspects of one's life. Healing involved identifying parts that were out of balance and taking action to restore harmony, such as apologizing to someone you'd offended or appeasing a specific *aitu*.

I knew a little about *aitu*—local legends and lore abounded with tales of these spirits that stuck their noses into all sorts of physical and social phenomena. But I'd never given much thought to how to stay healthy, with or without the help of spooks. That might seem odd, given that I grew up in a household where medicine was a dinner-table topic: my father discussing episiotomies and breech births as casually as he talked about rototilling the garden; my older brother, once he got his M.D. degree, debating with our dad the pros and cons of Panalba.

Oh, there was plenty of talk about *medicine* in our household, about techniques and challenging cases and finding the right fix for a given ailment. But even when my mother got cancer, family conversations centered more on how her doctors would treat the disease than on what caused it, or how to keep it from happening again, or what parts of my mother—besides her afflicted breasts—might need healing. Now, considering this new concept that staying healthy involved more than taking your vitamins, getting your shots, and following doctors' orders, I wondered if something was out of balance in my mother's life and how her equilibrium could be restored.

Awed by the staggering difficulty of keeping one's social, natural, and supernatural aspects properly aligned, and surrounded by potential perils, I took comfort in knowing at least *I* was invincible.

Chapter 12 — Heat

E manatua pule, 'ae le manatua fa'alaeo.
(Compassion is remembered, destruction forgotten.)
— *Samoan proverb*

Sitting cross-legged on my bed, I peeled a sheet of notebook paper from my sweaty leg as if picking at a sunburn. It was the beginning of Samoan summer — a season that stretched from October to May — and temperatures were edging upward from balmy to broiling. Trying to do homework in that kind of heat was maddening; if my papers weren't sticking to me, they were fluttering off the bed like startled pigeons whenever the electric fan turned its head their way.

As I struggled to solve chemistry problems, my very brain seemed a bubbling flask poised to explode with the slightest nudge. It wasn't just the heat and flapping papers that had me feeling off-kilter; it was the fuzzy way my mind had been working lately.

Schoolwork never had been hard before; I'd always been able to pick up what I needed to know by paying attention in class and drilling with flashcards when memorization was required. But now I was floundering in chemistry and calculus, staring blankly when Mr. Hieronymus droned on about Avogadro's number or when Mr. Oster scrawled derivatives on the blackboard. I tried taking notes, but found myself preoccupied with my teachers' peculiarities: the way Mr. Hieronymus's nose narrowed and flattened at the very tip into something resembling a pencil eraser, and the similarity of Mr. Oster's bulging eyes to Ping-Pong balls. When I wasn't mentally caricaturing my teachers' features, I was daydreaming. About Danny and Dick and now Peki, and weekend parties where the Vampires played their libidinous music and the air smelled of ginger blossoms and coconut oil and the ocean's brackish bouquet.

At test time, I stared at equations that might as well have been written in hieroglyphics. My cheeks reddened. My mouth went gluey. My thoughts darted around like a madwoman racing from room to room, searching for a misplaced item that never was there in the first place. I guessed at answers or left blanks and prayed for better grades than I deserved or ultimately received.

Already I could imagine my parents' reactions when report cards came out. No melodramatic scene, just the conspicuous absence of the usual praise and pride. My mother would frown, but a frown of concern, not disapproval. My father would say grades aren't everything and try to cheer me up with a joke. Later I'd hear voices through their bedroom door, too faint for me to make out anything but my name.

Academics weren't pushed in our household; brainpower was simply a family trait that my parents—and I—assumed I'd inherited. My mother and her sister had always excelled, so much that their parents sent the girls to the big high school ten miles away from their rural hometown while their brothers—no mental lightweights—stayed home to work on the farm. My father started college at sixteen; my brother was a Rhodes Scholar candidate. In a galaxy so bright, how could I not shine?

But now my star was burning out before its time. As I stared at pages in my textbook, chemistry formulas wavered and shimmered, mirages on the blistering asphalt of my brain. The noise coming through the screens didn't help my concentration. Our apartment was the end unit; behind it was the Hospital of American Samoa, where my father worked, and the wing that housed the men's ward was so close I could peek through its screened walls from our bathroom window. Every night I heard whatever TV show the men were watching: reruns of *Gunsmoke*, *Adventures in Paradise, Hawaiian Eye,* and *Bonanza* on the single channel that carried evening programs.

I heard the closing theme to *Adventures in Paradise* — strings and a swaying rhythm that suggested trade winds and swelling emotions, a song the Vampires played so often at Goat Island Club dances it seemed like the soundtrack to my own dramas — and I waited for the American Samoan anthem to close the evening's programming. Once again, my chemistry problems remained unsolved. Maybe I'd feel smarter in study hall the next day, I told myself, knowing I most certainly wouldn't. I'd have to get help from Abe, a brainy Samoan kid who tutored me on balancing equations and drawing electron dot diagrams. I turned off the light, pulled the sheet over myself and, after tossing for what felt like half the night but was probably only minutes, fell asleep.

An hour or so later, I awoke, tangled in my sweat-soaked sheet and chilled by the fan. I thought about turning it off but knew the heat would be more intolerable than the chill. I could get up and retrieve a blanket from the spare bedroom. No, that would require more effort than I was willing to expend. I lay awake and watched the clock's hands make their rounds as I remained stubbornly immobile. When I couldn't stand the discomfort any longer, I threw off the sheet and clomped into the next room. I didn't bother turning on the overhead light; the constantly-burning, wire-caged bulb at the bottom of the closet — the one that kept things from mildewing — shone bright enough for me to see what I was doing. I yanked a thin coverlet from the top shelf. Another came with it and fell into a heap on the closet floor. I briefly considered picking it up, refolding it and putting it back on the shelf, but I was in no mood for chores.

Inches from my face, Mr. Hieronymus's nose metamorphosed. From pencil eraser, it transformed into Silly Putty, pinky-brown and elastic, creeping amoeba-like across his

cheek and sliding toward his mouth, which opened and formed
words: *Nancy . . . wake . . . up.*

"Nancy! Wake up!" My chemistry teacher's voice became
my father's, taut with alarm. His hand gripped my shoulder, and
he rolled and shook me as if I were an obstacle he was trying to
dislodge. I turned away and covered my head with the sheet.

"Get up! Hurry!" He was shouting now. "Fire!"

I rolled over to see my mother pulling on a housecoat as she
rushed into the hallway. I jumped up, grabbed mine, and
followed my parents down the hall, the three of us holding
hands, a chain of trained animals in nightclothes. We passed the
spare bedroom on the way to the stairs, and I saw flames. Every
molecule of air seemed displaced by radiant orange liquid that
moved as if alive, advancing and retreating, sending tentative
arms upward, grabbing hold with fluttering fingers, and
spreading higher. Heat blasted toward us in waves: an
incandescent ocean at high tide. The smell reminded me of
winter afternoons in Oklahoma, when all the chimneys in the
neighborhood spewed smoky plumes. But this was no cozy
blaze behind a fireplace screen; our house was burning.

For a moment the spectacle mesmerized me. Then scenes
from every safety film I'd seen in grade school flashed through
my mind: families crawling through smoke-choked hallways,
whole buildings flaring up like campfires and collapsing into
heaps of charred timber. Pulsating terror overtook me. *We could
die in here!*

With the fear came this horrid realization: The fire was my
fault. That blanket I'd been too lazy to pick up? I remembered
seeing it land on the wire cage around the burning light bulb in
the bottom of the closet. I'd thought the cage would keep the
blanket from catching fire. Wasn't that why it was there? Now
the bedroom was a bonfire and the whole apartment complex
was in peril, all because of my carelessness. As we clambered
down the stairs, the bite of remorse gave my fear an acrid taste.

The fire truck arrived, and the scene that unfolded might have made me laugh if I'd been watching it in a movie. Instead, each mishap and ensuing delay made my skull tighten and my stomach twist. First, the firefighters started the pump. The hose lay flaccid in their hands, no water shooting out. It wasn't connected to the hydrant. The firemen connected the hose. It was too short to reach the fire. The bedroom windows glowed orange and hot as we stood helpless, and the firemen frowned and shouted to one another in brisk Samoan. Finally, someone thought to connect the hose to a closer hydrant at the hospital. The hose reached, windows were smashed and the firefighting began. Thank goodness there was water to be pumped. Until the week before, we'd been on water rationing, and the water supply had been turned off all night, every night.

We watched from the courtyard as streams of that precious water tamed the flames. Smoke clouds, dark and foreboding as tornadoes, billowed from a shattered window, and the grassy odor of wet pandanus mats overlaid the smell of burning wood. *My fault. My fault. My fault.*

"Looks like it didn't spread beyond the spare room," my father said, his voice still pinched. "There was nothing in that closet but extra bedding and toiletries, right?"

Nothing but extra bedding and toiletries. I knew my parents had spent months assembling all those things to ship from the States with our clothing and household goods. We could find replacements on the island, but at twice the cost.

"But all that water!" my mother wailed, her usual restraint breached. "What if it floods the first floor?" I knew she was picturing those streams cascading onto her electric organ, which had just arrived from the States with the rest of our things and now sat directly below the sodden spare room. My smoldering anguish flared at the thought.

Neighbors heard the commotion and came out to watch and to console us. When they asked how the fire started, my parents shook their heads and said they didn't know. I looked away and said nothing. Along with the fiery closet's contents, my self-esteem was melting into something unrecognizable. The good student was failing chemistry; the dutiful daughter, lately turned rebellious and heedless, had set the house ablaze; the intrepid adventurer didn't have the guts to admit responsibility. This kind of thing could get you in a heap of trouble with an *aitu*, maybe enough to make you sick.

My meditation on that thought was cut short when Pam and Sarah Baker, schoolmates who lived across the courtyard, dashed over in their nightgowns, keyed up from the hubbub and the discombobulation of being roused from their beds. Their mother — plump, hennish — followed in her robe. After the girls asked the obligatory questions and, with obvious excitement, watched the firefighters for a while, Mrs. Baker asked if I'd like to come back to their apartment until the fire was out. Her kindness magnified my shame, but I said okay, that would be nice.

Sitting in the kitchen with the Baker girls, I kept my attention trained on the scene across the courtyard. Pam, the slimmer, prettier sister, with long blond hair that dipped over her forehead, tried to distract me with chatter about school. I answered in monosyllables. Sarah, fleshy like her mother, with brown hair that always looked unwashed, scooped a cat off the floor and held it out to me. I took the animal on my lap and stroked it. Its purr and the feel of fur through fingertips soothed me a little.

Mrs. Baker fussed around the kitchen, checked the refrigerator, opened cupboard doors, and peered inside.

"Would you girls like some cocoa?"

The idea of drinking hot chocolate in the middle of a sultry, tropical night when my home was being reduced to charcoal struck me as ludicrous — and perfect.

I nodded, still mute with self-loathing.

When Mrs. Baker set the steaming mugs on the table I waited until Pam and Sarah drank from theirs. I took a sip and another, guilty at the pleasure of sweet liquid spilling down my throat and settling in my hollow belly. The night's events looped through my mind: the struggles with homework, the fitful sleep, the fateful decision to leave the blanket on the closet floor, the smoke and blaze. I set my cup down and hung my head.

"It's my fault."

The girls and their mother looked at me with identical expressions of bewildered concern: heads tilted, eyebrows knitted, lips pressed together.

"No, no, dear, don't say that," Mrs. Baker said, apparently thinking some general sense of self-reproach had compelled me to assume the blame. "How could something like this be your fault? Bad things just happen sometimes; it's no one's fault."

Unsure how much more I wanted to say—could I let it go at that, or did I have to elaborate?—I didn't respond at first. My mind ran the scenes in reverse: fire . . . smoke . . . blanket . . . homework. From homework, my thoughts wandered to my friend and tutor Abe and how, when I'd get stuck on a chemistry problem, he'd coax the answer out of me: "You *know* this, Nancy. You know the right answer—it's in there, just pull it out."

Not only was Abe the smartest kid in school, he was also the most respected for his levelheadedness and upright character—a good guy who knew right from wrong, and not just on Mr. Hieronymus's quizzes. More than once I'd sought his advice when some ethical dilemma baffled me as much as the laws of thermochemistry. Now I asked myself what he'd advise in this situation, but all that came to mind was this cryptic counsel: "You know the answer, Nancy—it's in there."

I fortified myself with another sip of cocoa and finally spoke.

"No, it really *is* my fault," I said. "See, I got up in the middle of the night to get a blanket off the shelf. I *think* I may have knocked another one down, and *maybe* it landed on top of the light bulb." There. I'd come clean, as I knew I should. But even in my confession I couldn't completely own up to what I'd done. I could see *aitu* elbowing each other and rolling their eyes.

"Oh dear," Mrs. Baker said. "Well, I'm sure you didn't mean to do it."

My lower lip twitched. Mrs. Baker patted my shoulder.

"You just sit right here and drink your cocoa and don't worry about anything. I'll go see how things are coming along across the way."

She crossed the courtyard and approached the silhouettes of my parents. She took my mother aside and spoke to her, their heads bent close. Now and then Mrs. Baker gestured toward the apartment where Pam, Sarah, and I sat—silent now—with our cups of chocolate. I strained to pick up words through the screened walls, but all I could hear was the rise and fall of the women's voices. After a few minutes, my mother turned to my father and spoke to him. He looked toward the Bakers'; then together they walked toward the apartment.

Head, heart, and every pulse point in my body thudded. I took another sip of cocoa but couldn't swallow. My mouth was a flannel-lined pocket with an emery board for a tongue. I thought of bolting for the back door, but my parents were inside the apartment before I could move. I couldn't look at their faces; I trained my eyes on the floor and watched their feet, scuffling on the pandanus as they moved toward my chair.

Not even bothering to concoct a defense, I braced for a tirade. Whatever they were about to dish out, I deserved. Recalling every bitter exchange I'd ever had with my parents, which admittedly had been few up to this point, I envisioned their usual displays of anger—my father's reddening face and caustic criticism, my mother's rigid silence—and felt chastised without their having spoken a word.

Then my mother touched my shoulders, and my father cleared his throat.

"Honey?" His sympathetic doctor voice. "It was an accident. It could've happened to any of us."

I looked up. No trace of anger or even disappointment showed in my parents' faces.

"It's all right," my mother said. She stroked my hair as if I were a pet. "We all got out safely, the fire is out. Everything's going to be okay."

Cool rivulets streamed through me, but traveling with them, a load of confusion. Only days before, my father had practically disowned me over pronunciation. Now I'd nearly burned down the house, and not even a scolding? It made no sense at first, but then it did, sort of. Some things could be replaced; some were too precious to lose.

There was this, too, behind my parents' reaction: compassion. Somehow, they could forgive my failings. Could I? Tonight, my self-esteem had come close to being incinerated, but if I'd learned anything about heat in chemistry class, it was that it didn't always cause destruction. Sometimes it acted as a catalyst, imparting energy to chemical reactions and prompting transformations that wouldn't otherwise occur. In the heat of this night, all elements of my character had come forth, both ignoble and noble. I wanted to believe they could combine into something new and better, something worthy of whatever adventures this paradise had in store for me.

Chapter 13 — Kinship

Ia ifo le fuiniu i le lapalapa.
(May the cluster of nuts bow to the midrib of the leaf.)
— *Samoan proverb interpreted as "The individual is responsible to the family."*

If one word can sum up a culture, that word, for Samoan society, would be *aiga*. Peki hadn't covered it in our lessons, but already I'd begun to understand its meaning, or at least the literal translation and the contexts in which the word was used. A fuller comprehension would come later.

The definition of *aiga* (pronounced ay-EENG-uh) in my *Teach Yourself Samoan* book was simply "family," yet Samoans used the word to describe things I never would've associated with the mother-father-sister-brother unit that meant family to me. There were *aiga* buses — open-air jitneys painted gaudy colors — and *aiga* baskets, woven from palm fronds and used to carry leftovers home from feasts or funerals. The common connection was the extended family — parents, siblings, aunts, uncles, cousins, grandparents, and others related by blood, marriage, or adoption — and the sense of shared responsibility, whether operating a family bus service or divvying up pork and *palusami*.

The spirit of sharing, the habit of pitching in, the sense of sacred obligation that is not a burden but a duty rooted in respect and devotion, all of that is infused into the meaning of *aiga* as perfume is into a petal. And because *aiga* in its broadest sense is such a central concept in their society, Samoans seem not to care where the edges of their families overlap with others; they spread their generosity clan to clan, village to village.

On the night of the fire, my little nub of a family felt the expansive embrace of *aiga* even before we'd finished assessing the damage. Fibber scrambled down from his mountain shack and roused his cousin Gus; together they mustered more boys, some related to them, some not, and as soon as the fire was out and it was safe to go back in the apartment, they were all in our living room, along with most of our *palagi* neighbors, moving furniture, rolling up soggy pandanus mats, mopping floors, and wiping down smoke-streaked walls with the efficiency of a professional clean-up crew.

Barry, the amiable Texan who lived in the next building, came to help, too. "Kinda going to extremes to get out of your chem quiz, aren't you?" His eyes glinted through the lenses of his glasses. "Couldn't you just fake being sick like a normal person?"

"My dad's a doctor, remember? I have to get creative." I laughed and was surprised to hear myself laughing, even if it was more from relief than amusement.

Standing there joking with Barry, I realized I was in my housecoat, my hair tangled like beached seaweed, in a room full of teenage boys. Oddly, I wasn't as self-conscious as I usually felt fully dressed, coifed, and made-up for a party. The atmosphere in the room felt so relaxed, so *familial*, like Christmas mornings when my brother still lived at home, all of us in pajamas with sleep-puffed faces and bed-rumpled hair, my father aiming the movie camera's blinding light bar at each of us, me prancing from coffee table to Christmas tree, my brother ducking behind his hand like a criminal leaving a courthouse, my mother sipping coffee from a Currier & Ives-printed cup. Even though *this* morning we were cleaning up a real mess, not cast-off ribbons and wrapping paper, and the wood-smoke smell was not from a blazing hearth but from a house fire, I couldn't shake that incongruously homey, holiday feeling. And then it hit me:

Fibber and his gang weren't just boys from the tennis court and dance hall anymore; by crawling out of bed to come to our aid in the middle of the night, they'd become like kin.

Barry felt like family, too, though not everyone understood that. Girls at school had been asking his girlfriend Bev how she felt about him spending so much time with me—we walked to school together most mornings and often, after Bev had gone home to Tafuna, spent idle afternoons and evenings hanging out in the apartment courtyard. Barry assured me Bev wasn't jealous, and for the sake of our friendship I hoped he was right. I didn't tell him that I was the envious one, watching the two of them at parties where they danced only with each other, Barry wrapping his ursine hulk around Bev's small frame, her stubby, blond pigtails jutting out like clumps of dry grass as she rested her head against his chest. Stable, devoted, and apparently basking in parental approval, they seemed a different species from the rest of us, with our embattled, on-again, off-again romances. Val and I nicknamed them Mom and Dad. We called each other Sis.

Our real parents had found kinship on the island, too. My mother and Mrs. Puckett, as different in style and substance as two women could be, bonded over bridge games and the challenges of raising teenage daughters in a land where life sometimes seemed a little too free and easy. When the two of them weren't commiserating, my mother headed off to beaches or hilltops with Phyllis Hieronymus, my chemistry teacher's wife, to collect seashells or wood roses, flower-shaped seed pods that formed on climbing vines. Phyllis was at least a decade younger than my mother, and her tell-it-like-it-is attitude contrasted with my mother's finesse, but they shared Midwestern sensibilities. Other days, my mother crossed the courtyard to visit Char, a young mother whose toddlers became surrogate grandchildren.

Not all of my mother's new friends were *palagis* who hailed from the heartland, though. Tiva, who managed the airport restaurant, and Mere, a school principal, were island born and bred — and as gracious and genteel as any of my mother's country club friends back home.

As for my father — who'd once confided that his only real friend in Stillwater was the rough-edged but sympathetically attentive owner of the Conoco station where we had our cars serviced — he'd already found comrades in two co-workers. "Doctor Paul" Godinet was a warm, cultured Samoan with wavy, gray hair who'd received medical training in Fiji — not enough for an M.D. degree, but enough to impress my father with his knowledge of both Western and traditional Samoan medicine. In the hospital hierarchy, he was a medical practitioner, lower in rank than a physician, but in my father's eyes he was every bit an equal.

Dad's other crony was Manley Donaldson, that peculiar little man who'd chauffeured us around the island when we first arrived. Together, the two of them jounced over rutted roads to visit clinics in outlying villages, passing the time with talk of art and music, my father's orchid collection and Manley's travels in Algeria and other exotic places. It was the first time I remembered my father having a true peer — another man with whom he could be completely himself, neither of them making any pretense of being manly in the narrow sense in which the rest of the world defined the word.

It would be weeks before our relatives back home got word of the fire, even longer before their genuine, if helpless, expressions of concern made their way back to us. But here on this island, where a month or so before no one even knew our names, we had all the family we needed.

Peki was conspicuously absent from the clean-up crew on the night of the fire. I supposed it was because he lived too far away for Fibber to recruit him, though exactly where he and his family lived was a mystery. Whenever I asked, he made a vague gesture and said, "On the mountain."

Had Peki even heard about the fire? It was hard to imagine he hadn't; *The Samoa Times* carried both Samoan and English versions of the story:

Fire at Doctors Apartment

The loud siren that awakened town residents Tuesday midnight was a response to a fire call from Utulei. The fire was mostly smoke, but according to reports, it destroyed valuable personal belongings of Dr. and Mrs. Sanders, occupants of the Apartment I-7 where the fire was.

Reports say that something inflammable must have touched a very hot light bulb. There were no injuries.

I was grateful the article didn't go into detail about exactly how that "something inflammable" happened to come to rest against the very hot light bulb, but word got around anyway, even up on Peki's mountain. This I learned from a note Fibber delivered during lunch period a few days after the fire. (Apparently, *aiga* duties included acting as your bashful cousin's emissary.)

He was waiting for me outside the Standard Academic Program building, leaning against the schoolyard's inexplicable centerpiece: the rusted hulk of a once-blue Chevy sedan that commanded the space the way statues of school mascots do on other campuses.

"Hey, Nasty! Hey, little sister." Fibber waved the folded piece of paper as if enticing a child with candy. "Peki told me to give you this." He handed me the note, written in blue ballpoint pen on lined paper from a school tablet, then stood by, picking bits of rusted metal from the car's scabbing surface as I opened and read the letter.

Dear Nancy,

I'm not dropping any more food on your floor, and you be careful not to set your house on fire again.

*There is something that I want to ask you about. I wonder if
you can have me for your friend, in all cases, as long as you
want. To me, you are the only nice little babe for me.*

*Well, I guess that's enough talking. Anyway I have a poem
here ready for you to make yourself happy.*

*What matter if
The world turns sour
Thorns are a part
Of the sweetest flower.*

*When the wind blows high
The storms breaks through,
Lucky I am
In having you.*

I hope you will like my letter.
— PT

I refolded the note and stuck it in my notebook. "Did Peki
write this?"

"The letter? Sure, who else?" Fibber flicked a piece of
corroded metal from his fingers like a cigarette butt.

"No, the poem."

"Poem?" Fibber shrugged and raised his eyebrows.

"Come on, brother, I know you read the note." I swatted
him with my notebook. The letter fell at his feet. He snatched it
from the ground and read aloud, his voice syrupy: "*Thorns are a
part of the sweetest flower.* That's you, Nasty girl — a thorny
flower!" Strangling with laughter, he handed the note back to
me. "Peki didn't write that poem. We had to learn it in school."

I didn't care. In my mind, any boy who sent romantic
words to a girl had the soul of a poet. Danny was always giving
me verses he said he'd composed, though most were about hot
rods and drag racing (cribbed from a car magazine, I suspected).
He did give me one poem I was sure he'd composed for me,

ending with "Please for me keep the light alive, and always remember '75," a reference to the year we planned to marry. I kept that one in my scrapbook with our sketches of palm trees and grass shacks.

Yeah, I was a sucker for romantic types. And even if Peki's poem was something he'd memorized in school, the thought of him sitting in his mountainside *fale* — or shack or whatever he lived in — scratching out words by the light of a single, bare bulb or kerosene lantern made me feel cherished in a way that both thrilled and unsettled me.

"Tell Peki I liked his letter very much, and I hope to see him soon," I told Fibber.

Fibber pushed himself off the rusty fender and started walking in that slow, rolling gait of his, toward the Samoan side of campus.

"Don't worry, my sister," he said, looking over his shoulder. "You will."

My father turned off the paved road, guiding our Pontiac Tempest down a bumpy lane that was hardly more than two ruts plowed through dense forest. At a clearing, he turned off the engine.

"This is the end of the line for this *aiga* bus," he said. "We'll walk the rest of the way."

Val and I gathered up beach towels; my father popped open the trunk, and he and my mother unloaded tote bags filled with suntan lotion, camera gear, and snacks. Then we all headed down a narrow trail that disappeared into a jungle dark as a backstreet alley: the path to Larsen's Beach.

On an island where postcard-perfect stretches of sand lay around every bend in the road, it might seem odd that we had to drive ten miles and then hike through thick jungle to sunbathe and frolic in the surf. But most other beaches were right next to villages, and plopping a towel on one of them would be as boorish as invading a neighbor's backyard pool. What's more, a woman wearing swimwear in public was a serious breach of Samoan standards of modesty. My friends and I could get by with it when we swam off the docks in Utulei and Fagatogo, where townspeople were accustomed to *palagi* transgressions, but out in the villages where tradition was taken more seriously, we'd offend entire communities by splashing around in even demure bathing suits. Larsen's Beach nestled in an isolated cove, so we could swim there without giving offense.

No matter how many times I hiked to the beach, the experience of being so deeply immersed in vegetation always filled me with awe. Even on the brightest day, sunlight barely penetrated the canopy. Looking straight up or to either side of the trail, all I could see were tangles of vines, arching branches, and assorted shapes and sizes of leaves, all the same deep emerald hue. Yet for all the dark and isolation, there was nothing scary about this forest. Its enclosure felt secretive in a cozy way, like the tunnels of blanket-draped chairs my brother used to build for me in our family room. Even the sounds enchanted me: the purr of doves, the string-section chorusing of cicadas, the swish of leaves as we brushed past them.

At the trail's end, the shushing of waves on shore muffled the jungle's music, and the ocean's fishy tang prickled our noses. We stepped out into blinding sunshine and the kind of scene that, before coming to Samoa, I'd seen only in travel magazines: an ash-white beach free of footprints. At both ends of the horseshoe-shaped expanse of sand, steep walls of black lava cloistered the cove. There was no one else in sight.

We spread our towels on the beach. Val and I raced to the water, kicking at the froth of surf and wading in up to our waists. On an earlier trip to the cove, Marnie had taught me how to body surf, aiming just so to slip through spaces in the reef and avoid being shredded on the coral. I showed Val how to do it, and we took turns riding the waves to shore.

"God, I love it here, don't you, Sis?" I whooped after one swell deposited me on the beach.

"Yeah, Kalamazoo never came close to this."

"Do you think you could live here forever?"

Val stared past the breakers to where the water turned from turquoise to sapphire and stretched as far as we could see, and beyond. "Nah. There's too much stuff I'd miss after a while — like French fries and TV shows that aren't two years old."

"Yeah," I said. "Me, too." I wasn't sure I meant it.

Driving out to the beach that afternoon, we'd passed through half a dozen villages, still alien to me, but increasingly attractive. Church services were in session, and through the open doors of the whitewashed sanctuaries, voices carried all the way to the road. The sound didn't so much waft as saturate the air. Sung *a capella* by a full congregation in strong, nasal voices, Samoan hymns sounded more assaultive than sweet to my ear, yet in spite of that, the close harmonies, steady tempos, and strangely wistful melodies entranced me. Each time we passed a church, I imagined myself inside, immersed in music and washed in rainbow sunlight. After church, there'd be a feast with roast pork, *palusami*, and taro, foods I was starting to crave as much as foot-long chili dogs and tater tots. I still wasn't sure I could handle the communal lifestyle and lack of privacy that Samoan family life required, or the extreme sharing that the *aiga* system demanded — it was considered stingy and cruel not to hand over anything a relative asked for — but the food and music might make up for all that.

Granted, most of my understanding of Samoan family life had come from Margaret Mead's nearly forty-year-old book. Still, many customs hadn't changed much over the decades. In reading the book, I was struck not only by the strangeness of some practices, but also by how similar some aspects of Samoan daily life were to life everywhere, including our household, with everyone reflexively pitching in to tidy up living spaces and help with cooking, gardening, and other chores. Even my family's weird habit of asking in the most roundabout way for someone to pass the potatoes had a Samoan counterpart, at least in the times Mead documented. A Samoan, she wrote, wouldn't just show up at a relative's *fale* and bluntly ask for something; he'd hang around all day making himself useful while the host tried to guess what he wanted, and only at bedtime finally make his polite request.

"Got any candy bars?" Val asked, clearly not schooled in Samoan protocol. We headed back to our beach towels, and I dug a Caramello bar out of one of the tote bags. We savored it square by square, nipping off bits of milk chocolate and letting the liquid caramel swirl around our tongues before taking another bite. Tongues: what strange things they were when you stopped to think about it—organs of taste and touch, utilitarian yet erogenous.

"So who do you like best: Dick, Danny, or Peki?" Val wore an expression of mild interest, not the suspicious squint from our early conversations about Danny.

I poured a pool of baby oil into my palm and spread it on a cordovan thigh. "Hard to say. Peki's sweet, but I don't know . . . Dick, I'm crazy about of course, but that's doomed. And Danny—I don't know if he'll even be the same person when I see him again. His letters are getting weird."

"Weird how?"

I wiped my oil-slicked hands on the towel and leaned back on my elbows. "Dark. Moody. Always some drama going on with his dad or sometimes things he won't even discuss. He just drops these bombshells, like he's been thrown out of the house or he's joining the Marines, and then he gets all secretive. Drives me crazy."

"You sure he's not making stuff up to get your sympathy?" The squint was back. I countered it with a glare.

"You don't even *know* him."

Damn her. She might be right. How very sister-like of her to zero in on a sore point.

I steered the conversation away from my boyfriends. "So how're things with Li'i?" Li'i was Val's new beau, a Samoan high school senior whose fawnish eyes and palm-frond lashes gave him a feminine beauty. Li'i was as shy as Peki, and at social events the two of them were usually side by side, creating through synergy the confidence that neither alone possessed. Together they embodied the Samoan proverb, *So'o le fau*, a literal description of joining two pieces of cord with a knot, interpreted to mean "There's strength in numbers."

"Li'i? He's okay, I guess." Val broke off another Caramello square. "He doesn't say much, but he's a good kisser."

My parents had wandered away from our sunbathing spot and were picking up seashells, appraising them like estate jewelry before depositing the most perfect ones in the pandanus basket my mother carried on her arm. As always, they seemed two parts of an inseparable whole, moving, stopping, bending, and straightening in unison, but I knew the appearance of consensus could be deceiving. In my last letter to my Stillwater girlfriend Cindi I'd written, "*I think my parents like it here pretty well, that is, my dad likes it real well and my mother is liking it better.*" The adjustment had been harder for her than for my father and me. Cooped up in our tiny apartment with its ambient soundtrack of crowing roosters, barking dogs, and blaring radios from passing cars, she took refuge in bridge games and dinner parties. Lately, even those had become tedious. Still anemic from the cobalt treatments, she tired easily, and she didn't tolerate the heat well. On shopping days, when she had to make the rounds of the general stores and stand in long lines at the agricultural market, she came home completely wrung out.

Watching my parents together on the beach, I wondered what other sacrifices my mother had made to keep my father happy and whether I could ever be the sort of wife who surrendered her own desires to her mate's—or to her whole family or village, as Samoan women did.

Hours passed in sun-doped lassitude. From time to time I emerged from torpor enough to lift my head and scan the opening in the trees where the trail broke through from the forest. Finally, late in the afternoon, I saw motion and a striped shirt I recognized.

"We've got company," I whispered to Val.

Peki and Li'i sauntered toward the beach as if they'd just happened upon our little party. In truth, Val had told Li'i about the planned excursion and figured the boys would find a way to join us.

"Well, look who's here," my mother said. "How do you suppose they knew where to find us?"

"Word travels fast on this little island, Mother," I said. "Everyone knows everyone else's business. Surely you and Mrs. Puckett know that." Her blink of hurt made me regret the remark. In the wake of the fire, I'd been trying to be more respectful of my parents, but I couldn't always rein in my sarcasm.

The boys sat on our beach towels, and Val and I tried to tease them the way we did at the tennis court. But even banded together, Peki and Li'i were struck dumb by their shyness. Before long my father announced that we'd better be getting back to town. He said the boys could ride with us.

We hiked back to the car. Peki and Li'i crowded into the back seat with Val and me; we wriggled onto their laps. The boys dropped their heads and shifted in their seats, but their lips curled into the slightest smiles and held those expressions through the long, silent drive back to Utulei.

After school the next day, Fibber handed me another letter on the same ruled paper.

Dear Nancy-Moreen, Peki had written, misspelling my middle name in a way that seemed sprightlier than the turgid Maurine. *Next time we go for a swim, don't let your parents go.*

Aiga apparently had its limits.

Chapter 14—Hard Rain

It was not like soft English rain that drops gently on the earth; it was unmerciful and somehow terrible; you felt in it the malignancy of the primitive powers of nature. It did not pour, it flowed. It was like a deluge from heaven, and it rattled on the roof of corrugated iron with a steady persistence that was maddening. It seemed to have a fury of its own.

—W. Somerset Maugham, "Rain"

Peki ran the roller through the pan of cream-colored paint, careful to load just the right amount onto the nappy surface. With long sweeps, he applied latex to the cinder block wall, his arms easily reaching from floor to ceiling. I followed behind with a paintbrush and touched up spots he missed. As he worked, tiny spatters spun off the roller and left pale flecks on his brown cheeks, like reverse freckles.

"It's really nice of you to do this." I bent down to dip my brush into the pan. "My parents usually take care of this kind of stuff themselves, or else hire a painter. I don't think we've ever had *friends* come over to help around the house—until we moved here, I mean."

Peki frowned. "No?"

"Things are a lot different here, Peki," I said. "*Fa'a Samoa* isn't *fa'a everywhere else.*"

He drew the back of his hand across his face, wiping off sweat and smearing the paint flecks into a shower of shooting stars across his cheeks.

"Better here," he said.

"Much."

In the days following the fire, Peki, Fibber, and Li'i had spent more and more time at the apartment, helping out or just hanging out. Peki was still teaching me Samoan, and in return I typed his school reports, correcting his English in the process. Many nights, Fibber sat at the table sketching, but not just idle doodles; his drawings now had purpose. I was running for vice president of SAP's student council, and he was designing campaign badges and posters with my caricature — turned-up nose, turned-under hair, and all. I loved the drawings but had to edit his captions; "Vote for Nasty" didn't send the right message. Li'i usually sat quietly doing homework until he worked up enough nerve to quiz me about the depth of Val's devotion. The easy camaraderie among the four of us was something I'd rarely experienced with boys back home and hardly ever felt with the *palagi* boys on the island. Though I still frequented the tennis court and get-togethers at the Jorgensens', evenings at home with the three boys were a welcome counterpoint.

These guys are so much fun, I wrote to Cindi in a letter that carried the heading: *Live, from Pago Pago, Samoa!*

They're really sociable, too — they don't go off by themselves like some boys. They're so considerate and polite and friendly — they always talk to us and treat us real nice. Like today I was walking along and Peki and Fibber both offered me rides on their Hondas. Think anyone would ever offer me a ride in the States?! And they act so concerned! They say, "Can I take you anywhere?" "I don't want you to have to walk by yourself." "Are you sure it's not too far?" And they're really sincere. I just love the guys here!

When Peki and I finished painting the wall, we cleaned the pan, brush, and roller in the utility sink just outside the back door. Along with the washer and dryer, the extra sink sat in a small, roofless enclosure where our house girl Malo — a woman about my mother's age—hung shrub-sized bunches of green bananas that she lopped off a few at a time and boiled for her lunch, leaving us the perfectly-ripened rejects. At first it had seemed ludicrous hiring a housekeeper when we lived in such small and easy-to-clean quarters. But Mrs. Puckett, for whom Malo also worked, told my mother that all the *palagi* families employed house girls, and it was expected that we would, too. With my mother's constant fatigue, a little extra help around the house couldn't hurt.

Malo was no taller than my five-foot-two-and-a-half, but like most Samoan women she was round as a breadfruit, thanks to Polynesian genes and a steady diet of boiled bananas, taro, and canned corned beef—the fatty staple Samoans call *pisupo*. (As the story goes, the first canned food brought to Samoa was pea soup, but islanders assumed the name applied to any food in tins. When corned beef displaced pea soup in the Samoan diet, the name *pisupo* stuck.)

Malo dressed in *puletasis* and wore her hair in a squat bun that added to the impression that she was wider than she was tall. When she ran out of household chores, she made flower arrangements, attaching hibiscus blossoms to the ends of slender reeds that bobbled in the breeze, or she carved whole pineapples into spirals almost too artful to eat. She spoke little English and communicated with my parents and me mainly through eyebrow flashes and gap-toothed smiles, though we suspected she understood more of our conversation than she let on. One sentiment she conveyed quite clearly without words was her disapproval of my closeness to the trio of Samoan boys. When Peki, Fibber, and Li'i were around, Malo scowled and banged pots and pans. The boys just laughed, but once or twice I overheard them having terse exchanges in Samoan with her in the courtyard.

I paid no attention to Malo's insolence. It was *my* home, and my Samoan friends were welcome there.

~ ~ ~

That afternoon, after Peki left, I sat at the table and opened an issue of *Newsweek* that was several weeks old, yet still the latest we'd received in our weekly mail. As usual, I flipped through the magazine's front section, skipping most of the stories on world affairs, stopping only when a grisly photo from the war in Vietnam caught my eye. I seldom read the articles about the war, couldn't make sense of them, couldn't keep straight all the names of places—Da Nang, Chu Lai, Bien Hoa— couldn't understand what the fighting was about. Still, when I came to the national news, I lingered over stories about antiwar rallies, especially when they happened in California, the epicenter of all that was cool and cutting edge. When I read about peace marches in Berkeley, where the poet Allen Ginsberg talked about "flower power," I yearned to be one of those long-haired, blossom-adorned girls who smiled with slightly unfocused eyes from the accompanying photographs, taking a stand, urging the world toward a gentler way of settling differences.

For similar reasons, I pored over stories about the civil rights movement. Earlier that year, Martin Luther King and some 2,600 supporters had been arrested in Alabama, Malcolm X had been shot to death in Harlem, and Negroes—who now preferred to be called Blacks—had rioted in the Watts section of Los Angeles. Unlike the war, the issues behind civil rights protests made sense to me. What I didn't understand was the hostility.

I'd experienced it firsthand in Oklahoma. There'd been no race riots or even demonstrations in my hometown, but in high school I'd noticed an undercurrent of tension among my black classmates, most of whom I'd known since junior high. Up through grade six, they'd gone to their own school, Washington Elementary, in the part of Stillwater white people called "Colored Town" when they were being polite ("N----- Town" when they weren't). At the beginning of seventh grade, I'd made a point of being friendly to the black kids, just as I would with anyone new, saying hi in the hallways even if I didn't know their names, and joking with the girls in my gym class. They were friendly in return, with a few exceptions, most notably Connie, a muscular girl with wild, comb-defying hair and an unrelentingly fierce countenance. But Connie's belligerence crossed all boundaries of color, gender, and age. She was mean as a snake to everyone.

With the other black kids, I gained traction after Douglas Lawson spread the word that years before, back when he was called Bunny and his mother was hired to help mine with housework, I had come to his house to play. I remembered sitting on the linoleum with him and his cousins, taking turns rolling a toy car across the floor as my father talked with his father, a minister I was instructed to call Reverend Lawson, even though I was allowed to address Bunny's mother by her first name, Irma.

On the way home, I'd asked my father why Bunny's family and all the other colored people lived in one part of town and why no white people lived there. I don't remember his answer; I do remember that it didn't satisfy me.

It was years after that, in high school, that cordial relations with my black classmates broke down. My hallway hellos were as likely to elicit glares as smiles, and every rebuff hurt my feelings. I could understand animosity directed at people who blocked schoolhouse doors and shouted racial slurs—I felt it, too—but hating all white people didn't seem fair. Then again, maybe my classmates' bitterness and the discomfort it caused me were necessary parts of the process of change, the sort of thing Bob Dylan meant when he wrote that song about hard rain. Maybe a thunderous, lightning-charged downpour was the only way to wash the world clean enough to start fresh. But like those flower-child girls in the *Newsweek* photos, I wanted to think there was a kinder way.

~ ~ ~

I looked up from the magazine when my father came in from the market carrying a bag of fruit and looking pleased with himself.

"Close your eyes. I brought you a surprise."

I shut my eyes until he said to open them. Atop my magazine sat an egg-shaped piece of produce with smooth, green skin. It looked like a green mango, but then again, not quite.

"Mahng-oh?" I pronounced the fruit's name the way Samoans did. "Oh, boy!"

I'd avoided green mangoes for a while after Dick's warning about mango rash, but after seeing my Samoan friends eat them with abandon and no ill effects, I finally got up my nerve and tried one. I liked the way it made my tongue tingle. When I didn't get a rash from that first taste, I became a green mango devotee, eating them whole like apples.

I carried the fruit to the sink and washed it with water that I poured from a pan on the stove. We couldn't use tap water without first boiling it; the island's sanitation system, though much improved in recent years, was still too chancy. I shook the water from the fruit and took a bite, anticipating the pucker. It was bland and watery.

"Mmmm," I said, sitting down at the table again. "Thanks, Daddy. My favorite fruit."

He smiled so broadly his ears shifted up a notch. "Nothing's too good for my Nanette."

I returned the smile but cringed inside, as if green mango juice had seeped through my skin. The pet name that once made me glow now made me squirm, especially when my father used it around my friends. Val took perverse pleasure in calling me Nanette just to annoy me. Suzi picked it up, too, and made a point of using it in front of the boys.

When I'd nearly finished eating the tasteless fruit, my father sat down across from me. He looked at the juicy, white flesh in my hand and then at me, with a mix of incredulity and embarrassment.

"That's not a mango, is it?"

"Um. Well. I think it's a *different* kind of mango." I held up the scrap, turned it this way and that, studied it from all angles. "But it's good. I like it." I took a bite and rolled it around in my mouth to demonstrate its lusciousness.

"It's a cucumber, isn't it?"

"Hmmm. I guess it could be." (I'd known it from the first bite.)

My father rested an elbow on the table and pressed his cheek against his hand. "There's something I've been wanting to ask you."

"What would that be, Daddy?" I finished the last bit of cucumber and wiped my hands on my shorts, expecting him to ask if I really preferred boiled taro to potatoes or if I thought his baked wahoo recipe needed improvement.

"You're spending a lot of time with those Samoan boys. Don't you have any *palagi* boy friends?" His tone was earnest, not confrontational.

"Oh sure, at school. And, you know, at the tennis court and Jorgensens'. I'm friends with all the boys who hang out there." I tried to mirror his chummy attitude, but I felt fluttery, unsure where the conversation was going.

"So why don't *they* ever come over here? Why is it always just Fibber, Peki, and Li'i?"

"Well . . . " I looked down at my magazine and turned a few pages, then raised my eyes and scanned the room, admiring the freshly painted wall, avoiding my father's gaze. The tiki, Double Ugly, stared at me with stony eyes from its post beside the front door.

"Well, Daddy, to be honest, the *palagi* boys are afraid to come over here."

I stole a glance at my father's face. Clearly, my answer had blindsided him as much as his question had me. Forehead pinched, he leaned forward.

"*Afraid?* Afraid of what?"

Paint fumes, pleasantly noxious, hung in the air. My stomach lurched, but it wasn't from the vapors. I was wobbling atop some new emotional precipice, dizzy from the unfamiliar perspective and the options before me. I could leap into the air of truthfulness and risk crashing against my father's anger, or I could creep backward into the shelter of my usual white lies, preserving the peace and his image of me as an obedient child. Before, the choice had always been easy, automatic, but now something else was at stake—not just my father's feelings, but new loyalties, new values.

"They're all friends of Dick's, Daddy. They know he's a good guy, and they know you and Mother won't give him a chance. They figure you won't approve of them either, so they don't come around." I was surprised at how freeing my candor felt. I'd leapt off that cliff and now floated high above the rough coast of my father's ire.

I could always gauge the intensity of his anger by how long it took him to respond. If he paused a few seconds or more, he was calm enough to give some thought to the issue at hand and choose his words carefully. But if he shot back an immediate retort, he was already over the brink of rationality and flailing away with whatever verbal weapons he could find to wound me as much as he felt wounded.

This time there was no hesitation.

"Well, maybe they're right." The words spattered out like raindrops at the height of a storm, stinging as they struck. "If they're on his side, they're the wrong kind of friends. As far as I'm concerned, they can just stay away. And those Samoan boys, too. They don't need to be hanging around here all the time."

The balloon of my euphoria collapsed into cold, flat resentment. Bitter thoughts shoved tenderness aside, outrage withered sympathy, and my mind clogged with caustic retorts I would hoard for future confrontations.

Within a couple of days my father had calmed down, and we were speaking again, if only about trivial matters. When I asked if he'd drive Val and me to a school dance in an outlying village, he readily agreed. I stressed the fact that the school's *palagi* teachers would chaperone and glossed over the reason Val and I were so keen on going. Val had been invited to the dance by Uili, who played guitar with the Vampires and competed with Li'i for her affections. For me, there'd be a new contingent of polite and sociable Samoan boys to check out.

When party time arrived, we piled into the Tempest and headed west from Utulei to that bend in the road where the light made the waves fluoresce. But though it was still daylight, the sky was dim, and instead of glowing, the ocean's silvered gray shimmered like the skin of some enormous fish. Farther down the road, past palm groves and *fales*, we came to the village—a cluster of concrete houses, a boxy, white church, and a school built in the same design as all the new village schools that had cropped up since Governor Lee took office: a round, *fale*-like central building with detached, flat-roofed classroom wings. The wing that faced the parking area reminded me of a roadside motel, each classroom with its own door opening to the outside.

After confirming the presence of chaperones in the round building where the dance was being held, my father left. The dance got underway: lights dimmed, a local band began playing, and the room filled with teenagers from nearby villages. Right away, Val and I were whisked onto the floor, where boys lined up for turns to dance with us. Uili kept cutting in to dance with Val, but I gyrated and spun with a succession of smiling young men, some wearing garlands of flowers around their necks, all with hair preened to high gloss with coconut oil. The more we all danced, the warmer and closer the room, and the stronger the scent of all those oiled heads. What was at first mildly pleasant now made me queasy. I was relieved when the band took a break and I could step outside.

I sat on the edge of a paved walkway that circled the building, inhaling moist air that smelled of ocean spray, breathing contentment in with the scent. I'd lost sight of Val on the crowded dance floor and hadn't seen her since. I wasn't concerned; I knew Uili wouldn't let her wander far. I wasn't nervous being among strangers in an unfamiliar village, either. If danger had existed, I'm sure I would've been oblivious to it in that heedless way that all adolescents miscalculate risk, but there truly seemed to be nothing to fear here or anywhere on the island. The only crimes reported in *Samoa Times* were petty larcenies and bar fights, and neither seemed likely in this setting where even the breeze was so gentle I barely felt it on my skin.

The band started up again, I went back inside, and a flower-festooned boy pulled me onto the dance floor. I didn't see Val, but I still wasn't worried; maybe she'd slipped out the back door to sneak a smoke. When she hadn't shown up after half a dozen songs, I started asking around.

"The *palagi* girl, Valerie, have you seen her?"

Shrugs.

"She came with me. She was dancing and now she's gone. Where'd she go?"

More shrugs. Finally, one boy remembered seeing her leave. "With Uili." He gestured toward a classroom wing. I considered searching for her but didn't want to intrude, so I kept dancing, watching for her return and glancing at my wristwatch as the hour neared ten o'clock, the time my father had said he'd pick us up.

At nine-thirty, headlight beams swept the parking area like flashlights scanning a crime scene. I took one more look around the room, but all I saw were strange faces, happily unaware of my plight. Threading through the tangle of dancers, I found the boy who said he'd seen Val and Uili leave. I gripped his shoulders and fixed my widened eyes on his.

"Find . . . *palagi* . . . girl . . . Valerie. NOW!" The boy hurried out the door and ran along the walkway, banging on classroom doors. I headed for the parking area, hoping to distract my father and give Val a chance to slip unnoticed through the back door and pretend she'd been at the dance all along. But just as I stepped outside, my father got out of the car. At the same moment, the door of the classroom directly in front of him opened, and a disheveled Val and Uili emerged. Val made a feeble attempt at slinking along the front of the building, but it was pointless.

My father glared at Val and Uili, then at me. His eyes were hard as the tiki Double Ugly's, his lips so tightly pursed they looked stitched together. Even in the darkness I could see the shade of his skin deepening.

"Get in the car," he ordered.

Val turned to give Uili a surreptitious wave. I shoved her into the back seat and crawled into the front, where my father sat staring at the windshield. A light rain was falling; the droplets looked like sweat beading up and trickling down the glass.

On the ride back to town, the car was silent except for the sounds of quickening rain on the ragtop and wipers sweeping the windshield. I wanted to talk to relieve the tension, but I knew better. Instead, I picked at a scar on my wrist until the skin peeled away. Even Val, who never took parental wrath as seriously as I did, had enough sense to keep quiet until we dropped her at her house. She spoke up only to thank my father for the ride and then whisper to me as she crawled from the car, "Call you tomorrow."

My father had barely backed the Tempest out of the Pucketts' driveway and turned it toward Utulei when he unloaded on me.

"How could you let her leave the party?" It wasn't a question, it was an accusation. "She's younger than you. You're responsible for keeping an eye on her."

"Sorry." I tried to sound meek, but the word came out snippy.

"That girl's headed for trouble if she doesn't watch out. It makes me sick, seeing her carry on with those . . . nnn—" The next word stuck in the back of my father's throat.

My head snapped toward him. *Those what?* What was he going to call Uili and his friends? *Natives?* Or was he about to use another, even more offensive, word? I waited for him to expel it, but he pressed his lips together and stared through the rain-streaked windshield.

The drops hit harder now, pelting the roof with hostile force. I drew my knees up and huddled against the passenger door; the armrest pressed into my spine like a gun at my back. Thoughts tangled as I tried to reconcile my father's outburst with what I knew of his attitudes toward people of other races and cultures.

He wasn't a racist. He *wasn't*. Was he?

Back in Stillwater, where scholars from various African, Asian, Middle Eastern, and Latin American countries came to study at the university, he was one of the few physicians in town who welcomed their families as patients, taking pains to learn about their countries and show respect for their customs. Our family had been guests in some of these people's homes; they'd given us gifts and treated us to delicacies, and I'd been proud that my father's kindness and open-mindedness made them think so highly of him.

Where had that father gone? Who was this man beside me in the car? I didn't want to look at him, yet I felt compelled to study the face I so often explored for clues to his state of mind. I looked but didn't know how to interpret what I saw. The twitch of his jaw and set of his mouth—did they signal resolve or regret? Was that steeliness in his eyes, or shame?

More memories crowded my jumbled thoughts. It wasn't just international visitors my father treated respectfully. Whether talking with Irma or Reverend Lawson or the yard man

Clarence, or any of the admittedly few local black people whose lives intersected with ours, he seemed to take a real interest in their lives and treat them as equals, and he stressed to me the importance of doing the same.

That's not to say I'd never heard him use a racial slur. He reserved the term, though, for a few "lowlifes" who repeatedly showed up in Stillwater Hospital's emergency room on Saturday nights, tanked up and bloodied from quarrels that turned nasty when somebody pulled a knife. The way he used the epithet made me think it had more to do with conduct than color. (Though now that I thought about it, I couldn't recall him ever using the word to describe a white person.)

Was he lumping the Samoan boys into that category? The boys Val and I found so courteous and charming? The boys who treated us the way our parents constantly reminded us we deserved to be treated? And if he was, why? I knew it wasn't their Samoan-ness—or at least not *just* their Samoan-ness. In spite of his unthinking references to "natives," he'd never said anything negative about other Samoans. He had nothing but praise for the Samoan medical practitioners and nurses he worked with, and he and my mother enjoyed the company of Samoan friends. What made those people so different from the boys who'd now become UA SA – FORBIDDEN?

For the first time in memory, I had no idea what my father was thinking and feeling. I wasn't sure I wanted to know.

Chapter 15 — Reconciled

O le upega e fili i le pō, 'ae talatala i le ao.
(The net that was tangled at night will be straightened in the morning.)
— Samoan proverb interpreted as "The dispute will be settled."

reconcile
- *to compose or settle (a quarrel, dispute, etc.)*
- *to win over to friendliness; cause to become amicable, e.g. to reconcile hostile persons*
- *to bring into agreement or harmony; make compatible or consistent*
- *to accept or be resigned to something not desired*

Steam coated the bathroom mirror and hung in the sodden air. I picked up a towel and wiped away the haze, careful not to bump two geckos that clung to the mirror's surface. The little lizards no longer repulsed me; I'd come to think of them as secret, silent friends, diaphanous as fairies — ever present, always watching, never judging, even now as I stood wet-haired and naked.

"It's not fair," I hissed. Reflected in the mirror, the geckos' wide eyes and upturned mouths urged me on. "Just when I'm starting to feel like I belong, he wants to cut me off from everyone."

One gecko cocked its head as if needing clarification.

"My dad, I'm talking about," I said. "As far as he's concerned, nobody's good enough — except maybe *Prince Carlson*." I spat the last two words so forcefully the geckos skittered to the top of the mirror. Days had passed since my father's flare-ups, but my resentment still festered.

A knock at the bathroom door interrupted my rant. I wrapped a *lavalava* around myself and opened the door a crack.

"Mind if I come in?" My mother seemed unusually buoyant. Christmas was three weeks away, and she and my father had been to a pre-holiday soirée at the governor's house the night before. I was sure she was about to bust wanting to tell me how grand it was. I wasn't in the mood to hear about it—just a bunch of *palagis*, no doubt, partying in Government House, high on a ridge, far above the "natives." I beckoned her in anyway. She leaned against the vanity and watched me comb snarls from my hair. Her fingernails, polished in Revlon "Fire and Ice" pitter-pattered against the countertop, echoing rain on the roof overhead.

"What's up?" The interest in my voice was slack as the strands that framed my face.

She quit the fingernail tap dance and gave me an earnest look, sixteen years of maternal concern engraved around her eyes. "Christmas. Just wondering what you'd like for Christmas—a new dress, something for your room? There's not much to choose from here, we have to make do, but—"

"Peace on Earth," I said, erasing the last trace of inflection from my voice. "That's all I want for Christmas." *Or at least peace in this family.*

I tugged the comb through my hair and pulled at the ends, trying to straighten the waves. Val had been right, Dippity-do was not to be found on the island. I'd had to resort to stretching my hair taut and Scotch-taping it under my chin until it dried or setting it with beer, which worked pretty well except on rainy days (almost *every* day now that rainy season was underway), when the dampness made my head smell like Pago Bar.

My mother picked up another comb and fussed with my hair, restoring the waves I'd just smoothed. I swatted her hand away. She gave me the forbearing-mother-of-a-trying-teenager look and changed tack. "We were thinking about a cable car ride

the day after Christmas. Daddy has the day off. Maybe Peki
would like to come along."

Peki? I shot a look at the geckos to see if the suggestion
surprised them as much as it did me. They blinked, impassive
little blinks I couldn't read. My eyes traveled to my mother's
reflection. Her expression was just as inscrutable.

"Haven't you heard?" I said. "There's a Samoan boy ban in
effect. Along with the previously-imposed *palagi* boy ban." I
opened a drawer and flung my comb into it, just to hear the
clatter.

"Oh, honey. You know Daddy gets worked up sometimes
and says things he doesn't mean. We just worry about you girls.
Val's parents do, too. It seems like we're the only parents on the
island who do. But Peki's a good boy. He doesn't have to stay
away."

I looked again at the geckos. I could swear one of them
shrugged. Everybody said teenagers were hard to understand,
with our up-and-down moods, but parents were just as screwy,
acting one way one day, changing direction the next. I still
wondered what was going on in my father's head—and heart.
Had he blurted something uncharacteristic in the fury of a
protective parental conniption, or were there parts of him I
hadn't seen—hadn't wanted to see—before? I wanted to stay
angry at him until I was sure he deserved mercy, and to be pissy
with my blameless mother for good measure.

Anger heated me up and gave me a righteous glow, but its
sour taste curdled in my stomach. As much as I wanted to rage
against my parents, I had to admit they *were* the same parents
who tolerated my flaws and still loved me, even when I set the
house on fire. Besides, it was the holidays. Yes, but . . .

Conflicting emotions whipsawed in my mind. Fury.
Forgiveness.   Indignation.   Indulgence.   Resentment.
Reconciliation. Outrage. Outreach. If only I could separate my
belligerent and benevolent sides like the Samoan twin goddesses
Taema and Tilafaiga. Born conjoined, the sisters split apart when

a scrap of wood shot between them as they swam in turbulent waters. After traveling together and slaughtering warriors on Tutuila and Savai'i, they agreed to separate for good, with Tilafaiga remaining warlike on their home island of Ta'ū and Taema pursuing a more peaceful path, forever protecting the island of Tutuila from strife.

But I was no goddess, and I couldn't split in two. I was one very mortal girl, indivisible, with loving and hateful impulses wrestling inside me. Only I could decide which would prevail.

I unclenched and let my mind fill with soft-focus pictures: childhood Christmases with heaps of presents and a feeling like candy dancing in my veins; magazine photos of my mellow, flower-child idols flashing two-fingered peace signs. My hostility shut down for the holidays.

"So." I turned to my mother, and my voice brightened like a lit-up Christmas tree. "Tell me about the party."

Back in good graces, Peki seemed more a part of our *aiga* than ever and now visited several nights a week without Fibber or Li'i for support. Some evenings, he'd hang around even after I'd gone to bed, sitting in the living room with my parents, not saying a word, just reading magazines until my mother suggested it was time to go home.

So gracious were my parents, Peki decided he wanted to buy them a special Christmas gift. Carried away with the peacemaking spirit, I suggested going in together on a basket or carving from the tourist *fale* in Fagatogo, never considering that giving a gift as a couple – to my parents, no less – might imply a degree of attachment I didn't intend.

I should've known better. As much as Peki seemed like part of the family, he didn't want to be my brother; he wanted to be my boyfriend. I knew it and didn't know what to do about it. I liked him well enough – what was there not to like about such a sweet, unobtrusive boy? – but he wasn't the boyfriend I wanted, if I wanted a boyfriend at all. Dick still was, and even though he'd become resigned to our enforced separation and now treated me more like a kid sister than girlfriend material, I knew he still wanted me on the back of his Honda.

Christmas morning, my parents exclaimed over the handmade gifts I gave them—a housecoat for my mother and an empty brandy bottle for my father, decoupaged with a mosaic of colorful magazine-page triangles like the ones we'd used to make the beaded curtain. But they *gushed* over the gift from Peki and me. We'd splurged on a fifteen-dollar, tabletop replica of a *fale*, with shells and woven pandanus around the base, crushed coral on the floor, wooden posts, and a carved roof that looked like real thatch. I couldn't wait to tell Peki, who was home celebrating with his family, how much my parents loved the gift.

But first, I had my own gifts to open. From Oklahoma friends, nail polish in pop-art colors, a selection of frosted lipsticks packaged like watercolors in a paint box, and a record album; from cousins, perfume and nylons; from each of my grandmothers, a five-dollar bill; and from my parents, two dresses, three pairs of flip-flops, a dust ruffle for my bed and— the best—a tortoise shell bracelet with S-A-M-O-A spelled out in inlaid metal. The bracelet matched the ring I now wore on the middle finger of my right hand: a tortoise-shell band with an inlaid circle of iridescent shell that changed color when I turned my hand this way and that, and my initial, "N," embedded just above the pearly circle. Samoan girls wore rings like this. At first I'd tried wearing it alongside my silver Tri Chi ring, but the two rings rubbed and clacked against each other and didn't look right together. Without ceremony, I'd taken off the Tri Chi ring and stashed it in a box in my dresser. Now the island-girl ring was my talisman and worry stone.

Rubbing its polished surface, I took my time before reaching for one last package. Wrapped in green and red with my name printed in ballpoint pen on the paper, the gift was from Peki, and as much as I'd shaken and prodded it, I had no clue what was inside. I always hoped for boys to give me jewelry at Christmas—heart-shaped rhinestone pendants or engraved bracelets—but this box was too big for a trinket. It could've held a blouse, but whatever was inside was too heavy and rattle-y to be clothing. I imagined some delightful assortment of crafts from the tourist *fale*—shell necklaces, seed-pod garlands, a shark's tooth pendant, a miniature kava bowl—a uniquely Samoan selection chosen just for me.

I laid the box on my lap and peeled off the paper, slowly, as if undressing the present. Peki's was the only gift I'd gotten from a boy this Christmas; I needed to savor every step. I lifted the lid, just enough to peek inside; then all the way. I commanded my fingers to remain calm, but they raced ahead, impelled by a momentum all their own, scrambling through layers of tissue paper to reveal—*what??* No shells, no seeds, no kava bowl. Inside the box, under the tissue, lay a vanity set, a fancied-up plastic comb, brush, and mirror, the kind girls gave each other at pre-teen birthday parties. I picked up the brush and ran it through my hair. The handle didn't fit my hand. The bristles scratched my scalp. I laid it down, picked up the mirror and caught a glimpse of a face devoid of delight.

Peki didn't know what I wanted. How could he know? He was a Samoan boy guessing at what would please a *palagi* girl, unaware that authentic Samoan creations were finer treasures than American junk. But Peki's gift was my only gift from a boy this Christmas. I would try my best to love it.

The day after Christmas, my parents, Peki, and I drove up Solo Hill to the cable car station, excited to embark upon the most stunning, palpitating ride in the South Pacific—maybe in the whole world. The tram that swayed above cruise ships and showered blossoms on tourists was the same one that ferried passengers from the Solo Hill terminal, across Pago Pago Harbor, to the top of Mount Alava, some sixteen hundred feet above the bay. The yellow car hung from a single cable that stretched six thousand feet from terminal to terminal, making the cableway the longest single-span aerial tramway in the world at the time.

Stepping into the elevator-sized car took some nerve, but once we were on our swinging, soaring way, I put my faith in the cable and the operators, men who took pride in their positions. Like many Samoans in this time of transition, they appreciated the government jobs that allowed them to leave the taro fields and *rise above*.

As we crossed the bay, I pressed against the car's side wall, my face as close to the window as I could get it without smooshing it against the glass. From this angle, my parents, Peki, and the other passengers disappeared; tram and girl merged, and I sailed solo across the harbor. The water below, sparkle-flecked at the surface, deeply, greenly shadowed beneath, reminded me of the eyeshadow my mother wore to parties. I was swamped with love — for mother and sea and everything in sight.

At the far edge of the bay, the tram climbed straight up the mountainside, and the view through the front windows got me thinking about perspectives. From afar, I'd seen the mountains as uniformly green cushions, but up close, the variety of textures, shades, shapes, and heights of greenery blanketing the hillside looked more like the creation of a delirious florist, everything thrown together in a mix that somehow came out just right. The view out the back was just as mind-bending. All the large-as-my-life settings of my daily routines — our apartment building, the high school, the Turtle, the tennis court, Centipede Row, the shops of Fagatogo — had shrunk to rice-grain size; cars were moving specks, people too tiny to see, too tiny to distinguish Samoan from *palagi*. A smooth pulse of harmony coursed through my heart. I hoped the whole island felt it.

No longer flying solo, I now was aware of Peki and my parents with me in the car. Were they viewing the island the way I was? I couldn't find words to articulate the question.

"Wow," was all I said. "Wowwwwwwwww."

My parents and Peki smiled, at me, at one another. Maybe they did see what I saw.

We reached the top, exited the tram, and followed a paved walkway through a park-like setting of natural and landscaped vegetation, toward an outlook pavilion shaped like a *fale*. Everything was clean and new and bright. Two television transmitting towers reached skyward, steely arms in a hallelujah gesture. I felt like throwing my arms toward the heavens, too. Glory, glory, glory all around.

"Can you believe this place?" I said to Peki. "That we *live* here?" He gave me a *crazy-palagi-girl* look and shook his head, but he smiled. Did he know how lucky he was to grow up here? To be able to stay as long as he wanted? Sure, Samoa was changing, but it still was a wondrous place to be.

I leaned over the guardrail and took in the vista, a landscape dominated by volcanic peaks heaved from the ocean a million and a half years before and now necklaced with buildings, some left over from Navy occupation in the first half of the twentieth century, others from the latest influx of Americanism. An island ordained by the goddesses as a haven. From this vantage point, the mountains where Taema and Tilafaiga left their footprints appeared as drowsy giants, unconcerned with all the activity and commerce at their bases. But I knew better. Those mountains watched what went on. They breathed and moaned and sang in concert with the lives beneath them. They *listened*. Once I'd understood this, I'd made them my friends, more trusted than even the geckos. Now, every day on my walks to school, to Val's house, to Fagatogo, I confided in those mountains, asking them questions I couldn't ask anyone else and quieting my mind to hear their answers.

The railing was painted the color of overripe papaya, the color of heat. I leaned harder against it and transmitted a message to the mountains: *I'm in love with this place! Is this where I belong?*

I looked down on trees where flying foxes roosted. Wild ginger spiked the air. Peki, eager to explore the rest of the mountaintop, tugged at my hand.

"Go on," I said. "I'll catch up with you." He shuffled off to the outlook, where my father snapped pictures. I waited and listened, waited and listened, but the mountains were mute. My question was one they'd been asked before, but one they couldn't presume to answer.

On the way back to the cable car, my father shot more pictures, individual close-ups of me, my mother, and Peki against a scrim of distant sea blending into sky.

"Now you and Peki together," he said.

Interesting. In our three months on the island I couldn't recall him taking a single shot of me with anyone else, except my mother. Certainly not with a boy. Was this just another slide for his travelogue—caption: *Nancy with native boy*? Or did it signal some new level of acceptance?

I stood beside Peki, a modest gap between us. Was *this* where I belonged? Another question the mountains couldn't answer.

INTERLUDE—EPHEMERA

*T*hat dream again. The one I've been having since—when, exactly? Pinpointing when it began is like extracting a raindrop from a river: its haunting impressions meld with images from my waking life.

I'm walking on the gravel path toward Fagatogo, upstream against the current of hearty men and women with flashing eyebrows and baskets of bananas. My gaze meets theirs but then is drawn to the distant mountains. I mentally trace the contours of their slopes, as if running my fingers over a lover's sinews and soft spots.

I'm home.

But no. Only visiting, and not for long. The moment I feel embraced by familiar sights, the instant I take a breath of frangipani-charged air and sense my heartbeat synchronizing with the pace of island life, I'm aware of an opposing impulse demanding that I hurry, hurry, reminding me my time is running out. And though I'm still here on the island, I yearn for it.

Was it the recurring dream or the reality of this impermanent island life that changed the way I experienced my days? Time had always seemed limitless—it does when you're young—with days that sometimes felt unbearably long and a future that stretched over the horizon like that highway I used to stare at from the Sonic parking lot. But in Samoa, my perception of time shifted, as if I were at the opposite end of life, aware of time's all-too-rapid passage and my utter powerlessness against its progress.

The reminders were hard to ignore. In nearly every conversation, someone mentioned a kid whose time on the island had expired before mine began.

"Oh, that's right, you never knew Reggie—he left before you came. Man, what a blast we used to have with him." Or, "You never met Barb, did you? We all hated to see her go."

The comments were vague enough to leave me wondering exactly what I'd missed, but so tantalizing I was sure I'd missed *something* by arriving precisely when I did. And with that realization came an awareness, like the shadow of a predatory bird, of how ephemeral the Samoa experience was for my friends and me.

In Oklahoma, my friendships were so constant I never considered they might not last a lifetime. Here, transience was a way of life. Except for the Samoans among us, we were all short-timers whose parents' two-year contracts dictated our tenures. I knew my friends' projected departure dates as well as I knew their birthdays, and all the while we were growing closer, we were doing the mental math and detaching by degrees, preparing for the inevitable separation.

Ephemerality wasn't lost on my Samoan friends, even those who expected to spend their lives on Tutuila. In fact, they reveled in an annual celebration—as eagerly anticipated as Thanksgiving—that owes its existence to a fleeting phenomenon. Every October or November (the exact timing depends on lunar cycles and other factors), sea worms known as *palolo* unhitch the back ends of their bodies like freight trains uncoupling cars. The long, segmented sections, which look like twirling spaghetti and contain the worms' reproductive equipment, rise to the surface en masse, where they dissolve, releasing eggs and sperm. Unless, that is, they're scooped up first by hungry Samoans who consider the aquatic vermicelli their ambrosia.

I'd witnessed the annual spectacle, seen the reefs twinkling with the lanterns of Samoans netting *palolo,* heard my Samoan friends rave about fried *palolo* on toast. Never tried it myself, figuring something so rare, so relished by the islanders, shouldn't be wasted on someone who might not appreciate its salty tartness and scratchy texture. Or maybe I just didn't want to get attached to one more thing I'd never taste again.

Though I never tried *palolo*, I regarded my whole life now as a delicacy to be scooped up and devoured, throwing myself into beach parties and dances, exclaiming over parades and fireworks, following romantic leads, exchanging intimacies with girlfriends, geckos, and mountains, taking in as much Samoa as I could. Gobbling it all down before it was gone.

Chapter 16 — Attached

Ua numi le fau.
(It's more complicated than it looks.)
— *Samoan proverb*

The boyfriend thing was getting sticky. Peki not only made himself at home in our living room, he also stationed himself by my side at every party, like a Fita Fita guard standing duty. One night, emboldened by beer, he'd whispered "*Alofa* Nancy," and not as part of a language lesson.

Did I reply "*Alofa* Peki"? I'm not sure. His company and devotion were rock beneath my fidgety feet, but sometimes I felt like that rock was fastened to a chain around my neck. That was the thing about attachment: it grounded you, but it weighed you down. Narrowed your options. Obliterated your identity if you weren't careful. Right now, even in my conciliatory mood, I was detaching from my parents, trying to become my own person. Why tether myself to someone else?

Especially now, when my options were so uncommonly kaleidoscopic. For the first time in my life, I had not just *a* boyfriend, but boys, boys, boys, boys lining up to dance with me, walk me home, date me, kiss me. So what if my desirability had more to do with being one of a handful of *palagi* girls on the island than with my shiny hair or kissing skills? I was loving the attention, the fizzy thrill of never knowing who I'd end up with at a party.

In my diary, in tiny backhand script, I detailed encounters with the many young men I believed to be infatuated with me: student council president Eric (of the long limbs and skewed smile), Vampires bass player Poloka (of the Dylan-esque hair and scowl), drummer Pili (Beatle-ish swoop of bangs), governor's son Carlson (limo and freezer full of hamburger patties), new kid Wayne (half-Hawaiian, hyperkinetic, marginally annoying), two-years-younger Lane (twerpy, too, but with redeeming Burt Reynolds looks), plus the ever-present Peki, and Dick, always Dick.

As for my own affections, they shifted from day to day, hour to hour, minute to minute. "Stringing along" was not a term I liked to apply to my current state, but for now, neither was "attached."

Not to boys, at least. My island, my mountains, those were another matter. Those were attachments I didn't mind, attachments that demanded nothing of me. But the more attuned I became to my island home, the more I noticed *its* growing attachments: to American dollars, goods and habits. Those connections did come with strings, strings that were hard to see at first, like a spider web you don't notice until you walk right into it and feel the cling of its strands.

They'd grown slowly during much of American Samoa's sixty-five years as a U.S. territory. For most of that time, the territory was left to its *fa'a Samoa* ways, except during World War II, when the place swarmed with sailors and Marines and serenity was shattered with guns firing practice rounds and even one shelling from a Japanese sub. After the war, decades passed and not much happened until the early 1960s, when, embarrassed by a *Reader's Digest* article titled "Samoa: America's Shame in the South Seas," the U.S. government coughed up some cash and appointed a new governor.

Enter H. Rex Lee, Carlson's dad and former deputy commissioner of the Bureau of Indian Affairs. When Governor Lee took charge of the territory he described on first encounter as "a melancholy vista if ever I saw one," he shook loose more funds from Congress, recruited help from the Navy, got island chiefs onboard with his vision—new schools, educational TV, roads, tourism — and transformed Tutuila so completely that when the *Reader's Digest* reporter came back to see the results, he wrote a glowing sequel to his first story, titled "Samoa: America's Showplace of the South Seas."

That second article had just come out, around the same time the new luxury hotel opened with a grand celebration, and now the whole island was basking in the blinding sunshine of acclaim and expectation.

But sunshine makes for shadows, and the modernization campaign had a darker side. With all the public works projects underway, jobs were plentiful and traditional ways of making a living — fishing and farming — weren't so attractive. More and more, Samoans now relied on paychecks instead of age-old skills, and because most of those paychecks came from government projects, Samoan society depended more and more on its U.S. connection. Who could foresee the day when funds would dry up, roads and buildings would corrode and crumble in the salt air, and there'd be no resources to maintain everything that had been created and dedicated with great fanfare during the current building boom?

Governor Lee always insisted that "All we do is aimed at keeping Samoa Samoan." But really, how could American Samoa hold on to its identity with all its new entanglements?

Like I said, attachment can get sticky. Sometimes, though, you can't resist. Case in point: New Year's Eve.

Carlson had the limo and Tuke's services for the entire day and night and recruited a gang of us to party with him. After swimming at Larsen's Beach and stopping for ice cream and Cokes at the governor's house, we piled back into the car and headed for a party in Tafuna, where Peki, Dick, and others waited.

The mood at the party was flirty and convivial, everyone exchanging New Year's kisses like dime-store hearts on

Valentine's Day. After giving and receiving a few, I turned to Peki, who stood in his usual spot beside me.

"You'd better get busy. A lot of girls are waiting for your kisses." I gestured toward the floor where Marnie, Suzi, Kathi, and a few others sat in a circle, smiling in his direction.

Peki looked at his feet, spilling over the sides of his flip-flops. "No. I'll only kiss you," he said.

"Have it your way." I flounced to a sofa in the next room, where Val sat with Dick.

"Peki's missing out on all the fun," I told Val. "Go give him a kiss." She went off to find him, leaving me alone with Dick.

"Silly boy. Peki says he won't kiss anyone but me." I meant to sound playful but realized too late it came off conceited. Dick looked away, then back at me with eyes like small oceans.

"If everything had gone the way I wanted it, I'd be the one saying that."

His words whirled in the pit of my stomach and set off vibrations as stirring as the Vampires' music. I gave him a long, appraising look. He hadn't gotten any better looking. No matter; some deeper appeal kept drawing me back. Was it just the drama of forbidden romance? The self-centered pleasure of knowing he was tormented with unfulfilled desire for me? Or was it something about *him* – his outrageousness, his motorcycle-fueled sex appeal, his refusal to shape himself into anyone else's notion of what he ought to be? It was all those things and the way they were mashed up together. And it was also the simplest thing: when he wasn't spewing profanity or pissing off grown-ups, Dick was a genuinely nice boy who cared about me and treated me with respect.

Also a helluva good kisser.

"Say it anyway." I pulled him off the sofa and into a corner.

We kissed, and I vowed I'd make it work with Dick this time, parents be damned, Peki be damned, detachment be damned. I didn't tell him about my intentions; I didn't see the need. We were attached.

Chapter 17 — Wind

Ua liua le vai o Sinafatunua.
(Sinafatunua's river has turned around.)
— Samoan proverb used when someone loses an advantage and another acquires it.

The waters where my friends and I took our after-school swims were growing warmer by the day. The breeze, just a sighing presence until now, was becoming as assertive as the Oklahoma winds I despised. Of all the weather extremes I'd endured in my home state — summer days in the hundreds, January ice storms, tornado-spawning thunderstorms — the relentless wind always caused me the most distress. No, distress is not a strong enough word. The wind drove me stark raving mad. In winter it whipped at my ears and poked its witchy, frigid fingers through my warmest parka; in spring, its pollen-laden gusts sent me into sneezing frenzies; in summer it kicked up dust swirls that scoured my face and left my hair gritty. I reacted as if every draft were a deliberate attack on my sanity. I slammed doors and screamed into gales. The gales howled louder and drowned out my cries.

Now, Tutuila's wind infuriated me just as much, launching me into tirades when it snatched schoolwork from my fingers and scattered my papers down the street. I hated how it twisted things around, wrested control from my hands, tore apart what had seemed orderly and secure.

The windy days made everyone else edgy, too, especially Dick, whose eruptions boiled out of proportion to the minor frustrations that triggered them. His anger never was directed at me, but I took responsibility for quelling his inner furies. I had cleaved myself to him; I was his mainstay, his tie-down in the tempest.

He should have been in better humor, given recent developments. Though I still hadn't mentioned my resolution to devote myself to him, I'd been sending unmistakable signals: winks, smiles, appreciative laughter, fingertips on his forearm. And as of New Year's Day—an auspicious beginning if ever there was one—my parents had even eased up on him.

That evening a bunch of us, including Dick, had gone to a party at a Samoan kid's house in Pago Pago. The band that was supposed to play had gone fishing instead, so the party was called off. Still in a social mood, we all traipsed over to my house to play records. I raced inside ahead of everyone else to ask if it was okay for Dick to come in. My mother gave me a quizzical look and said, "Well, of course," as if I'd asked permission to mop the floor. My father offered no resistance, either. I hustled Dick inside before they could change their minds.

The evening felt surreal: Dick in my house, drinking the Fanta my mother offered, shooting me a grin as he picked out a Beach Boys album, settling into the rattan easy chair as if he'd always been welcome to stretch out there. My secret plan was off to a promising start. Yet by the time school resumed after the holidays, Dick was a vortex of agitation.

In typing class one afternoon, he swore under his breath from the desk behind mine as his fingers stumbled during a timed test. At the desk beside his, the class star—a pixie-faced Samoan girl named Ramona—fluttered her tiny hands across the keyboard, logging eighty-plus perfectly-typed words per minute. The faster Ramona typed, the more flustered Dick became, and the louder and more frequent his expletives. The Royal typewriters on our desks were manual models as big as window air-conditioners, with keys that balked unless struck with tendon-snapping force. I hammered at my keyboard with as much pressure as my piano-conditioned fingers could muster, adding to the classroom clatter I hoped would mask Dick's outbursts.

Blasts of wind swept through the screened windows, rattling the papers in our copy stands and blowing my hair into my face as our teacher, Mrs. Counihan, patrolled the aisles, announcing minute by minute how much time was left until the kitchen timer on her desk rang like a fire alarm. With her spool-like, silver curls and her Naturalizer shoes, Mrs. Counihan looked like she should be crocheting afghans, but she ruled the classroom with the steeliness of a schoolmarm who'd been putting up with adolescent exuberance far too long. Mrs. Counihan tolerated no fooling around, no impudent attitudes, no distractions from the QWERTY keyboard and the interminable transcription of disembodied paragraphs. And because Dick personified distraction, impudence, and fooling around, Mrs. Counihan detested him. Her disapproval meant nothing to Dick and wouldn't have mattered to me if Mrs. Counihan hadn't belonged to my mother's bridge club. I knew she reported Dick's offenses with the exactitude of a probation officer, and now that my parents were at least tolerating him, I didn't want to lose ground.

The timer sounded—a drawn-out jangle that ended in a shudder. All around the room, fingers stopped mid-stroke, except at the desk behind me, where I heard *tap-SHIT!-taptap-SONOFABITCH!-taptaptap.*

Mrs. Counihan's glare was a gun precisely pointed at Dick's head.

"Richard!"

I flinched at the sternness of her voice, but it had no effect on Dick. Another gust invaded the classroom and sent papers flying in all directions. My sympathies were blowing every which way, too. Sure, Dick was frustrated—I got that—but why couldn't he just act right, at least in front of grown-ups, instead of giving them more reasons to distrust and despise him? Was that really so hard? What was I signing on for in pledging myself to this boy? I gave him a harsh look.

"Richard Whitaker, you will stop typing when the timer sounds, or you will receive an automatic F." Mrs. Counihan bounded down the aisle and ripped the paper from Dick's typewriter, spinning the platen so hard it kept whizzing after she walked away. She tore the typing test in half, wadded the two pieces into a ball and strode toward the trash can at the front of the room.

There was silence for a moment, then scraping as Dick pushed his chair back from his desk, followed by rustling around the room as we all swiveled in our seats to see what would happen next.

Dick stood, lifted the typewriter off the desk with both hands, and with a huff, heaved it onto the floor. The crash reverberated like a felled tree, and right behind it came Dick's grand finale.

"I hate Jesus Christ!" he roared like a furious beast. Rage reddened his face. My face burned, too. He hated *Jesus*? I *loved* Jesus. Everyone loved Jesus. Did he really hate Jesus, or was that just the most outrageous thing he could come up with?

Dick turned and ran from the room, his sneakers yelping on the wooden floor. I listened as his footsteps reported his path — through the hallway, down the stairs, out of the building.

Then there was no sound at all but the slapping of screens against the window frames.

The winds and warm waters were signs that hurricane season was upon us. More senseless fury waiting to be unleashed with the slightest provocation. With the changing weather, some savvy islanders stocked up on food and kerosene for lanterns and lashed coconut fronds to their *fales*, but my girlfriends fortified themselves in a different way, with a sudden new interest — in a sailboat, of all things. In the months I'd lived on the island, we girls had loitered at the tennis court, hung around the cruise ship dock, and explored every shop in town, but never had anyone suggested visiting the marina that lay beyond Fagatogo, near the village of Pago Pago at the harbor's apex. Now every after-school shopping trip required a detour past the small-boat basin, where a twenty-four-foot sloop had been anchored for several days.

The draw was not really the boat, but its sixteen-year-old skipper. Robin Lee Graham, a California kid with pluck and unbelievably trusting parents, had set off from San Pedro the previous July, intending to sail around the world. Now it was January, and after encountering a mast-buckling gale fifteen miles from Tutuila, he was sitting out hurricane season in Samoa.

I'd read about his voyage before we left Oklahoma—how he'd ventured out on *Dove* with only two kittens and a guitar for company and $75, some secondhand clothes, and a bunch of ballpoint pens for currency—and I'd wished I could meet such a daring boy. Here was a kid who was doing in real life the kind of stuff I'd playacted in my childhood backyard dramas. And here was a boy who, unlike Dick, channeled his thirst for excitement and independence into real accomplishment, not pointless defiance. Now chance had deposited us both on the same piece of rock in the Pacific.

"Has anyone seen him yet?" I asked as our troop made another pass by the marina.

Suzi and Kathi exchanged smug looks.

"Seen him?" Suzi's smile was feline. "We've been on his boat. Karl went down to meet him as soon as he heard he was in port. So Lee—that's what he likes to be called—invited Karl aboard for a beer last night, and Karl said we could come along."

It was bad enough that Suzi had something to gloat about, but Kathi, too? She'd been getting under my skin since I'd noticed Dick paying attention to her shortly after the typewriter incident, though I found her harder to dislike than Suzi. That was just the problem: nothing about Kathi was unappealing;

everything was—I hated to use the word—*adorable*, with those shining eyes and that pinch of freckles strewn across her nose. There *was* something in the slouch of her stance and the shadows around her eyes that made her seem vulnerable and a tad insecure, but instead of acting tongue-tied and awkward around boys as I often did, she sparkled.

I first observed her in action one afternoon when one of the older Samoan boys took a bunch of us for a ride in the back of his pickup to the east end of the island. As I hunkered down in the truck bed and watched the rolling backdrop of white sand beaches and picturesque villages, Kathi stood pressed against the cab, face to the breeze, laughing as her hair streamed like wisps of smoke in a wind tunnel. At one point she turned toward the rest of us and began singing: *I want to go back to my little grass shack in Kealakekua, Hawaaa—iiiii.* She knew all the words, even the tongue-twisting Hawaiian lines, and when she ended with . . . *where the humuhumunukunukuapua'a go swimming by,* I secretly hoped the truck would hit a pothole and she'd go flying out and land head-first in the *sami* to sleep forever with the *humuhumunukunukuapua'a.* Instead, she launched into another song, the spirited Samoan tune "Minoi, Minoi" (Wiggle, Wiggle), swiveling her hips as she sang. I tried to join in, but I knew only a couple of lines, couldn't carry a tune, and had no hips worth wiggling, so I went back to staring at the scenery.

So now, this little Gidget, this kitten-girl, had Dick under her spell and a head start on Lee, the boat boy. I told myself that a young man who was out on his own in the world, who had to contend with sharks and squalls, wouldn't be beguiled for long by a fourteen-year-old's patter, however charming it might be. And neither would Dick, right?

Val and I spent the next afternoon exploring the *Australis,* the biggest ocean liner Samoa had ever seen. The thousand-passenger ship was so enormous we kept getting lost in its labyrinth of passageways, becoming so disoriented we forgot to speak to each other in pseudo-Samoan. When we emerged late in the day, Kathi and Suzi were waiting at the end of the gangplank.

"Guess what!" Kathi's face was luminous. "Lee's having a little party on his boat tonight. We're all invited."

I hurried home to get ready for the evening, debating whether to make up some phony destination—a Rec Hall dance or a movie at the club—or tell my parents where I really was going.

My mother was setting the table when I walked in the door, my father putting finishing touches on a bowl of fresh pineapple, mango, papaya, and banana slices. I looked around for something to do, not so much to maintain the usual flow of our family's cooperative efforts as to shore up my image as a helpful, obedient daughter.

"How was the boat?" my mother asked.

"Boat? I haven't been on anyone's boat," I blurted, forgetting, in my quandary over Lee's invitation, all about the *Australis*. Then trying to cover my fumble, "Oh, you mean the *ship*. It was fine. Big. Pretty. Fine."

"Say," my father said, "speaking of boats, you'll never guess who I met today. That boy who's sailing around the world. He was down at the market when I was buying fruit. Seems like a very nice young man. He asked if I knew where there was a Laundromat, and I told him he could come over here to use our washer and dryer any time."

Whatever remaining resentments I had toward my father swirled away like dirty wash water, and in flowed a new current of fantasy material. In my mind, I was still pledged to Dick, even if he didn't know it. But Dick was *work*, Dick was *trouble*, Dick was *flirting with Kathi*. Lee, though I hadn't met him yet, at least had the advantage of my father's approval. No harm in exploring the possibilities while I worked things out with Dick.

After dinner I changed into denim shorts and a red-and-white striped pullover that came as close to looking nautical as anything in my wardrobe; then I headed to Val's to meet the other girls. On the way to the boat basin, Val and I bombarded Suzi and Kathi with questions about the young mariner. The authoritative tone of their answers irritated me.

"Oh, and you didn't ask, but his cats are named Suzette and Joliette," Kathi volunteered.

I thanked her for the information instead of smacking her like I wanted to.

It was dark when we reached the marina, but Kathi and Suzi had no trouble leading us to the slip where *Dove* was moored. Dick, Eric, and another schoolmate, Ed, were already aboard the sloop, which seemed scarcely larger than the rowboats my cousins and I used to paddle around the lake where their parents had a summer cottage. Sitting with the other boys, wearing a blue-and-white flowered Hawaiian shirt and tattered pants, was the sandy-haired "Schoolboy Sailor," as newspapers called him.

He flashed the smile I'd memorized from magazine photos: unassuming and lopsided. Then he disappeared into the cabin and popped up with bottles of beer in both hands. The boys took them; we girls all declined. Lee crawled back onto the deck and squeezed between Suzi and Kathi, who'd inserted herself beside Dick before I could claim the spot. The boys continued the conversation they'd started before we arrived, asking Lee all about the boat and his adventures at sea.

Dove's sway felt like the little dance that mothers do to soothe their babies, shifting from one foot to the other. For accompaniment, riggings clanged against masts, and waves sloshed against the sailboat's sides. The motion and repetitive sounds put me into a trancelike state. Dick acted calmer, too, nodding and smiling as Lee talked. I wanted him to smile at me. I directed one of my subtle signals his way. He didn't notice.

I tried to focus on the boys' conversation, groping for a sentence or phrase onto which I could attach a tiny barnacle of intelligent comment. But I knew nothing about sextants and genoas, and any question I could think to ask about Lee's voyage seemed shallow and fawning. Finally, I blurted, "Where are your cats?" and immediately wished I'd come up with something better.

Lee, still caught up in boy talk, barely looked my way. "Down below, I guess."

Then Kathi spoke up. "Hey! Do you know what a cat's favorite color is?"

Lee gave her the magazine smile. "No, what?"

"Purrrrr-ple."

Dick, whose arm rested on the back of Kathi's seat, slipped it around her, gave her a squeeze, and laughed like she'd said something truly hilarious. Ed smiled and nodded. Eric said, "Good one, Kath." Val and I exchanged eye rolls.

"Okay, how about this one?" Kathi's eyes shone in the glow of Lee's kerosene lantern. "What do you call a cat that likes to dig on the beach?" She paused for effect, then chirped, "Sandy Claws!"

I stared up at the stars and for the rest of the night, sent no more smile signals.

Val sat at the kitchen table, scraps of colored paper splayed before her like a hand of cards.

"How do you like my invitation design?" She held up a bit of orange paper cut into a shape that resembled a tombstone with feet. On the tombstone's slab, she'd drawn an amusing face and stick-like arms that held a square sign on which to write the invitee's name.

"It's an Ug!" I said, recognizing the cartoon character she'd invented. "I love it!"

The Ug cartoons had started as a distraction for the two of us on afternoons when the wind kept us indoors. We'd retreat to Val's bedroom or mine and draw comic strips dramatizing events of our lives—or, more accurately, our fantasy lives—populated with Ug versions of our friends and family. Ug-Dick, who starred in many of the strips, had a sweep of blond hair. Ug-Wendy wore a stylish bob and a permanent blush. Shy Li'i was represented by an Ug facing the opposite direction, and Peki's Ug kept its arms folded across its chest in Peki's usual stance. Eventually, Kathi and Suzi saw a few of the cartoons, and word spread. Now Val was famous around school for representations that, with only a few features, perfectly caricatured our classmates and teachers. Ug-shaped invitations were ideal for her fifteenth birthday celebration, a party we were planning together and, with typical adolescent delusion, expected would resolve any social and emotional difficulties we were experiencing.

Parties in Samoa weren't like the basement rec-room get-togethers I'd gone to in Oklahoma, where a couple dozen kids gathered to play records and drink Cokes on a Saturday night. That kind of event was an everyday occurrence here—with Fantas standing in for Cokes—but real parties, which someone threw every weekend, had live bands and guest lists of seventy-five to a hundred kids, *palagi* and Samoan. Val's invitation list included all the usual gang, plus a slew of Samoan kids from Fagatogo, Utulei, and Pago Pago who had invited us to their parties, and of course Robin Lee Graham. In the days since the boat party fiasco, Val and I had run into Lee and his friend Jud—who'd flown down from California to keep Lee company—once or twice in town. We'd even managed a bit of conversation, enough to feed our crushes on Lee and to convince ourselves that, though he was difficult to read, there was a good chance he found us irresistibly witty and attractive.

I picked up a pair of scissors and started cutting out Ugs as Val inked in their faces and wrote the party time and place on their blank backs.

"Just promise me one thing," I said, "that you won't sneak off to deliver Lee's invitation without me."

On party night, Val and I wore dresses we'd made just for the occasion: hers a white piqué shift, mine an empire design with puffed sleeves, in a blue-and-green print of mod-style daisies as big as dinner plates. I'd fashioned a headband from the same fabric and wore it with my bangs peeking out from beneath. The other girls had gone to extra lengths to look good, too. Kathi and Marnie wore floor-length *holomuu*; Suzi and Wendy, floral prints; Sylvia, satiny pink with a matching bow perched like a skittish butterfly between bangs and teased bubble. Amazing that she'd kept it in place on her way to the party—the wind was so fierce we could feel it indoors, blasting through the screened walls and flapping the canvas curtains.

Boys showed up in pairs: Karl and Nat, Eric and Ed, Fibber and Gus, Li'i and Peki, Carlson and his best friend Riley. Wayne, the hyper kid who'd moved to Samoa a few months earlier, arrived with his sidekick Tau and Tau's brother David, who was visiting from the States. David, like Tau, was quiet and mannerly, with a smile that never quite seemed to reach its full potential. But all three boys talked excitedly about their plans to go surfing that weekend at Nu'uuli, one of the few places on the island where coral reefs weren't a hazard. The crazy winds should whip up some killer waves, they figured.

The Vampires, set up in a corner of the Pucketts' living room, began playing from their repertoire of Ventures-style surf music—"Walk, Don't Run;" "Diamond Head;" "Slaughter on 10th Avenue"—tunes with cascading glissandos that brought to mind boys like David, Tau, and Wayne riding boards down waves as high as Solo Hill. As the dance floor grew more crowded and the dancing more frenetic, I regretted my headband—my head was sweltering—and was grateful for the strong breezes through the screens. The tempo slowed, and the band launched into "Blue Star," the plaintive melody they'd played on my first date with Dick at Goat Island Club—the tune with bass notes that resonated in some aching chamber inside me; high, vibrato strains like transcriptions of my own stirrings, and a wistful ending that sounded like raindrops plinking into a pool.

Carlson asked me to dance. I accepted but kept looking over his shoulder at the doorway. Just as the music came to its most heart-twisting crest, Dick walked in. He wore his usual party outfit: short-sleeved shirt tucked into tight wheat jeans, shiny black Beatle boots. His hair, combed straight back but not slicked down, brushed his collar. Had he ever looked better? My heart wound itself into a tight little knot, and I drew a sharp breath. I tried to catch his eye and send one of my signals, but Kathi caught it first, and he made his way to her side. I crumpled. They'd been keeping steady company since that night on Lee's boat, and I was completely thrown by the development. Even when Dick and I had been forbidden from seeing each other, and I'd run around with every other boy on the island, *he* had never shown any interest in other girls. Even when I'd had misgivings about him, *his* affection for me had never wavered. But now he was tying up at another port, and I was adrift. That was another thing about attachment, I realized now: the pulling away could tear you up.

The music stopped. I told Carlson I needed a drink of water.

"I'll get you a Fanta." He made a move toward the refreshment table, his hair flapping like a silken flag.

"No," I said, "water. I'll get it," and I walked away. I stopped short at the kitchen door when I saw my parents sitting at the table with Val's mother and father. My mother and Mrs. Puckett were laughing, but the men wore serious faces, and their heads were bent in deep conversation. As they talked, my father swigged orange Fanta from a bottle; Dr. Puckett, a lean, dry-witted counterpoint to his wife's ample boldness, drank from a can of beer. I knew they were talking hospital business, commiserating over their frustrations: the opposition they encountered when they tried to introduce a birth control counseling service, the temperamental physicians they had to deal with daily. Val and I had heard our fathers blowing off steam about their troubles at work, and our mothers worrying about the toll the stress was taking on them. If even parents couldn't control the turbulence in their lives, how could we? My old protective impulse — the one I'd recently diverted to Dick — kicked in, and my temporary escape from the party seemed less important than my father's venting session. I might not be able to smooth things over for him any more than I could for Dick, but right now he seemed more worth the effort. Instead of interrupting to get a drink, I returned to the living room and found Val tidying a stack of napkins on the refreshment table.

"Party's going well," I said. "Is Lee here yet?"

Val nodded toward a distant corner.

Lee, in his blue Hawaiian shirt, leaned back in his chair, an expression of mild amusement on his face. It was as though he was observing all of us for a sociological study, interested in our habits in an academic way, but not engaging in our rituals. The difference between his life and mine was so vast I could hardly stand to think about it. Here I'd thought moving to Samoa was a major adventure, but all I'd done was tag along with my parents. What I truly longed for was an experience that required real bravery and tested my fortitude. It occurred to me then why I'd felt attracted to Lee. I didn't want to date him; I wanted to *be* him. Sure, even he had to sit out hurricane season, but in other ways, he was in control, sailing his own ship, making the winds work for him instead of railing against them.

Was that also the root of my attraction to Dick? Wanting to be like him — bolder, more outrageous (not the throwing-typewriters, making-people-hate-you part, but the oh-yeah-who-says-I-can't part)? Did I think that by attaching myself to these boys I'd be transformed into someone who could do things my way, too? No matter. The romance with Dick had been blown off course, and the one with Lee had never left port.

I looked out through the screens at palm trees waving their fronds and lights winking from across the bay, sending signals I didn't know how to read. I couldn't make out the mountains in the darkness, but I'd stared at them so often I could see their shapes like after-images. I knew they were resolute in the wind.

The wind. How it changed everything, and how I hated it. Just weeks before, I was on top of the world—or at least on top of Mount Alava—in love with everything around me and absorbing the love flowing to me from all directions. Now everything had twisted and turned, as if the papers on which I'd so neatly sketched out my life had been ripped from my hands and scattered down the street, the wind hooting at my distress.

But those mountains. No matter what might blow in and out of my life, those mountains would not fail me.

Chapter 18 — More Wind

Ua tagi le Fatu ma le 'Ele'ele.
(The stones and the earth wept.)
— Samoan proverb

Rain was pelting the tin roof like buckets of BBs, and the sky was still black when Val and I dragged ourselves out of bed around noon the next day. The revelry had gone on until one-thirty in the morning, and my parents had let me stay to help clean up and then to spend the night.

Rain was an everyday occurrence in Samoa, but most showers were brief mistings from a sky that didn't bother to cloud up, or sudden downpours that eventually yielded to bright skies. This rain was unrelenting, with a darkness that swallowed up morning and refused to let even a rivulet of light seep through its pores.

Val's mother was in the kitchen when we went to make coffee.

"Radio says there's a hurricane headed straight toward us," she said with no alarm in her voice. "But it's supposed to hit the other side of the island, and not until four o'clock this afternoon. You should probably get home, though, Nancy. I'll drive you."

In the short time it took to drive to Utulei, the forecast was revised, and by the time I got home the cyclone wasn't expected until evening. My parents had the radio on listening for updates and were busy making preparations, as the broadcasts advised. As always, they worked in sync, knowing instinctively what needed to be done and setting to work with no discussion of who should do what. My father rounded up a flashlight, batteries, and kerosene for the one small lantern we owned. I pitched in unprompted, following my mother around the apartment to search for candles. We found only half a dozen, but they'd have to do; all the stores on the island had closed.

Next, we stockpiled water. We had no bathtub, so we filled the washing machine tub and every empty pot, pan, can, and bottle in the house. Usually, when I helped my parents with chores, we chatted to take our minds off the work. This afternoon, subdued by the pounding and squalling outside, we hardly spoke.

"Now what?" I asked my mother when we'd finished with the water, hoping she'd come up with another chore to keep us occupied.

"Just hole up and wait, I guess," she said. "There's not much more we can do." She slumped a little, just for a moment, then straightened her spine and smiled at me. "Guess I'll finally get caught up on those back issues of *Ladies Home Journal.*"

I'd seen my parents in scary situations before: when tornado sirens blared and we had only minutes to take cover, when nurses wheeled my mother away for cancer surgery, and of course, the night of our apartment fire. They never panicked, never showed their fear, always took appropriate action without a lot of fuss, and then hoped for the best. They were brave.

I wanted to be brave, too, like I was in my imaginary life. But I didn't feel it. We were in a house with screens for walls, on an island with few other substantial buildings. If the wind, my old adversary, took out its rage on us, what would become of my family, my friends, my glorious island, that sense of harmony I was trying to hold on to? There was no way of knowing. There never was, was there, when scary things happened? You just had to search every corner of your soul, gather up as much courage as you could find, and hope everything would turn out all right. Or at least not all wrong.

~ ~ ~

Cloistered in my room, I tried to read but couldn't concentrate with rain hammering the roof and wind like an insistent, uninvited guest rapping at the tightly-closed louvers. I peeked out the narrow window beside my bed and caught glimpses of palm trees whipping like wheat stalks. I found Mike, a smoke-colored kitten I'd adopted from the Baker sisters after the fire, cowering under the bed. I pulled him out and tried to hold him on my lap, not sure which of us needed comforting more. He slithered from my grasp and retreated to his hiding place.

My mother looked in and asked how I was doing.

"This is getting scary, Mother. What're we supposed to do?"

"Just sit tight," she said. "I guess they'll tell us on the radio if we have to go to higher ground."

"How would we do that?" No roads snaked up the mountains, and I doubted the cable car to Mount Alava was operating in this tempest.

My mother didn't answer. I looked around my room, mentally gathering up treasures I'd take with me if we had to flee: the oversized, brown leatherette-covered photo album filled with snapshots from the past four months; Danny's letters, stacked and bound with blue satin ribbon; my Every Day Diary; as much tortoise-shell jewelry as I could cram into my purse.

My father stuck his head in the door.

"I'm going down to the marina to see if that Graham boy wants to stay with us tonight. I can't stand the thought of him sitting out there in that little boat in this kind of storm."

He put on his raincoat and left. My mother and I busied ourselves making up the bed in the spare room, grateful for the distraction. Just as we finished tucking in the last corner, my father came in the back door—alone. Lee had appreciated the offer but declined it, saying he preferred to stay with *Dove*. I wondered if Suzette and Joliette were as frightened as Mike.

The lights flickered. Around six-thirty the power went out altogether. My mother lit a candle. My father clicked on our transistor radio. The three of us huddled in the living room and waited—for what, we weren't sure. In a way, it was like sitting out tornado warnings back in Oklahoma, the waiting and listening to weather reports. The difference was that when tornado sirens sounded and we ran for shelter, we always felt safe once we were bunkered in the cellar. We'd sit wrapped in quilts, talking and playing cards by candlelight, certain that if a tornado touched down, we'd be protected. Here, in a house with only two solid walls and some flimsy shutters, there was no such sense of security.

After a couple of hours, the radio reported that the hurricane wasn't likely to hit until early morning, so we went upstairs to bed. I coaxed Mike into curling up with me. He was asleep in an instant, his little chest softly rising and falling against mine. I lay awake listening to the storm's sounds, my pulse battering the walls of my arteries in concert with the rain against the roof. Just as I started to doze off, my breathing finally attuned to Mike's, my father woke me. His voice had the same urgent tension as the night of the fire.

"It's sounding pretty bad out there. We'd better get back downstairs in case the roof blows off."

I tucked my blanket and pillow under one arm, scooped Mike into the other and hurried downstairs, my bare feet drumming the wooden steps. My parents carried the dining table into the living room and pushed it against the cinder block wall.

"Get under here," my father directed my mother and me. "You'll at least have something over your heads if things start caving in."

"Do you think that'll happen?" My voice sounded feeble against the bluster and roar outside.

My mother slipped an arm around me, slender as string but strong in its intention. "Just a precaution, honey. But do what Daddy says."

We both crawled under the table, and my father packed pillows around us. I called to Mike and held up a corner of the blanket I'd wrapped around myself. He darted under it and scrambled up my thigh and onto my lap like a mountaineer hell-bent on reaching a summit.

Outside, the rain was no longer just battering the roof, it was being driven sideways into the walls, slapping against the screens and shutters with tremendous *whump*s. Even louder were the crashes of trash cans, tree limbs, and anything else that wasn't firmly attached being blown against buildings and parked cars. Something smashed into the shuttered wall behind the sofa with a splintering sound. I jumped; Mike spat; my father, sitting with his back against the cinder block wall, scooted closer to the table, reached for my mother's hand, and gripped it tight. She bowed her head.

Was this the worst of it, or just the beginning? There was no way of knowing. My mind ran helter-skelter, inventing what-ifs more frightening than what we already were enduring. What if the louvered walls gave out and the rain and debris blew right into the house? There'd be no escaping in this cataclysm. What if the roof did blow off? I'd brought only Mike, my pillow and blanket downstairs. My pictures, diary, letters, clothes—all my possessions—were still in my room. With the upstairs exposed like the rooms of a dollhouse, all my things would be scattered, shattered, or soaked. Except for my memories, every trace of my existence on this island would be wiped out. That thought roiled my gut more than fear of physical harm.

I pictured Lee out in the marina and imagined how the wind and rain must be pummeling *Dove*. More awful images came to mind; I shook them away and focused instead on his courage. If he could face this storm in a twenty-four-foot boat being tossed and battered in the churning harbor, surely I, with a sturdy wall at my back and a table over my head, could weather the roaring, the whumping, the crashing, the splintering, the prospect of losing my most cherished possessions.

The hurricane raged on for hours, so strong at times our eardrums felt like we were on an airplane or high atop a mountain. Even when our ears weren't about to burst, they were assaulted: more roars, whumps, and crashes. Would it *ever* end? Around 2:30 a.m., the radio went off the air (because the tower blew down, we later learned). From then on, we knew nothing about the storm's progress, only that as of the last broadcast, the wind was already clocked at 100 miles per hour.

Could this be the test of fortitude I'd longed for? (And *why*, exactly, had I longed for it, I wondered now.) Or might this be only a warm-up for greater challenges ahead? There was no way of knowing. Strangely, though, once the radio died and we were alone with our thoughts, mine stopped running wild. I couldn't know what was coming; I could only see this trial through and deal with difficulties as they came up, the way I imagined Lee would do.

Near dawn, the storm sounded less ferocious, and it seemed the worst was over. We all went back upstairs and slept for a few hours under a roof that had stood up to the wind and endured. When I awoke, the wind had stopped, and a light rain was falling. *Everything would be all right now.*

I sat up in bed. Gray mud covered my bedroom floor. Streaks of the same ashy silt ran down the inside of the louvers. I slopped across the room and onto the balcony, expecting to see rainbows or shafts of sunlight through retreating clouds.

The courtyard was flooded; some of the palm trees that lined the road had snapped in half like masts of shipwrecked schooners, others were stripped of fronds and left standing like telephone poles on some forlorn stretch of highway. Everything was fouled with the same dingy mud that invaded my room. Was the whole island such a mess? And if everything on solid land was so torn up, what about Lee in his little boat on the water? His bravery had gotten me through the night; had it been enough to see him through, too?

Moving automatically, the thinking part of my brain numbed, I dressed, slipped my feet into flip-flops, and summoned the nerve to stagger downstairs and out the back door. I had to wade across the yard to survey the rest of the neighborhood. The roof of a nearby apartment building had blown off and crash-landed on my father's clinic; one hospital ward had lost part of its roof, too. A section of steel roofing the size of a desktop was embedded in one louvered wall of our living room like a knife in a corpse. That explained the splintering crash we'd heard.

I scanned the slope behind our apartment, where *fales* and shacks were in shambles, and drew a ragged breath at the sight of Fibber's house—barely standing. All over the hillside, Samoans milled around, picking up scraps of wood, palm thatch, and metal roofing, looking as if they had no idea where to begin putting things back together. If I thought of scrambling up the mountain to help, as Fibber had scrambled down the night of the fire, that urge was swamped by a stronger desire.

Guided by some indefinable impulse, I walked toward the mountains that were the backdrop to my daily episodes and encounters—those icons of stability in my stormy world. In my intimate exchanges with them, I'd come to know their every curve and shading, the location of each coconut palm that stood sentry on their ridges. I surveyed the scene, searching for my favorite promontory and the single palm it wore like a plume in a courtier's chapeau. The ridge now was battered and brown, the tree vanished.

Until that moment, the devastation had seemed so unfathomable I'd been unable to react, except by instinct. But seeing that particular patch of land ravaged, I felt a tide of grief rise in me, and with it a wave of tenderness.

Would Samoa ever be the same? There was no way of knowing, and in a way, it didn't matter. I'd thought I loved the island for its perfect, perfumed beauty. But now, scarred as it was, with the underlying ugliness of its rocky slopes exposed and its flowers stripped from their stems, I wanted more than ever to embrace this place and its people.

Chapter 19—Waves

In traditional Polynesian belief, the soul at death leaves the body from a tear duct and begins a tentative, instinctive journey into the uplands for a time and then proceeds along the path of the spirits to the place on each island where the souls jump off into the land of the dead. If a soul expert feels the person should not have died, he or she can find the soul, "snatch" it between cupped hands, and reinsert it.
— Encyclopedia of Death and Dying: Polynesian Religions

Later that morning, I made my way to Val's house, searching at every turn in the road for signs the storm had shown some mercy. But everywhere I looked, the landscape was a bleak skeleton of its former self, a leaf stripped to its veins by a ravenous insect. Palm fronds lay scattered, resembling lifeless soldiers on a battlefield; an uprooted tree blocked the stairway to my school's front door; metal roofs were peeled back like banana skins. Even the ocean reeked with death smells. By the time I reached Centipede Row, I wanted only to hole up in Val's room and escape the awful scene.

Val sat on her bed, her eyes like a statue's, staring but not seeing.

"Pretty scary last night." Her voice came out hoarse and whispery, as if the winds had scoured her vocal cords.

I crumpled onto the other bed. "Yeah. Worst hurricane to hit the island in thirty years, everyone's saying."

"Did Lee . . ."

"My dad checked on him—he's okay." How that was possible, given the clobbering the rest of the island had taken, was beyond me. Had spunk and skill saved him, or was there more to it than that?

"Have you looked around outside yet?" I asked Val.

She nodded slowly, and for perhaps the first time since we met, we could think of nothing else to say.

Val's mother appeared in the doorway. I reflexively sat up straighter, certain we must be doing something wrong but not sure what it was that we were supposed to be doing.

"Don't get too comfortable, girls," Mrs. Puckett said. "We may have to head to higher ground in a hurry—there's a tidal wave coming."

"But how. . . I mean, where. . . " I recalled my mother's unease when I'd pointed out the lack of roads into the mountains.

"We can drive up the hill to the cable car station," Mrs. Puckett said. "That should be high enough." I wanted to ask how many people could crowd onto the little hilltop and how many vehicles the station's small parking lot could hold, but Mrs. Puckett's flinty expression stifled me. "Put on warm clothes; then you can help me get Rex and the other girls ready."

Val waited until her mother left the room.

"Put on warm clothes? It's a tidal wave, for godssake, not a blizzard!" Her acerbic tone was back, and she snorted out a little laugh.

I laughed too, but nervously. "C'mon, Val. If she comes back and finds us goofing around, she'll knock us both across the room."

Val, the embodiment of recalcitrance, slid off the bed and ducked into her closet. I heard her muffled voice: "Put on warm clothes. Put on warm clothes."

She emerged a few minutes later with five cardigans layered over her blouse, a pair of long pants under her skirt, two knit scarves wound around her neck, and a stocking cap pulled over her eyes. Why she'd brought her Michigan woolens to Samoa I couldn't imagine, but there they were. She looked like a toddler bundled up to build a snowman.

A stack of sweatshirts sailed toward me.

"Here—put on warm clothes!" Val plopped down beside me, and we fell back onto the bed, laughing. A tickle feathered through my rib cage; hula girls shimmied in my belly. Oh, the relief, the normalcy of laughing again, of being our goofy teenage selves instead of the grown-ups we'd had to emulate for the past twenty-four hours. We were still wriggling and convulsing when Val's mother appeared at the door again. I jumped off the bed and stood rigid as a GI at a surprise inspection. Val, stuffed like a scarecrow, struggled to get up.

"We're putting on warm clothes, Mom," she mumbled through knitwear.

I drew in my breath and waited for Mrs. Puckett to detonate. To my complete astonishment, she broke into laughter.

"Oh, Val!" she said and turned to leave the room, shaking her head but still smiling.

By the time we were ready to evacuate, the tidal wave, too, had turned away, as if rebuffed by our laughter, and the warning was called off. It was hard to wrap our heads around such sudden turns of events: the night before, devastation; now, in the face of another disaster, reprieve. It was harder still to shake the lingering sense that we shouldn't get too comfortable—another catastrophe might be about to hit.

The usual soundtrack of playful shouts, laughter, and snatches of music from open car windows was absent; the only sounds were the scuffle of feet on crushed coral and the rasp of tires on wet asphalt, as Val, Marnie, and I watched the passing procession on the thoroughfare just beyond Marnie's living room windows. The house was so close to the road and path that you could sit in the front room and talk through the screens to people passing by. Usually that was fun, but now, the third day after the hurricane, people's faces still bore imprints of shock and sadness, and observing them at such close range felt intrusive, like seeing them naked.

When three boys pulled up in a Toyota pickup, we welcomed the diversion. Wayne, his buddy Tau, and Tau's visiting brother David were jammed into the cab, their surfboards lined up in the bed. Surely they weren't going ahead with their surfing plans, were they? Then again, who could blame them for trying to carry on with life as usual?

Wayne, the flirt, leaned out the passenger-side window and wolf-whistled.

"Hey, ladies! We're off to Nu'uuli — incredible waves out there. Better come with us. Surfer boys always need a few beach bunnies watching from shore."

I'd seen Nu'uuli the day before, on a drive to Tafuna with my parents to pick up a parcel at the airport and survey the island's damage. The waves were high, all right — scary high. The palm forest of Nu'uuli's Coconut Point lay in splinters, and the battered shoreline hardly seemed the right setting for a beach party.

"In the movies, maybe, or your dreams," Marnie shot back, smiling. "We've had enough excitement for a while. We're staying right here."

"You don't know what you're missing!" Wayne's brown face crinkled, and his eyes disappeared behind mounds of cheekbone. As the truck sped away, Marnie laughed and called after it:

"So long, surfer boys."

Sitting on the front porch of our apartment later that day, staring at broken palm trees across the road, I saw a familiar blue-and-white flowered shirt. Lee, laundry bag slung over one shoulder, walked toward me, wearing that famous smile.

"Your father said I could use your washer and dryer," he said when he reached the porch. "I hope I'm not imposing."

"Are you kidding? We were all set to take you in the other night. We couldn't believe you wanted to stay out on the boat. What was it like out there?"

Lee told me how he and Jud, along with the cats Suzette and Joliette, had spent the night in *Dove*'s cabin, whooping like rodeo cowboys as the boat bucked on the waves, watching through portholes as the tops of palm trees brushed the ground and lights blinked out from one end of town to the other. He made it sound like an amusement park ride. This kid was beyond gutsy.

"Boy, and I thought spending the night under a table was exciting," I said. I didn't tell Lee how I'd trembled in that pillow-lined shelter, steadied only by the thought of him riding out the storm. I didn't ask if he, like me, had prayed for protection.

My father came to the door and invited Lee inside, but just as we turned to go in, shouts caught our attention. A gang of boys, led by Pili, the Vampires' drummer, and Poloka, the bass player, sprinted across the courtyard toward our apartment.

Out of breath, Pili panted between snatches of information. "Tau's truck . . . just saw it . . . at the hospital . . . think someone's hurt."

My father rushed out the door and took off in a trot toward the hospital. The boys and I paced on the porch. I stroked my tortoise shell ring, twirling it slowly around my finger. The familiar fragrances of frangipani and ginger still clung to the air, but they were different now. Bruised. And instead of comforting me, the weighty, almost edible scents made my heart feel like it was trapped under heavy timbers. I kept seeing Wayne's face grinning from the truck window and hearing Marnie's dismissive sendoff: *So long, surfer boys.*

"Those waves were too big," Pili said. "They shouldn't have been out there."

The kindest of the boys in our crowd, Pili had a gift for lightening tension and sadness. More than once, he'd cheered me up in study hall with jokes and silly stories when I was brooding over a chemistry test score or moping about the latest roadblock to my romance with Dick. But he was somber now.

"Maybe it's nothing serious," I ventured. "Maybe one of them just got scratched up on the coral." I pictured bleeding knees and elbows in an attempt to deflect more frightening images. I scanned the boys' faces for signs of agreement. They all looked away.

"Never should've gone out today," Pili said.

I turned to Lee, who knew the ocean better than any of us. He'd defied waves and winds at their most fearsome; surely he wasn't afraid for the surfers. But Lee wore an uncharacteristically stony face. He shook his head.

Then, at the edge of the courtyard, my father appeared, walking slowly toward the apartment. His shoulders were square as shirt box corners and he held his head erect, but his face sagged around his mouth. The boys and I surrounded him before he reached the porch. He looked around the circle, meeting each pair of expectant eyes with a grave expression. The doctor's bad-news face.

"I'm afraid it's not good," he said. "The boys were all out on their boards, and the waves overpowered them. The one boy, Tau, he's all right; he made it back to shore, but he lost sight of the other two." He took in a breath and exhaled a heavier one. "The Coast Guard has a rescue team out there looking for them now, but they're not hopeful. I'm sorry."

One by one, Pili and the other boys drifted silently away, bits of flotsam on an ocean of incomprehension. I sat on the porch and tried to reconcile what had happened with what little I knew of loss. Both my grandfathers had died years before, and an uncle I rarely saw had succumbed to a heart attack out in Oregon. But they were old by my childish standards, and though their deaths were unexpected and sad, it was common knowledge that older relatives eventually passed away. But schoolmates, friends—no. They didn't disappear, didn't . . . die. I had trouble even thinking the word.

Sure, accidents happened: Betty McCollum fell from the second story of a construction site where we weren't supposed play; Sue Ann Tolleson ran her forearm through a plate glass window; Danny broke his arm learning how to pole vault. But those mishaps resulted in stitches or plaster casts that friends could autograph. Everything got fixed. Put back together, good as new. Nobody died. Nobody's soul went flying heavenward, defying anyone to catch it and stuff it back inside the body of one too young to be taken.

With the enormity of absorbing the loss came a creeping guilt. It wasn't just Marnie's flippant dismissal that echoed in my mind, but also things I'd said and done to Wayne. Lately, we'd flirted a little when I wasn't preoccupied with Dick, Danny, Peki, or someone else, but whenever Wayne got too serious, or just plain got on my nerves, I pushed him away. On New Year's Eve, he'd walked most of the ten miles from Fagatogo to the party in Tafuna, expecting to connect with me. But when he got there, I was all wrapped up with Dick and barely acknowledged him. Just days before the hurricane, he'd run into Val and me at Tropic Isle and told us he was organizing a get-together at his house. "If it all works out, I'll come down and get you girls," he'd said. I'd fired back: "What makes you think we'll want to come with you?" I was teasing, but he was wounded, and I never said I was sorry.

My mother came out onto the porch, sat down beside me and took my hand. I waited for her to say something soothing, the way she always did when she knew I was sad or hurt. For the longest time she said nothing. Then, gently: "We're going to the hotel for dinner. Come along."

I crawled into the Tempest's back seat and stared out the window as my father drove us to the hotel. As we passed Penicillin Row, I caught glimpses of dark ocean through the gaps between houses and wondered if the Coast Guard was still searching, and if in their search they'd encountered any displaced souls waiting to be returned to their rightful owners. Then I pictured Wayne and David, weak but still clinging to their surfboards, bobbing out there in the blackness. As we turned into the hotel driveway I noticed one first-floor room where the curtains were open and the lights blazed. Just then someone walked in front of the window — someone with a lanky frame and an energetic stride that looked so much like Wayne's I did a double take and allowed myself, for a moment, to believe he was alive and safe.

But no, he couldn't be. We would've heard.

The hotel dining room's curved wall of windows overlooked the bay. We took a table by a window, and though it was too dark to see anything but squiggles of moonlight on the water, I stared out through the glass for the whole meal and ate only a bite or two of my hamburger.

When we returned to the apartment after dinner, I sat in the darkened living room and tried to make sense of everything that had happened over the past four days. Why had the hurricane hit our island and bypassed others? Why had the tidal wave changed course? Why had Lee and Tau been spared, but Wayne and David lost? Were these random, disconnected happenings, or was God weaving the dark and bright strands into some magnificent fine mat that only He could envision? And if He was, could we petition Him to tweak the design into something more to our liking?

I pondered these mysteries until my head ached and my thoughts blurred. When I finally stumbled to bed, I fell into fitful sleep, filled with dreams of sinking through green liquid that stung my eyes and burned my lungs. Then, near dawn, came a different dream, one that seemed more real and replayed the previous evening in vivid detail. In the dream, I drove to the hotel with my parents, saw the figure in the window, returned to the apartment, and sat alone in the living room. But this time, the phone rang. Just as I picked up the receiver, I woke from the dream. I lay in bed, in that dusky state between sleep and wakefulness, trying to re-enter the dream and find out who was calling. In a sort of phantasm, I saw Wayne in the hotel window, holding a telephone receiver to his ear and waiting for me to answer.

But then, as desperately as I tried to hold on to my half-sleep fog, it dissipated and left me in the glare of full consciousness, where the reality of Wayne's disappearance and death was undeniable. I forced myself out of bed and downstairs to join my parents, who were making breakfast.

"Good morning!"

The cheeriness in my father's voice made me blink as if I'd walked into a too-bright room. My mother beamed, too.

"They found Wayne," she said. "Alive."

"He's fine," my father added. "The Coast Guard heard him whistling out there in the water and followed the sound."

I sat down at the table, feeling as if my parents had flung open the window slats to reveal a scene unscathed by the hurricane: mountains reupholstered in greenery, palm trees erect and leafy. I wavered between relief and disbelief.

The day before, I'd struggled to comprehend how, in less time than it takes a wave to break on the shore, an entire life — the sum of first steps, first grade, first kiss, boyhood dreams, teenage desires — could vanish like that singular palm on my favorite ridge above Utulei. Now, it was almost as hard to accept that someone who was supposed to be dead was alive after all.

Wayne had been taken away, but miraculously snatched back, body and soul intact, leaving me with remnants of grief and guilt I didn't know how to unload, but also a shred of reinvigorated faith. I thought about that moment when, passing the hotel window, I'd allowed myself to believe that Wayne was safe. Had my belief, transient as it was, improved the odds of his rescue? Had my prayers been picked up on some divine telecommunications line?

"What about David? Is he okay, too?"

My mother's smile flatlined. She pressed her lips together and shook her head. "They haven't found him. The Coast Guard has called off the search."

"But maybe he's still alive. Like Wayne. Maybe they just haven't heard him whistle." I searched my parents' faces for the brightness I'd seen moments before.

My mother laid a hand on my shoulder. "Maybe, honey. We can hope. But I'm afraid it's not likely."

I thought again about my wishes and prayers. In my guilt over hurting Wayne's feelings, had I prayed harder for his rescue than for David's? Did I value David's life less because I'd met him just days before? A new burden bore down on my psyche, and I found myself hoping that if there was such a thing as divine intervention, it didn't involve me in any way. As much as I wanted to believe we all can summon the power to turn tides, to wrestle souls back into place and send death out to sea, I wasn't sure I could handle the responsibility.

Chapter 20 — Samoan Follies

Pago is . . . cloudy weather and
Pago is . . . rain
Pago is . . . very windy
A big hurricane
Pago is a barren island where
Trees are blown away
Drier every day
No breadfruit or taro (pause)
We'll cook the wheelbarrow
— Larry Broquet, "Pago Is!", Samoan Fales, 1966

After the hurricane, David's drowning, and Wayne's near-death, I would've given anything to plunge right back into the social swirl, to wash away the fear, the grief, the guilt, to go on with life as usual. But Samoa was different now. Life was not as usual.

The whole island is practically gone, I wrote to Cindi, dispensing with my usual obsessive recounting of romantic woes. *In places where the jungle was so thick you couldn't see two feet in front of you, now you can see for two miles . . . It makes me so sick to see how the island was ruined in just one night.*

That one night — and its awful aftermath — had changed my friends and me, too. Though we'd all endured our own, separate hurricane ordeals, we'd lived through something momentous together. We now were connected in a way we'd never been with our stateside cohorts. We were wiser, too, in ways we'd rather not be. Already all too aware our days on the island were numbered, we now also realized our youth offered no protection against time running out altogether. David had died. So could we.

Far more than our personal sense of safety had been shattered. We had only to take an *aiga* bus ride around the island to witness the fragility of our surroundings. Debris and fallen trees littered clearings, rocks were strewn across roads, *fales* lay tattered. The hurricane's winds, which reached 120 miles per hour before breaking the gadget at Tafuna that measured their speed, had also flattened breadfruit, banana, coconut, and mango trees and ripped up taro fields, wiping out the mainstays of the local diet. Shipments of government surplus food — mostly butter and cheese — helped a little, though islanders weren't accustomed to that kind of fare. The butter was fine for making banana bread from all the rotting fruit scattered on the ground, but processed cheese? My Samoan friends and their families had no idea what to do with the stuff.

Their hardship only compounded my guilt. Food shortages were a concern for my family, too, but for now we had meat in the freezer and canned goods in the pantry. If things got too bad, we could fly back to the States. For most of our Samoan neighbors, leaving wasn't an option.

We could handle only so much despair. For relief, my friends and I threw ourselves into an upcoming musical revue — *The Samoan Fales*, a spoof of island life written and produced by some of the *palagi* adults. (The name played on the similar pronunciations of *fale*, the Samoan word for house, and the English word *folly*.) When posters went up around town announcing auditions at the Turtle, I marked my calendar and recruited friends to try out for the chorus line.

Val, Suzi, Kathi, and I showed up early and sat cross-legged on the cobblestone sidewalk, waiting for Wendy, Marnie, my neighbor Pam, and Toni, the *palagi* girl from the *fiafia* village.

"Do you think we'll all get in the show, or will they only take the ones with boobs?" Suzi asked. It was so like her to already be cooking up an excuse for possible rejection. The comment did make me wonder, though, if my modest bra size might be a liability. I was glad I'd worn a loose T-shirt that made a mystery of my actual dimensions.

It hadn't occurred to me until then that I might not qualify, but once Suzi raised the possibility, I sized up the competition. Like me, Pam and Toni had taken dance classes in the States, and they both got bonus points for their long blond hair. Wendy, Val, and Marnie lacked dance training but trumped the rest of us in the boob department. Suzi was no threat in any way, but Kathi was—well, Kathi was Kathi—and now, incidentally, wearing Dick's ring.

The other girls arrived, looking cuter than I recalled any of them ever looking before, and we entered the auditorium as a singular tangle of tanned legs and pastel cottons. A portly man named Mr. Wiley bustled about, handing mimeographed sheets to the other hopefuls, who sat in folding chairs or on the edge of the stage, dangling their legs like poolside sunbathers.

"Wonderful, wonderful, what a marvelous turnout," Mr. Wiley exclaimed.

My companions and I, hands on out-thrust hips, exchanged *puh-leeze* looks, with eyes rolled toward the ceiling and lips expelling little huffs of disdain.

"Is he for real?" Val said it louder than she should've.

Ignoring the remark, Mr. Wiley beamed like a cartoon sun, "OK, people, let's get started." He bounced to the piano bench and sat down with unexpected delicacy.

"I'll play you some tunes from the show, just to get you in the mood." His fingers raced like scrambling geckos over the keys, and he rocked from one butt cheek to the other in time with the music. After a *buh-dump-buh-dump-bump-bump* intro that sounded straight out of vaudeville, he began to sing:

Pago is . . . lots of coconuts
Pago is . . . beer
Pago is . . . roasted taro and

Pago is . . . here
Pago is the open market where nothing much is free
Buy it C.O.D.
Look at the bill, and you will be ill, oh!
Pago is . . . flower ulas and
Pago is . . . dogs
Pago is . . . crazy buses and
Pago is . . . frogs (hogs!)
Those guitars are always strummin' and
Big mosquitoes always hummin'
You can get to town by thumbin' 'cause
PAGO . . . IS!

The song went on with verses about cups of kava and Mount Alava, *Hawaiian Eye* and *Bonanza*, the hurricane, and water shortages. The guy was over the top for sure, but I had to admit the song was clever. Mr. Wiley played and sang a few more songs; then came time for chorus girl auditions.

We all popped out of our seats and moved en masse onto the stage, joined by several other *palagi* and Samoan girls from our school. Mr. Wiley directed us to line up according to height. Then: "Who knows how to do can-can kicks?"

My hand shot up. I'd been in a chorus line in a ninth-grade talent show and still had a photo the school photographer had taken of me backstage in leotard, fishnet stockings, high heels, and excessive eyeliner, looking like an underage hooker, but rather enjoying playing the part.

"Fantastic!" Mr. Wiley's face glistened and his bald head reflected light like Pago Bay at sunset. "Please demonstrate for the other girls, Miss—"

"Sanders," I said, stepping forward and thrusting out what chest I had, wondering if the oversized T-shirt had been the right choice. "Nancy."

"All right, Miss Sanders, here we go!" Mr. Wiley launched into a lively rendition of the familiar can-can tune, and I began hopping on one leg and kicking the other so high I feared it might rip right out of its socket. Midway into my third kick, I had another memory from that ninth-grade stage show. On performance night, we'd come to the part of the dance where we executed our highest kicks while the chorus line traced out a circle like the second hand of a clock. I remembered how the klieg lights had made me feel: warm, but not overheated, radiating an incandescence of my own into the audience, which in the glare I saw not as schoolmates and parents but as rapt admirers and talent scouts. In that glorious moment, I imagined myself on a Broadway stage.

The line swept around in the circle pattern we'd practiced for weeks, but the music seemed faster than in rehearsal, and the soles of my high heels so much slicker than the ballet shoes I'd worn during practice sessions. There, on the end of the chorus line, I felt like I was in a game of crack-the-whip. I clutched the shoulder of the girl beside me, but in one sickening split-second she slipped away, my feet slid out from under me, and I landed on my ass, legs sticking straight out like a plastic doll's. Even dazzled by stage lights and dazed by the impact, I could see the whole football team in the second row, nudging each other, pointing and laughing. I was back on my feet in an instant, but my dignity was as dusty and bruised as my backside, and my dreams of onstage fame significantly dimmer.

With that memory playing, rewinding, and replaying in my mind, I no longer enjoyed my current moment in the spotlight; I only wanted Mr. Wiley to stop pounding on that damn piano before I humiliated myself again. Finally, he lifted his hands from the keys and raised one in a gesture like a policeman halting traffic.

"Splendid!"

How many more superlatives would we have to endure before the night was over? I started keeping a mental list.

"Now girls, let's see you all do that. Starting on your right . . . "

The can-can music rolled from Mr. Wiley's fingers, and fourteen pairs of legs hop-kicked like crazy, hopelessly out of sync and all at different heights. We resembled a chorus line less than a centipede with a neurological defect, but Mr. Wiley seemed delighted with our performance. He sprang from the piano bench, bounded to the back of the room, and conferred in low tones with two other men who'd been watching the auditions.

On stage, we fidgeted, gnawed at cuticles, and exchanged sideways glances.

After a few minutes, Mr. Wiley returned.

"Ladies—" His forehead creased into ripples. "We've arrived at a decision."

I glanced at Val. Arms crossed, she gave me a *who-gives-a-shit* look.

"Congratulations, you are all *Samoan Fales* chorus girls. We'll post rehearsal schedules in a few days."

"Marvelous!" Val said, again a little too loudly. "Stupendous! Phenomenal! Fabulous!"

I hissed at her, "Stop it!" and nudged her toward the door, burying my head in the crook of my arm to stifle my laughter.

"Oh, sorry," she said when were nearly out the door. "But really, isn't this all just too *terrific*?"

Out in the villages, in the real Samoan *fales*, life was far from terrific — or marvelous or any of the effusive descriptives in Mr. Wiley's vocabulary.

Samoa had been knocked on its ass.

And yet, riding through the wreckage with my parents, I'd heard shouts and laughter again as villagers got back on their feet, dignity unbruised, and picked up the rhythm of their lives. Women and children cleaned up rubble, and clans came together to lift whole thatched roofs back onto *fales*, all with good humor.

There was no withdrawing or isolating themselves in misery, no asking why one *fale* was hit while another was spared. Instead, I witnessed an acceptance that was not resignation or passivity, but a kind of grace. It was something to admire. Later I'd hear this typically Samoan reaction to misfortune described as a manifestation of *malosi*, a word that means strength, not only of the body, but of the spirit.

Malosi or grace or whatever it was, I wanted to tuck some away for the next time I stumbled and needed shoring up. For the next time misfortune tore through and left a mess in its wake.

As diverting as *Samoan Fales* rehearsals were, I couldn't stop thinking about life in the villages — the devastation, yes, but also the cheerful pitching in to make things right again. I felt like I should pitch in, too, yet what could I do? I had no idea how to thatch a roof or repair a tattered pandanus mat.

I did, however, know how to read.

When our principal announced that *Fia Iloa* elementary school needed teachers' aides to help with reading classes, I applied and was picked to work with a second-grade teacher, Mrs. Ieti.

Just a short walk from my school's front steps, *Fia Iloa* (the name means "I want to know") was the elementary equivalent of SAP, with a mix of Samoan and *palagi* students. So I wouldn't be teaching only Samoan children, and I wouldn't be working in a village. Still, doing something other than perpetual partying and playacting seemed better than doing nothing.

Two days after I was selected, I was dispatched — with no real preparation — to meet Mrs. Ieti in her classroom. Round-faced and round-bodied, with her hair gathered into a mound atop her head, she seemed even more nervous than I was. She spoke in a murmur and kept her gaze directed downward. School was over for the day, so she gave me a stack of papers to grade. When I whipped through them and handed them back, she finally looked me in the eye and smiled.

"*Fa'afetai,*" she said. "Thank you."

The next day, she let me work with the class on reading skills. Unlike Mrs. Ieti, the kids needed no warm-up. They flocked around me, eager for turns to read aloud, and their faces lit up when I smiled and nodded approval. I lit up too, inside, just as I always had when I'd played with my little nephews. My brother's sons were not much younger than these second graders, and when they were babies and toddlers and I myself was a grade-schooler, they'd been like little brothers to me. Could I really be feeling the same kind of affection for these schoolkids I'd met only minutes before?

As the days went on, one little boy charmed me even more than the rest. Tui had mischief in his eyes and missing teeth in a smile that was almost too big for his face. His reading efforts were valiant, but what he really loved was drawing. Whenever I saw him bent over a new creation, I made a point of complimenting it, just to see that smile.

One day, as I was leaving Mrs. Ieti's class, Tui ran up and handed me a sheet of rough paper. I turned it over to find a crayon rendering of a *fale*. I took it home and pinned it up in my room, along with other special souvenirs—a paper lei, postcards from friends, a magazine photo of Sonny and Cher.

I might not be rebuilding villages, but I was building something, and now I had my own Samoan *fale* to show for it.

Performance night came. The backstage bustle. The squeaks and rustles of the audience shifting in their folding chairs and fanning their programs. Broadway itself could not have felt more thrilling. Dressed in matching pink *lavalavas* and schoolgirlish white blouses, we chorus girls fussed with one another's hair and glopped on as much blue shadow and black eyeliner as our eyelids could hold. As we waited in the wings for the show to start, we ran through lyrics and traded lines of dialogue. We had only a few short songs and speaking lines, but after weeks of rehearsals, we'd memorized the whole script and score and felt their cleverness now belonged to us. Most of the songs and skits were innocent jabs at government officials and bureaucratic snafus or witty observations of life, fa'a Samoa. But a few were a touch risqué. Those, of course, were the ones we most delighted in reciting.

Chanting in a sing-song voice, Kathi launched into a talking blues piece: "Tafuna town is just like any other town . . . "

Suzi joined in: "The mountains are up, and the ocean's way down . . . "

Then the rest of us: "The people live at such a pace, I think they're gonna call it Tafuna Place. Yeah, Tafuna town is just like any other town, and I'm glad to call it home (I love my neighbors). I'm glad to call it home."

As if we hadn't heard the lines a hundred times, we all burst into giggles at the likening of Tafuna to Peyton Place, the fictional setting of a TV series whose characters' lives overflowed with illicit passion and hypocrisy. Most of us had watched the show in the States, and its parallels to the rumored infidelities and other unseemly behavior among the expats of American Samoa were unmistakable.

The show began, our cue came, we trooped onto stage and took our places on a set designed to look like a tavern, presided over by a salty cocktail waitress named, with a nod to Somerset Maugham, Sadie. We were no longer teenage innocents, and we were not Rockettes. We were B-girls in a sleazy tropical bar.

I'd known this in rehearsals, but it hadn't really sunk in until, before an audience of island bigwigs, neighbors, teachers, and parents, we danced and kicked our legs high and sang a song with lines about charming men into buying us drinks. Now, in place of the glow that lit up my stateside performances, I felt the burn of embarrassment coloring my cheeks.

This was different from dressing up in fishnets and high heels in ninth grade. Though my *Samoan Fales* costume was more modest than my talent show getup, my perspective was more revealing. As a ninth-grader, I hadn't yet been exposed to the seamy side of grown-up behavior—except in the occasional adult movie I'd slipped past my parents to see. Now that I was actually living among adults who drank too much and had secret affairs, grown-up naughtiness revolted more than titillated me.

I watched the faces of people in the audience turn red, not with shame, but with the exertion of uproarious laughter over references to their own hanky-panky. Certainly there were many upstanding adults—like my parents—in that audience, but viewed through my scandal-tinted lens, I saw only sinners. To my mind, these adults were no more mature than my friends and me—maybe less so, because instead of wanting to grow up, they still wanted to act like us, with our shallow, serial romances, secret drinking, and duplicity.

I smiled at the back row, as I'd been trained to do, but I didn't laugh anymore. As the lights stung my eyes and melted my makeup, I thought back to scenes in the villages after the hurricane. Samoans had shown us their best face. What kind of face were we showing them? What examples were we setting for the children in Mrs. Ieti's class and all over the island?

My anthropological observations were confirmed. My models were not to be found in the expat settlements of Tafuna and Utulei and Fagatogo; they were out in the villages where a different kind of adulthood was being played out. The kind where men and women, free-spirited and fun-loving as they were, acted their age and willingly shouldered responsibility. The kind with *malosi*.

Chapter 21 — Uma Lava Pisupo

Aua le tufia le popo pa'ū po.
(Don't pick up a coconut that falls at night; wait until morning.)
— Samoan proverb meaning "Be wary of disturbing news from an untrustworthy person."

L ife, post-hurricane, was moving toward normal, and then — another upheaval. This one had little impact on the island as a whole, but it rattled my world all to pieces.

I first heard of the impending disaster from Suzi, who acted all concerned with her *I-have-really-bad-news* opening, as we stood on the path where we'd stopped to talk — she on her way to Marnie's house, me on my way to Val's. But then she seemed to take unnecessary pleasure in watching my reaction to the punch line.

"So I guess you've heard Dick's leaving," she said, "and just when it looked like you two might get back together. Tough luck, eh?"

I stared at her and replayed her words. Sounds of passing traffic roared and blared in my ears. Had I heard Suzi correctly over the noise? Dick couldn't be leaving — not *now*. He'd just broken up with Kathi, and at a party the night before, he'd turned his attention back to me.

Now, less than twenty-four hours after that romantic rekindling, Suzi was telling me — *what*? I stepped off the path and asked her to repeat what she'd said.

"You heard me: Dick's leaving. Pretty soon, too." She sounded bored. "Too bad for you."

This time, the words buzzed in my ears and drowned out the traffic. I glared at Suzi. "You don't know what you're talking about. Why would he leave in the middle of his senior year?" I hoped she didn't notice the quaver in my voice.

She gave me that look, like a cat gives you when it's been purring on your lap and abruptly decides to swipe its claws across your forearm. "After you left last night, he told Karl his family is moving to Manu'a. He doesn't want to go with them, so he's moving back to California to live with relatives and graduate from his old high school. He had a girlfriend back there, you know."

I forced every muscle in my face to remain neutral. "So? I had a boyfriend back in the States, too. Big deal."

Suzi arched her eyebrows and shrugged. My stomach seized up.

Get a grip, I told myself. *Think this thing through like a chemistry problem or a math quiz. Start with the knowns.*

Okay. I knew this: Marnie had told me that before I came to the island, Dick was always saying he wanted to move back to California, but once he met me he stopped talking like that — except when one of those shadowy rumors about him circulated among the *palagi* parents. Now the rumors had died down, and my parents were letting him come to our apartment as long as other kids were there. And he was talking about leaving? I wasn't buying it.

"It's just talk," I told Suzi. "He's said things like that before, and he's never left."

"He's serious this time. Ask him yourself at the movie tonight," she said over her shoulder, continuing on her way as casually as if we'd been discussing what to wear to the next party.

I fumed and rationalized all the way to Val's house, kicking chunks of crushed coral from the path. This was classic Suzi. She couldn't stand to see things working out for someone else, so she had to make up lies to tarnish every lustrous moment.

Val was sitting at her desk typing on onionskin paper when I walked in.

"You won't believe what Suzi just told me — this has gotta to be her biggest whopper yet." Already the fib seemed so preposterous I was able to laugh as I related the conversation to Val. But then a shard of doubt pricked my certainty.

"You don't think it could be true, do you?"

"Are you *kidding*?" Val's expression blended empathy with impatience. "There's no way Dick's leaving this island until you do." She pulled the sheet of paper from the typewriter, added it to a pile on her desk and handed the stack to me.

"Here. I just finished typing up what we wrote last time."

The manuscript in my hand was our latest project, our own musical fantasy about life in Samoa. Once again proving her best-friend-worthiness, Val had agreed to make my romantic tribulations the focus, as she did with most of the cartoons and stories we co-authored.

"Oh, and I came up with another song last night. I wasn't going to show it to you yet, but it seems apropos." She rifled through notebooks piled on her desk, pulled out a page and laid it atop the sheaf in my hands.

I read the title: "That Whitaker Boy" (sung by ladies' bridge group). "Oh, this is going to be good."

I read on:

> *Of all the teenagers here —*
> *And we have a lot.*
> *The sly! The fat! The dumb! The queer!*
> *The sexed! The had — the got!*
> *We ladies of the bridge club*
> *Have a child we hold most dear*
> *We admit — for him, we'd try*
> *If our bods weren't all so shot!*

"Wow, Val, this is better than *Samoan Fales*! This is great — or should I say, 'marvelous'?"

"Keep reading. It gets better."

The next lines detailed Dick's *cigarettes called Kent* and *Honda with fender bent . . . his bouncy, sexy walk, his incoherent Air Force talk, his unindustrious habits in school, and his tendency to disobey rules.*

"Can I show it to him at the movie tonight? He'll crack up." I already had the paper folded and stuck halfway into my shorts pocket when Val nodded, smiling with the satisfaction of a heralded author at a standing-room-only book signing and the warmth of a loyal pal who'd just made her best friend happy.

Dick was waiting just inside Goat Island Club's back door when Val and I arrived that night. He reached for my hand and led me to a row of empty seats. The movie, *Island of the Blue Dolphins*, had sounded good from the review in the *Samoa Times*, and I expected its story line about an orphaned girl living in the wild on an isolated island to resonate with my own going-Samoan fantasies. But the plot was too simplistic and the dialogue too contrived to hold my skittery attention.

Dick seemed restless, too. When he suggested leaving, I shot from my seat like a breaching porpoise. As we walked behind the warehouses, toward Centipede Row, I debated whether to show him the song first or mention Suzi's remark. I hoped both would amuse him, so I decided to start with Suzi and save the song for the finale.

"Hey," I said, laughing in an attempt at lightness that came off sounding nervous, "I ran into Suzi today, and she told me — get this — she told me that you told Karl you're leaving in a few weeks. Is she pathetic or what?"

Dick looked away. I followed his gaze to the fishing boats on the other side of the bay, lit up like carnival rides.

"Shit!" he said.

"That's what I thought." The words rushed out faster than I meant them to. "I told her she was full of shit, that there was no way you were leaving now. I mean, really, where does she come up with these things?"

Dick turned back to face me. "I wanted to tell you myself." His face had that crumpled look, like the night we'd talked in the shadows outside the Rec Hall. "Yeah, it looks like I'll be leaving in a few weeks. Unless something drastic happens."

"Drastic like what?" Leaving was the most drastic thing I could think of. What could top that? I looked back at the lights across the bay, twinkly a moment before but now hazy blurs.

"Nothing. Never mind. It's pointless to even think about." Dick stopped at the bench behind the Jorgensens' house. We kissed, but instead of warm waves, I felt sinking stones in the bleakness beneath my ribs. *Loving and leaving. Loving and leaving.* It happened with Danny; it was happening with Dick. Wasn't there ever any loving and *staying*? Any holding on? Wasn't anything forever?

The mountains, shaded silhouettes across the bay, seemed more remote than usual as I begged them for answers. They'd weathered all sorts of upheavals, witnessed centuries of comings and goings, but *they* still stood strong. Or did their bedrock hearts crumble a little with each loss?

"I swear, if your parents would let me go out with you, I'd stay here as long as I could," Dick said. "But I don't see that happening."

"Maybe things are different now." I gripped his hand as if holding tight enough would tether him to the island, to me. "Maybe they'll—"

Dick stubbed out his cigarette on the back of the concrete bench. "You know they won't." I felt his hand on the back of my head, his fingers purposefully feathering strands of hair as if assessing their value. What would they have to be worth for him to stay?

"Don't leave." I said it without pleading, as though simply pointing out an option he'd overlooked. When he shook his head, my tone turned plaintive. "Not now. *Don't leave.*"

"It's not that I want to leave *you*. You know that, right?" He twisted the ring on his right ring finger—the ring he'd just reclaimed from Kathi. "Look, I offered this to you before, and I said you could have it any time you wanted. Will you take it now?"

All the times I'd played this scene in my mind, it never had played out like this.

Wordlessly, I took the ring and slipped it into my pocket. Beside it, folded in a tight square, its words concealed by layers atop layers, Dick's song remained unsung.

For the next two weeks, every fantasy I'd ever had about Dick came true—except the one where my parents realized how badly they'd misjudged him, and he canceled his plane reservation. We were a couple again, together every single day, like when we first met, before my parents butted in. Except for the hovering sense that time was running out and separation inevitable, life felt glorious, marvelous, spectacular, every one of Mr. Wiley's superlatives.

We exchanged pictures and wrote long, distressed messages on their backs. The only photo he could find to give me was a black-and-white snapshot of him at Tafuna beach popping a wheelie on his Honda. The whole image was a mere two-by-three-inch rectangle, and Dick and bike, midway between foreground and mountains, were the size of my thumbnail. But even in that minute likeness, the hunch of shoulders over handlebars and the wave of blond hair were so typically Dick they made me ache.

I told him to write small on the back, and his careful printing was almost microscopic:

I hope you can beleave [sic] *me that I don't want to leave
this place now because if things were O.K. with your father
I'd stay here with you just as long as I could.
All my love, Dick.*

Unlike when Danny and I parted, Dick and I made no mention of getting back together in the vague, eternally unclouded *someday*. Our one shot was now, and our now was about to be over. Except that maybe it wasn't. Every few days, he'd waver and say maybe he'd stay after all. Move in with one of the other boys until at least the end of the school year. I'd hold my breath, careful not to jinx his change of heart. But then the next day, no, he was definitely leaving, and there was nothing I could do about it.

My seventeenth birthday party, an indulgent fête at the new hotel, had already been scheduled before I found out Dick was leaving. Now it turned out his departure date was just a few days after my party night. My party would be his last on the island. But not his farewell, thanks to Marnie.

"We can't have your birthday celebration be Dick's official send-off," she'd said when I'd told her about the timing. "That just will not do." In a matter of days, she'd organized a *tofa* — goodbye — party for Dick at her house the weekend before mine.

Dick and Eric arrived at Marnie's after everyone else, having come from another party in a village on the island's west end. The boys wore leis of red ginger and frangipani, and when I danced with Dick, scents of flower and boy combined into a wrenching aphrodisiac.

Toward the end of the evening we sat on the front steps of Marnie's house, looking out at Mount Rainmaker's darkened contours. We talked for a long time, saying things we'd said before, but this time with more resignation than tortured yearning.

I gave Dick the song Val had written for him, but not the square of folded notebook paper I'd had in my pocket that night at the club. In the intervening week, Val and I had made Dick a booklet, with his song typed on onionskin and bound in cardboard from the back of a writing tablet.

He opened the cover, read the words and laughed at the end of every line. Then he laid the book on the step, and his face puckered.

"You girls." There was mild astonishment in his voice. "Nobody's ever done anything like this for me."

Some time that night he said he loved me.

Loving. And leaving.

Coke bottles—not Fanta, but genuine Coca-Cola—stood at attention in ice chests, like eager, tuxedoed waiters. Grills sweated in anticipation of frankfurters. The Vampires twanged guitar strings, tapped microphones, and prepared to reverberate eardrums. It was the eve of my seventeenth birthday, and on the hotel's poolside terrace, my party was about to begin.

Guests arrived, the boys in high spirits, the girls toting packages wrapped in the same candy-store colors as their party dresses. When I later unwrapped the gifts, I would find myself in possession of an enviable assortment of tortoise shell bracelets, enough lengths of printed fabric to satisfy my sewing needs for at least a year; and about a pint of Evening in Paris cologne, portioned up in one-ounce bottles of cobalt blue glass that delighted me as much as the toilet water's wood-tinged scent.

I should've been the happiest seventeen-year-old on the island—on the entire planet—and would've been if not for the penetrating melancholy and disbelief. Dick's departure was now just days away. How I could enjoy my birthday under those circumstances was beyond me, but I made up my mind to try.

The music started, that slide at the beginning of "Slaughter on 10th Avenue" that sounds like a hawk's cry terminating in a staccato chord, followed on its heels by jungle drums and a repetitive three-note bass line. And then the melody, wandering unexpectedly into dips and rococo flourishes and turning skippy-hoppy. Even with a sinking heart, how could I not dance to that?

I looked around for a partner. Carlson-the-governor's-son appeared as if cued for an entrance.

"Okay," I said before he even asked for the dance. We threaded between round, redwood tables and slatted chairs to a spot in front of the band, but before stopping there I made sure my parents had a clear view of us from the corner where they'd settled in to chaperone. My strategy for the evening was to conspicuously engage with as many parentally-sanctioned boys as possible in hopes that occasional disappearances with Dick would go unnoticed.

Those hoped-for connections were few. In photos from the party, Dick is a peripheral presence, his face at the edge of the frame or barely visible in the crowd. That's how he seemed to me that night: central in my thoughts but out of reach, nearly vanished.

"Slaughter on 10th Avenue" ended with a single, sustained chord. Carlson tried to stay attached to me until the last musical molecule evaporated, but I broke away. The Vampires paused just long enough for swigs of Coke before launching into "Walk, Don't Run," a danceably inviting tune that I chose to sit out.

The swimming pool, with its underwater lights, seemed filled with liquid radium that cast eerie, dappled reflections onto the faces of the boys who dove and splashed in it. (The girls, with hairdos to protect, kept their distance from anything damp or chlorinated.) Wayne was right in the midst of the aquatic exuberance, doing cannonballs off deck chairs and exploding out of the water like a missile shot from a submarine. After that terrifying night in the ocean, I'd have thought he'd have hung up his swim trunks for good, but either he'd put the experience behind him or he was facing fear head on. Either way, I gave the guy a lot of credit, but I'd also come to realize that even though Wayne had nearly drowned, his juvenile antics really got on my nerves.

Watching Wayne, though, a thought popped into my head. If the powers that control such things could reverse his death, then turning Dick's departure around should be a snap. That thing I'd said about divine intervention? I took it back on the spot and began praying: *Don't let him go, don't let him go, don't let him go. Don't let my party be the end.*

Maybe for once, I could be responsible for something good happening.

The rest of that night is a fuzzy memory that sharpens momentarily when I look at photos that show me whispering to Val, dancing with coconut-oiled Samoan boys, and standing with arms crossed behind my back and head tilted in an earnest display of interest as my favorite Vampire Pili demonstrates a guitar riff.

I have no photos of the last dance, but my memory needs no prompting to recreate that scene. Dick had put in his bid hours before, and at 10:45, when the drumbeat call and agonized guitar response of the opening strains of "Blue Star" signaled the party was drawing to a close, he made his way to my table, held out his hand, and led me onto the floor. It was the sort of moment that "Blue Star" was composed to orchestrate, with all the essential elements: love-struck teenagers, ramped-up hormones, a painful parting. It would've been clichéd if it hadn't been my own damn life.

"I wish it didn't have to end this way." Dick's face was so close I couldn't bring it into focus, but I could read his voice: resolute, not doleful as before.

He said it. He said "end." That's when I knew it really was.

The Samoan word for "over" is *uma*, but when something is so absolutely finished there's no hope of reprieve, Samoans say it's *uma lava pisupo* — "no more corned beef."

As "Blue Star" trailed off with those last, plinking notes, Dick and I were most definitely *uma lava pisupo.*

Chapter 22 — Mistaken Identities

Ua o le malu i Falevai.
(It is the protection of Falevai.)
— Samoan saying applied to disappointment at unfulfilled hopes

Val and I scuffed along the path to Fagatogo's shopping district. We had no specific destination or purpose; going downtown after school was just what we did. Once we got there we'd find something to make the trip worthwhile: Fantas to be drunk, hamburgers and donuts to be eaten, and, on good days, a new shipment of record albums to be pawed through at South Pacific Traders.

"I wonder where you'll see Dick today." Val asked the question as matter-of-factly as she might inquire where I wanted to shop.

Almost a week had passed since Dick's departure, but I kept catching glimpses of him around the island. Not that I actually saw blond, motorcycle-riding look-alikes, but my heartsick imagination converted anyone with the slightest resemblance into the boy I wished I could see. A blur of mannish shape on a passing motorbike, a flash of white jersey — that was all I needed to conjure him.

"Who knows?" I said. "He's everywhere — and nowhere." I dragged my feet, taking self-pitying pleasure in the scratch of flip-flops on crushed coral. A queue of basket-bearing Samoan men and women passed by, each one smiling, flashing eyebrows, and calling out the greeting, "*Malō!*" Each *malō* renewed my admiration for their *malosi*, even if I myself could manage only an arc of a smile and an eyebrow flash.

We reached the edge of the *malae*, an oval-shaped expanse of grass about the size of a football field. At the far end, bunched at the base of a mountain, sat the shops of Fagatogo, a collection of white frame, two-story structures with peaked-hat roofs, mixed in with larger government buildings. They all looked comfortable there, like they belonged, but they hadn't always. Some buildings dated back to the turn of the century, when the United States and Germany divvied up control of the Samoan islands, and the U.S. Navy moved in. Others were more recent, but all departed squarely from Tagaloa's sacred, rounded *fale* design.

Kneubuhl's was the largest, most modern store—almost like a supermarket, with shopping carts and self-serve refrigerated cases for meat and milk, along with the requisite shelves of canned goods, bolts of fabric, and housewares. But South Pacific Traders was the place I liked to shop. The small store sat behind the row of businesses that faced the *malae*, and to reach it you had to travel down a narrow alley where scrawny dogs whimpered for handouts and children from nearby *fales* scampered and yelled "*Palagi!*" A turn down an even narrower alley and a climb up a flight of stairs took you to the second-floor shop. Though it was probably only half a block from the *malae*, venturing back to South Pacific felt like wandering through a Moroccan bazaar.

As we cut across the *malae*, headed for the shops, I caught sight of a figure in the distance—a youthful frame and a head of blond hair. My mind playing tricks again, no doubt. But as we drew closer, the hallucination didn't disappear or meld into something more explicable. About that time, I noticed a flock of official-looking men and women—an entourage—surrounding the blond guy, and my brain made another flying leap.

"Omigod, Val! It's Steve McQueen!" Ever since I'd seen the macho movie star jump that barbed wire fence on a motorcycle in *The Great Escape*, he'd seemed the very archetype of male sex appeal. Now, here he was on my little island.

Val squinted. "I don't think so."

I picked up my pace, stumbling in my flip-flops. "Well, it's gotta be somebody famous—look at all the people around him. And look at the hair. Who else has hair like that? I'm telling you, it's *Steve McQueen.*"

I kicked off my flip-flops, scooped them up from the ground, and took off running barefoot toward the business district, the shoes flapping against each other like muted castanets. In the back of my mind, I remembered my father's stern warnings that going shoeless in Samoa was inviting parasites, but damn, that was Steve McQueen over there.

Val, trotting beside me, pointed. "They're walking away. No, wait, they're going down the alley."

We gained on the group. My calves ached. I hadn't run this much since I'd gone out for track in sixth grade. My armpits and the backs of my knees dampened, and I could feel my bangs, so sleek when I'd left home, forming ropy clumps. Weaving around startled-looking Samoan women in *puletasis*, we raced up the alley just in time to see the golden-haired man and his group ascending South Pacific's staircase. I stopped so abruptly Val crashed into my back.

"Sorry," I said, slipping my feet—undoubtedly parasite-infested by now—back into my rubber thongs. "Now here's what we do: we walk in nonchalantly and pretend to look at records. Then he says hi, and we say hi, and we strike up a conversation. See, that way we don't seem too fawning."

Val gave me the dubious slit-eyes. "What if he doesn't say 'hi'?"

I was already halfway up the stairs, pulling at my bangs in a vain effort at straightening and fluffing. "Just follow me and do what I do."

At the top of the stairs I paused, took a deep breath, and pushed open the door, prepared as any sweat-soaked seventeen-year-old could be to meet a movie idol. The shop was small—just a couple of rooms about the size of a living room and bedroom, with shelves and glass cases around the perimeter and tables of merchandise in the middle. The record bins were near the door, and because that's where the famous man and his contingent were gathered, we found ourselves in their midst as soon as we stepped inside.

Only then did I get a good look. If this was Steve McQueen, then the three years since *The Great Escape* had not been kind. The fair hair that lured me across the *malae* was actually a peroxided shade of yellow, more brass than gold. The overtanned face was all puff and pudge, nothing like McQueen's rugged movie-poster image.

As I stared at the man, trying to reconcile expectation and reality, one of the shopkeepers, a plump Samoan woman with a dramatic air, fluttered over.

"Girls! Do you know who that is?" Her stage whisper struck me as ridiculous; the putative star was standing right beside us. "That's *Johnnie Ray*!" She made a sweeping gesture that took in both the disappointing celebrity and a display of record albums on the table beside him. The name and the album cover photos triggered dim memories of a cornball entertainer who sang in a way that made it seem like he was crying.

I wondered where the shopkeeper had found the albums; to my knowledge Johnnie Ray hadn't released a record since the 1950s. I'd never felt one way or the other about the singer, but all at once I despised him, not for his maudlin performing style or his Hollywood has-been looks, but for failing to be the star I thought I was stalking—someone he was not and never had claimed to be.

With no flesh-and-blood movie star to follow around the island, we settled back into admiring the ones we watched on screen Wednesday and Sunday nights at Goat Island Club. There was boyish Doug McClure in *Shenandoah*, deeply cool Paul Newman in *Cat on a Hot Tin Roof*, suave Cary Grant in *Charade*, and the real Steve McQueen in *Love with the Proper Stranger*.

When we weren't daydreaming about kissing those handsome men, we fantasized about being the leading ladies they actually kissed: Natalie Wood, Elizabeth Taylor, Audrey Hepburn. It was a toss-up which actress I most wanted to resemble, but I thought I had the best chance of approximating Audrey Hepburn, even if oversized eyes and heavy eyebrows were the only features we had in common. At the movies one Sunday night, I studied her expressions and gestures, aiming to incorporate them into my own repertoire: the closed-lip smile, the coquettish head dip, the wide-eyed look of innocent astonishment. The character Miss Hepburn played in this film was ditzy and a bit awkward, but the actress was so lovely to look at, her clumsiness seemed all the more charming. I wondered if I was cute enough to be adorable, even when acting like a dipshit.

At intermission, the lights came on, and I stretched both arms upward, leading with the wrists and flicking my hands upward at the last moment, as I'd seen Miss Hepburn do. Someone tapped my shoulder, and I turned, chin lowered, eyes wide, to see Pili and Eric in the row behind me. Pili was every girl's dreamboat and no one's property. His features blended all the best traits of his *palagi* father and Samoan mother: almond eyes, the smoothest ecru skin, and straight, black hair with a kick of a wave in the swag over his eyebrows. But his looks were only half the package. Pili was also nice to girls, unfailingly, impartially so. He'd mastered certain social skills — the direct gaze, the thoughtful nod, the habit of frequently repeating your name when he addressed you — that made you feel you had his full attention. Yet, though he acted genuinely interested in all of us, he showed no enduring romantic interest in any of us, a situation we all, at every opportunity, tried to rectify.

Eric, a *palagi* whose father was my English teacher, was equally engaging and unattainable. Though not as good looking as Pili — his facial features and long, bony limbs were so irregular Val and I called him Crooked Man — he, too, was dependably amiable yet romantically aloof. We *palagi* girls all vied for his attention, as we did for Pili's, but he preferred Samoan *teines*.

So when Pili (or Eric—I wasn't sure who'd tapped me) made even this slight overture, it activated my eternal faith in the unlikely. This time it surely *meant something*.

As I turned to face the boys, Pili was smiling—whitely, evenly—and the highlights in his hair gleamed like starshine on the darkened bay.

"You know, Nancy . . . " (his usual, intimate opening) "Eric and I were sitting here watching Audrey Hepburn up there, and we came to the conclusion that she reminds us of you."

I dipped my head even lower and raised the corners of my mouth in a crescent-moon smile, trying to convey mild pleasure instead of revealing the hammering thrill I actually felt. Then parting my lips just enough to speak: "*Really?*"

"Oh, sure." Pili nodded vigorously, and Eric's head bobbled as if the two friends were wired into each other's circuitry. "I mean, not in looks, but the way she acts. That's *so* like you, Nancy."

If Suzi or Karl had made the comment, I would've known it was deliberately mean, but coming from Pili I had to assume it was an honest observation. I was no more Audrey Hepburn than Johnnie Ray was Steve McQueen, and pretending otherwise was as futile as chasing a falling star.

But who *was* I? Replaying scenes from the past five months, I saw myself as a range of characters with conflicting traits. A girl who carelessly started a fire—yet admitted her guilt . . . who criticized her father—yet defended him against criticism . . . who trembled through a hurricane—yet survived! Bold, cowardly, loyal, fickle, kind, spiteful, principled, deceitful, purely *palagi*, increasingly *fa'a Samoa*, I didn't know what to make of myself. I'd soon be even more confused when Suzi, in typical fashion, added another adjective to the mix.

~ ~ ~

I was still chewing over Pili's words the next afternoon when the girl gang assembled at Val's. We were listening to the Rolling Stones—jangly guitar and prickly lyrics of "Get Off of My Cloud"—as Sylvia, comb in hand, attacked Suzi's hair, undoing her pigtails and teasing with an intensity that bordered on maniacal. Val lounged on her bed; Kathi and Marnie shuffled Val's record collection, trying to decide what to play next.

"The Byrds?" Marnie held up an album. "The Animals?"

"Birds *are* animals," Kathi observed.

I ignored her and changed the subject. "I think Pili and Eric were flirting with me at the movie last night."

Suzi turned toward me, causing Sylvia to flail her comb at thin air.

"Don't get your hopes up. And don't count on any of the other *palagi* boys rushing in now that Dick's gone." Her lips curled derisively, and she turned away to face the mirror again. Sylvia's comb flitted back like a nesting bird to Suzi's ratted-out hair.

"Bullshit," Val said.

Marnie stepped between Suzi and me, a human shield. "Yeah, Suzi, why would you say something like that?"

Suzi turned to me again and lowered her voice. "Well, I shouldn't be telling you this, but I overheard the guys talking about you after Dick left. They said they all thought you were cute and cool when you first got here, but now that they've gotten to know you, they think you're weird."

"Weird? What do you mean?" Once again my mind rolled the tape of recent months, searching for examples of strangeness on my part. I saw myself acting awkward at times, like Audrey Hepburn in that movie, and having a few embarrassing moments, like the time a note I'd written to Val about Eric fell out of my binder and Eric picked it up and read it. But *weird*? No. I hadn't stalked anyone—well, except for Johnnie Ray, with whose fleeting popularity and failure to live up to expectation I now identified. I didn't dress funny, except for maybe the poufy dress and the open-toed go-go boots I'd found at a discount store in Stillwater and sometimes wore to parties. But everybody said those were cute. The girls, anyway.

"Weird in what way?" I prodded.

Suzi shrugged and turned back to check her hair in the mirror. "I'm just telling you what I heard."

I wanted to think Suzi's comment was just another mean-spirited fabrication, but her words burrowed into me like a parasitic worm. With no ready comeback, I was left to consider again the question of where, exactly, my true identity was to be found. Was it in gossip passed along by a so-called friend whose intentions were suspect? Was it in my parents' image of the ideal daughter, no better a match to reality than my expectation of meeting a movie star in a Fagatogo back alley? Was it in my own mind, stitched together from self-scrutiny, emulation, and wishful thinking? Or was my identity, like Samoa's, still being forged from fragments of past, scraps of present, and slivers of imagined future?

Chapter 23 — Snapshots

E le pu se tino i 'upu.
(Words do not pierce the body.)
— Samoan proverb meaning "Insults should not be taken too much to
heart."

Wendy studied the menu like a scholar extracting
universal truths from an ancient scroll.

"I was thinking hamburger, but — wow, banana split.
I haven't had one of those since I left the States. Yeah, banana
split. Or wait, do I want a milkshake? Hmmm. Yeah, yeah,
chocolate shake. No, wait — banana split."

I folded my arms across my chest to keep from drumming
my fingers. The view from our table at the hotel snack bar
fanned out before us like movie scenery: the pool of faceted
aquamarine, the low lava-rock wall edging the poolside deck,
and beyond that, breakers and the harbor's mouth, a welcoming
gap between mountains that stair-stepped down to meet the sea.
The sight usually made me feel serene, but this afternoon I was
keyed up and impatient to get to the matter at hand: my party
pictures.

Wendy kept staring at the menu, tilting her head this way
and that, squinching her eyes, mumbling to herself.

"Just pick something, okay?' I said. "It's only food."

The waitress, a young Samoan woman with upswept hair
and an eye that wandered independently of its partner, strolled
over from the bar and stood smiling between us. I ordered a
hamburger and a Coke with a side of breadfruit chips, tasteless,

tooth-defying disks I pretended to enjoy as much as the unobtainable Frito-Lay products I craved.

Wendy stammered, then blurted, "Okay, a banana split. But, um—chocolate? Strawberry? It's been so long I've forgotten—do you specify a flavor, or is it standard?" The waitress looked as perplexed as Wendy, but maybe it was just the eye.

"You're making this way too complicated." I sounded snappish and didn't care. "A banana split is a banana split."

Wendy reddened and fluttered her hands like she was fanning herself. "Okay, okay. Just plain banana."

The waitress scribbled on a pad, one eye tracking the movement of her pen while the other roamed skyward; then she ambled back to the bar.

"Finally." I reached into my purse and pulled out a thick packet of three-by-five color prints. After a two-week wait, my birthday pictures had at last arrived from the processing place in the States where we sent film. Val and I already had looked through them a dozen times, arranging them so the best ones of Dick came last, but Wendy hadn't seen them yet. I scooted my chair over so I could look on as she paged through the stack. She regarded each one deliberately, giving the photos the same attention she'd lavished on the menu, but without the indecision and dithering.

"See, there's you." I pointed to the middle of one print, where Wendy, in a white shift that made her tan look four shades deeper, bent close in conversation with Suzi. "And right there, behind Sylvia, that's Dick's arm. You can't see his head in this one."

"Hmmm." Wendy made the neutral expression sound sympathetic. Then, "Oh, look—that's unfortunate." She pointed to a circle of perspiration radiating from the armpit of one girl's pink party dress. "Why would she wear long sleeves? It was stifling that night."

I hadn't noticed the stain before, because when I looked at that picture I fixated on myself dancing next to the glistening girl, specifically on the childish puffed sleeves of my dress and the goofy angle of my arms: shoulders drawn back, elbows raised behind me, forearms hanging limp.

"I look like a chicken about to take flight. Tell me I don't really look like that when I dance."

"You don't really look like that when you dance." Wendy started to move on to the next picture.

"More convincingly, please."

Wendy laid down the pictures and turned to face me full-on. "Honestly, Nance, I don't know what you're worried about. You're cute and cool. Cute, cool, cute, cool, cute, cool. And maybe just a little weird, but in a good way. Okay?"

I took a moment to assess her response, trying to gauge whether she was offering a legitimate appraisal or just telling me what she thought I wanted to hear. I couldn't be sure — it was as hard to find the truth in her judgment as in Suzi's — but begging for more assurance seemed really pathetic so I simply said, "Thank you. Same to you."

The waitress returned. She set my hamburger, Coke, and breadfruit chips on the table and then, in front of Wendy, plopped a paper plate with a single, unskinned banana.

"What the . . . no, no, this isn't right." Wendy picked up the fruit and waved it at the waitress, whose eyes darted crazily, trying to follow it.

"But you said 'plain banana,' " the young woman protested. "This is plain banana."

"Banana *split*, plain banana *split*. Do you even know what a banana split *is*?" Wendy's flush deepened from crimson to maroon.

The waitress lowered both eyes. For once they traveled in concert.

I was surprised at Wendy's flare-up; she was usually more considerate. I had to believe her indignation had more to do with her own sense of disconnection from stateside life than with the server's blunder. She'd confided to Val and me that she worried she wouldn't know how to act when she moved back to the States at the end of the school year. She'd been in Samoa nearly two years now. That was a long time to be out of the loop on fads and fashions.

"Give the girl a break," I said. "Would you know how to make *palusami*?" I explained to the waitress that what Wendy actually wanted was the entire ice cream concoction. The waitress headed back to the grill to relay the revised order, Wendy calmed down, and we turned our attention back to my pictures.

The next one showed couples slow-dancing in the foreground, and towering behind them, grinning widely and gripping a bass guitar, a massive Samoan guy with a Mohawk haircut. He wore a calf-length black silk kimono, embroidered with an elaborate peacock design, open in front to reveal his bare chest and tight, black swim trunks. His name was Magalo, but everyone called him Bill Bigfoot, and though he looked imposing and had a belligerent streak, he was mostly a lovable goofball. The Mohawk and kimono were just part of his persona and didn't raise an eyebrow among our crowd.

After the picture of Bill Bigfoot came a shot of the hotel's poolside bar, overhung with dozens of glass fishing floats, each in its own form-fitting net of knotted, white cord. Down at the end of the bar sat sailor Lee with his Coke and his perpetual expression of friendly superiority. I wondered what he'd been thinking as he took in the revelry. It occurred to me that although my partying friends and I weren't engaged in any death-defying conquest, this time in our lives might end up being just as memorable for us as for the boy adventurer. For the moment, I was content to be right where I was, moored to a single, safe island, with no desire to venture out into an uncertain ocean. I sympathized with Wendy's anxiety over leaving Samoa. All of us *palagi* kids had similar worries and sought reassurance from anyone who'd already returned to the States.

As we continued looking through my pictures, I thought about a letter that was published in our school newspaper, the *Samoana Shark*, a few days before. It was written by Barb of graffiti fame, from Des Moines, where she now lived. The letter, which went on for nearly two mimeographed, legal-sized pages, described her reunion with four Samoan friends who were attending a community college in Muscatine, Iowa. It should've given me hope that leaving Samoa might not mean losing touch with everything *fa'a Samoa*, but instead it evoked quite a different response. The letter read:

REUNION IN DES MOINES, IOWA

Yesterday, Saturday, February 12, 1966, was Foreign Student Day. It was indescribably wonderful. I was down at the Veterans Auditorium at 8:30 a.m. and worked to set up the Samoa booth. Malae and Ne'e arrived first. We jabbered on and on till we were worn out. The whole auditorium was crammed with people from everywhere in the whole world. Everyone I talked to had a different accent, different color of skin, and different way of smiling. It was almost too much for the emotional capacity of any human heart. Next came Moega and Marie. Everyone was embracing, jumping, on and on, slapping each other on the backs, crying, and just plain bursting . . . They rattled on in Samoan for hours, and all welcomed and greeted me with unexplainable warmth and happiness, like I was one of them . . . We got a record player and had Samoan music going the whole day. We ran around the auditorium all day laughing constantly, joking, reminiscing, and just being glad to see each other. I, in no way, felt out of place, American or like a visitor. Everywhere they were asked to go, they took me too, by the hand. They wouldn't allow anyone to take their picture without me in

the middle, their arms around me. Several people stopped to
ask me, "you must be part American!"

We ate at the Auditorium at 6:30 p.m. and never stopped
talking long enough to really eat . . . I got a few funny looks,
being the only odd one among a crowd of foreigners! The
boys were in their brightly flowered shirts, while everyone
else was in suits. I felt like a queen. Of course, when the
band started, they couldn't sit still, so we all flew out to the
dance floor. It was the first time I had felt free and glorious
enough to dance since I left the land of love. At the end of
the night, I was red from exhaustion and wet from head to
toe, like the many nights in Samoa after a Goat Island
teenage party! We all left the dance, arm in arm, singing
"Amerika Samoa."

At first Barb's letter had triggered the same envy that had
gnawed at me since I'd found her graffiti in my bedroom that
first day on the island. There Barb was, all the way back in Des
Moines, still *Palagi* Princess of Samoa, and here I was—*yes*, it
dawned on me now as I leafed through my photos, here *I* was
living the covetable life Barb had left behind, a life she now
could only reprise for one sweet-sad day and night.

All at once I saw myself through a different filter. Even in
my poufy party dress, elbows akimbo, I was the smiling girl
surrounded by big-hearted Samoan friends and loyal *palagi* pals.
I hadn't seen it before, but here was irrefutable evidence,
captured in Kodachrome, that true friends embrace you in spite
of your eccentricities—whether Mohawk and kimono, or general
weirdness—and that I could claim plenty of such friends. If I
went back to my apartment and inscribed on that piece of
plywood my own social circle, it might rival even Barb's.

Chapter 24 — Family Matters

Quiet nights of quiet stars, quiet chords from my guitar floating on the silence that surrounds us

Quiet thoughts and quiet dreams, quiet walks by quiet streams

And the window looking on the mountains and the sea, how lovely
— Antonio Carlos Jobim, "Quiet Nights of Quiet Stars"

My father had good news. I knew it as soon as he came through the door, moving with dance-like steps, the whole lower half of his face upturned. With the hospital right next door, he always came home for lunch and spent the hour entertaining my mother and me with tales of interesting medical cases and jokes he'd heard from the other doctors. Lately, he'd been amusing us with reports on the current trend among Samoan mothers: naming their newborns after favorite television programs and characters. It was funny — and a little disturbing — to think that a child my father had delivered might go through life as Mickey Mouse Atuatasi or Bonanza Noma'aea. My favorite name, for a baby born at exactly 6 p.m., was Top of the News.

But this day, my father had no funny names or stories to relate, he had an announcement.

"Ladies," he said before taking even one bite of his wahoo sandwich, "prepare yourselves to live in luxury. Well, *relative* luxury."

My mother, whose threshold of tolerance for my father's drawn-out anecdotes was several notches below mine, brightened. "We're finally moving to Penicillin Row?"

"That's right." The corners of my father's mouth stretched practically to his temples. "Van Kolken's contract is up. He's leaving at the end of the month. We're next in line for the house."

My mother smiled the way I loved to see her smile. Giddy. Girlish. The way she smiled when she found a perfect seashell, when the surf caught her unaware and bathed her feet in brine, when she played "In My Merry Oldsmobile"—complete with honking-horn sound effects—on the electric organ. At those times, her doctor's-wife reserve dissolved, her fatigue lifted, and she was the farm child again, displaying the sort of joy that picnics and sunsets had more power to elicit than all the diamonds my father could heap upon her.

"Oh, I can just see myself sunbathing in the backyard, watching the ocean liners steam past," she said. "I'm going to go right out and get myself a chaise longue—I wonder if they have those at Kneubuhl's."

My immediate thoughts were more practical.

"Can I have the front bedroom?" I knew from visiting other doctors' children that the sole street-side bedroom in every Penicillin Row home was the prize, big and breezy, with actual walls and double-hung windows instead of screens and louvers like my apartment bedroom. The only other options in the new quarters were a stuffy inside room and a sleeping porch that offered no privacy.

"Fine with me," my father said. My mother, still dopily smiling, gave a vague nod.

The move was set for the first weekend in June, a couple of weeks before school let out for summer. I imagined the three months of leisure ahead: lolling in my new room with girlfriends, throwing parties in the spacious, screened living room (though the perpetual party life had lost some luster since the hurricane), and maybe even lying in the sun with my mother in the backyard, like we used to do in Oklahoma.

We'd done so many things together in Oklahoma. No matter how close I'd felt to my friends, my mother had always been my first choice for after-school company. Though older than my friends' mothers by at least a decade, she seemed more fun and energetic than her younger counterparts. She and I batted tennis balls on the driveway, tooled around town in the Tempest with the top down, shared dressing rooms at Bonnie's—a women's wear shop on Main Street—and swapped outfits like sisters. We laughed to the point of pants-wetting over jokes that no one else found funny, and her questions about school life and boyfriends felt more intimate than intrusive. I didn't tell her everything—she *was* still my mother—but I didn't tell my girlfriends everything, either.

That all changed in Samoa. Was it the place? Her dispirited moods? My passage into full-blown adolescence? Whatever the reason, spending time with my mother became far less appealing than hanging out with new friends who appreciated my sarcasm and didn't constantly compare me to my pre-Samoa self. Now, it pained me to reflect on how I'd abandoned her at such a lonely, vulnerable time. Maybe, starting fresh in our new home on Penicillin Row, I could make it up to her.

Floating in our separate thought-streams, my mother and I nibbled at our sandwiches and chewed absently, but my father, who still hadn't taken a bite, had more news.

"I just got the okay to go to a medical meeting in Chicago next month. We can all fly back to Oklahoma, and the two of you can stay in Stillwater while I go to the meeting."

"Stillwater? Next month?" The town I'd come to think of as painted scenery in a stage play about my previous life became pungently real. I heard the drone of cicadas and the *chk-chk-chk* of pumping oil wells. I smelled the sour-sharp mix of damp meal and chlorine that was the hallmark of Crystal Plunge, a public pool situated next to a grain mill. I tasted home-grown tomatoes, still warm from the back of a farm truck, and long-simmered pole beans, and cold watermelon. And tater tots! I was *there,* cruising Main Street with Cindi, honking *T-O-G-TOG, Hi-Tri-Chi.*

"How long can we stay?"

My father said we'd have at least ten days in Stillwater. Eager to share the news, I set up the portable typewriter on the dining table and pulled sheets of airmail stationery from a barkcloth folder. *Dear Cindi*, I wrote. *Guess what!!!!! I'm coming to Stillwater next month! I'm so excited I'm going to have to stop thinking about it! I'll bust my brain!*

I wasn't sure what excited me more: returning to my old home or sharing with my Stillwater friends all the details of my new life. They'd been getting blow-by-blow accounts in letters, but there was so much more I could tell them in person. And pictures! So many to show them. Oh, my friends were going to love it all.

My jagged excitement over the Penicillin Row move and the Stillwater visit had barely leveled into a gloss of pleasant anticipation when more big news arrived. One Sunday afternoon, just back from a sleepover at Wendy's, I was packing record albums into moving boxes when my father handed me a sheaf of letters from the now twice-weekly mail delivery. I sat on my bed and shuffled through them, scanning envelope fronts for Cindi's dependably forward-slanting cursive and Danny's cramped scrawl. In spite of my dalliances, my correspondence with Danny had remained faithful, and I still looked forward to his letters, especially now that Dick was gone. Cindi, too, was a touchstone. Nothing from either of them—a letdown. Maybe in the next mail call.

There was a letter from my same-age cousin Johnny, along with separate envelopes from my former Girl Scout leader, Mrs. Cooper, and her daughter Beth, to whom I'd written for advice on organizing a scout troop for Samoan girls—a project Sylvia and I had initiated around the same time I started working in

Mrs. Ieti's class. I set all three aside and continued rifling through my mail.

Then, at the bottom of the stack, handwriting that set me bouncing on the bed, a smile pushing at my cheeks. It was the precise printing of Tom, an older boy from New Mexico I'd met a few years earlier when he'd come to Stillwater for a summer science institute at the university. He and some other boys from the program had attended services at our church, and my parents had adopted the whole crew, inviting them over for steak dinners and backyard pool parties. The boys, in turn, made me their sidekick and let me in on their egghead inside jokes and dormitory pranks. I don't know how it got started, but the other boys called Tom "FR-2," which sounded like some android acronym, but actually was the prefix for Stillwater telephone numbers in the FRontier exchange (ours was FR-2-2741). With his quirky sense of humor and a grin that, disconcertingly, reminded me of Liberace, "FR-2" seemed as good a fit as "Tom" for the boy who became my parents' favorite—and mine.

There never was anything overtly romantic between us, but I had a crush, and the letters we exchanged after Tom returned to New Mexico were just enough to keep it simmering as my active romances flared and cooled. This missive was brief but mind-boggling. Tom, now a New Mexico State University student working on a satellite-tracking project, was being sent to American Samoa's tracking station for a six-month stint. He'd be here at the end of the month.

I popped off the bed, unable to contain the jiggles. Letter in hand, I flitted around the room, then stopped to read the words again. *At the end of the month.* Perfect. In the prospect of Tom's arrival, I saw a cure for the romantic doldrums I'd fallen into after Dick's departure. He might be a little geeky himself, but FR-2 was one *palagi* boy who surely would not consider me weird.

~ ~ ~

The rattan couch in our new Penicillin Row quarters was exactly like the one in our old apartment. Ditto the armchairs, coffee table, dining table, and dining chairs. But the new home, with its airy living room, lent the tropical furnishings a bit more cachet. Outside, palm trees framed a postcard view of Mount Rainmaker, topped with a coronet of clouds. My own private mountain. What wisdom would it whisper to me?

On the stereo, João Gilberto sang in a voice that personified gentle air and the rhythmic lapping of waves against seawall, and Stan Getz's saxophone exhaled notes like lovers' murmurs.

The album belonged to Tom, who sat beside me on the sofa.

"Sounds almost as good as your friend down at the hotel." Tom's face folded into the Liberace expression, creasing around his eyes and across the bridge of his nose. "Maybe if we're lucky he'll serenade you again today."

He was talking about Iakopu, a tour operator who sang and played the ukulele for tourists when ships were in port and spent the rest of his days cruising up and down the island's one road in his Checker limo, offering rides to my girlfriends and me and proposing to take us on picnics. We never accepted, but Iakopu, with perennial cheer that also was somewhat Liberace-like, never gave up.

On Tom's first day on the island, a few days before we'd moved to Penicillin Row, I'd shown him the sights of Utulei and Fagatogo, rhapsodizing all the way about the noble mountains, the fine men and women, the lively children in Mrs. Ieti's class. We'd ended up at the hotel snack bar, where Iakopu and his band were entertaining. As soon as Tom and I sat down, Iakopu made a beeline for our table and stood beside it, plinking away, until I acknowledged him. Tom found the serenade and Iakopu's ardor hilarious and wouldn't stop teasing me about it. I acted mortified but in truth enjoyed Tom's joshing, more tickle than taunt.

Teasing, however, was the only sign of affection Tom had displayed, except for a brief, arm-around-the-shoulders hug when we picked him up at the airport—a neutered squeeze, emptier than no touch at all. I'd thought we had something more special than that.

Within days, though, I realized we *did* have something special—something I needed more than another romance. Here was a boy friend who wasn't a boyfriend, and what a relief that was. True, I already had a couple of platonic male friends, but neither was a constant presence. My neighbor Barry and I only hung out together when his girlfriend Bev wasn't around, and lately Bev was nearly always around. Fibber still dropped by sometimes (Peki, apparently weary of my fickleness, rarely came along now), but Fibber had a girlfriend, too, and the heap of family commitments that came with being Samoan. Tom, on the other hand, had no clingy girlfriend, no *aiga* obligations, nothing to do except scan the skies on nights he was scheduled to work. The rest of the time, he was eager for companionship and open to anything I might suggest—except changing his footwear from leather loafers to something more island-appropriate.

His nose wrinkled as he regarded my flip-flops. João Gilberto was singing "Só Danço Samba" now—all bossa nova beat and slurry Portugese words, burnished with Getz's sax notes—as we lounged on the sofa. "How can you wear those things?" he said. "Don't you get blisters between your toes?"

"Not anymore. You get used to them." I slipped off my rubber thongs and propped a foot on the coffee table, spreading my toes to reveal the toughened space between the first two. "But I guarantee *you're* going to get blisters if you keep wearing those loafers in this heat. Plus, they look dorky."

"Not as dorky as you're going to look when you get parasites, and your leg swells up to the size of a pontoon." He hopped off the couch and crossed the room in a Quasimodo gait, dragging one leg like a cumbersome, inert attachment.

I doubled up laughing; my mother stuck her head around the corner from the dining room, where she was pinning pattern tissue to a length of fabric printed to look like tapa cloth. The move to the bayside house, her now daily sunbaths, and possibly our renewed rapport had transformed her. No longer complaining of exhaustion, she was a dervish of cheerful industry, stitching curtains and dresses and painting furniture bought secondhand from departing families.

"What are you two up to now, chasing frogs again?" she asked in a voice pitched like a giggle.

"No, ma'am; that's more of a nocturnal activity," Tom said, and his use of the word *nocturnal* and the memory of the night before, when we'd scrambled around the damp front lawn like deranged hounds, trying to round up the scores of toads that emerged every evening, struck me even funnier than his heavy-leg routine. I slid off the couch like soap from a bathtub rim, then pulled myself up and staggered toward Tom, drunk on hilarity.

"C'mon. Let's go look for Iakopu."

Instead of Iakopu, we found Daisy and Eti at the hotel. Daisy Jessop, older sister to Vampires' bass player Poloka, was slim and stylish—more Rio than Pago. Whenever I heard Astrud Gilberto's rendition of "The Girl from Ipanema," it was Daisy I pictured strolling the beach, tall and tan and young and lovely, oblivious to admirers' smiles. Eti, plumper, with hips perfectly proportioned for the Tahitian dancing she performed more fervently and skillfully than any other dancer on the island, was Fibber's most-of-the-time girlfriend.

The two girls were best friends, in addition to being related in some ambiguous way (Daisy called Eti her "auntie" but the actual relationship was more complicated). Lately they'd been treating me like a kid sister, which bewildered as much as thrilled me. Daisy and Eti were the most beautiful, sophisticated girls on the island; I was a toad on the lawn compared to them. But I made them laugh, and they appreciated my fascination with Samoan ways of life, so they included me in after-school gossip sessions at Daisy's quarters over the family store and Eti's house just up the alley from South Pacific Traders.

The two older girls gave me the lowdown on all the Samoan boys—which ones were "tauf" (Samoan-speak for "tuff," meaning cool or sharp) and which were "no-good-for-you-Nancy" and informed me about the intricacies of *fa'a Samoa* and the *aiga* system, which seemed mainly to involve a lot of complicated swapping of fine mats and *pisupo*. On several occasions they tried to coax my lank *palagi* hair into a beehive like theirs, but eventually they gave up and diplomatically insisted I looked cuter in a ponytail.

As Tom and I approached the umbrella-shaded table where the girls sat that day, Daisy waved and called out, "Hey, who's your new friend?"

Tom went red but aimed the Liberace beam straight toward her.

"Daisy, Eti, meet FR-2." I expected them to ask about the nickname, but apparently FR-2 was no stranger than "Top of the News," and neither girl raised a perfectly plucked eyebrow.

"Hey, FR-2—" Eti paused to swipe frosted pink lipstick across generous lips. "Want to come to a party tonight?" She pressed her lips together and opened them with a sound like a popping champagne cork. "You, too, Nancy. It's at Chris Grey's, down in Pago—you know, you've been there with us."

I said I'd have to ask my parents. Chris, an *afakasi* ground stewardess for Polynesian Airlines, wasn't part of the usual crowd, and her house was a little out of the way.

Tom, his bashfulness melting like coconut oil on sun-warm skin, winked at Daisy and Eti—or maybe he just smiled so intensely that one eye was forced shut.

"We'll be there," he said.

And so began an arrangement that suited both Tom and me and bound us together in a kind of surrogate-sibling symbiosis. Through me, Tom gained entrée to girls he was too shy to approach on his own. In return, he talked my parents into letting us go places they'd never have allowed me to go alone or with my other friends.

It was almost like having my real brother around again, the brother who — though already a teenager when I was born — was the hub of my small world when I was young. For the first seven years of my life, it was as if I had three parents: two of the conventional sort and an extra one whose sole purpose was amusing me and convincing the other two to go easy and let me have my way. It was my brother Ron who bought me my first Schwinn and taught me to pedal without training wheels, running alongside to steady me when I wobbled. It was Ron who took me sledding and fixed my cocoa when we came home pink-cheeked and chilled, who built me rocket ships from old packing boxes and drew me treasure maps showing where to find coins he'd secretly buried in the backyard.

His wedding day, when I was seven, was the day I first felt the cold and queasy desolation of abandonment — the rolling heaviness inside like being filled with bird shot, the grasping for something solid as the earth fell away. At the reception I sat alone on a sofa so deep my feet dangled from its edge, sat there in my floor-length, aqua organza flower-girl dress, sipping punch and eyeing my brother and his new wife as if they were petty thieves and I a wary cop.

Just before they left on their honeymoon, my brother and sister-in-law came to tell me goodbye. Ron knelt beside me.

"I'm not deserting you, Nan — you know that, don't you?"

I stared at the toes of my dyed-to-match slippers, not yet knowing love and loss would be an undercurrent in my life, only knowing this goodbye felt really, really bad.

"Nothing's going to change. You'll always be my sister. We'll still have fun — you'll see."

I know he believed it, and as I wrapped my pipe-cleaner arms around his neck in a near stranglehold, I tried to believe it, too. But my brother was making a promise that would prove impossible to keep. Sure, there would be frequent visits in the early years and charming, handwritten letters illustrated with stick figures. But before long, other children — his own — would vie for whatever attention he could spare, and by the time I was sixteen and he was thirty, we no longer would know how to talk to each other.

But now, in Tom, I was finding what I'd lost when my brother went away: a champion of my causes, an unfettered playmate, a confidant, a co-conspirator. This young man from the Land of Enchantment would not fill the shallow gully of my romantic longings; instead he would, for a time, close a chasm that ran to my depths.

Chapter 25 — Home

Ia manuia le Malaga.
(Blessings on your journey.)
— Samoan adage

The gauzy curtains on my bedroom windows, sea-green in daylight, were drained of color when I awoke sometime after midnight. Outside, a streetlight cast a bright circle on the lava-rock wall, the gravel path, and the edge of the roadway. Beyond the circle: the dark stillness of tropical nighttime. Silent except for the ocean's pulse, steady as a peaceful sleeper's. Pacific.

In the next room, my parents stirred. Time to get ready for the middle-of-the-night drive to the airport to catch our flight back to the States, by way of Hawaii. Soon I'd be back in Oklahoma, reconnecting with Cindi, the Tri Chis — and Danny, who'd promised to drive up from Alabama. My excitement was a hot wire running head to toe, sending currents to my skin, all prickly and alive.

I slipped into the bathroom before my parents, washed up, swiped on eyeliner, and ran a brush through my hair, which I'd shampooed and set on big rollers the night before. *Not bad.* Then back to my room to don the travel outfit I'd pressed and carefully hung in the center of my closet. Not the pinstriped dress and pumps in which I'd traveled to Samoa — I'd forsaken that get-up the moment I peeled it off that first day. For this momentous journey, I'd made a very different wardrobe choice. Though I rarely wore one on the island, I'd decided the perfect travel garb was a *puletasi*.

I slid the ankle-length *lavalava* from its hanger and wrapped it around my waist. Next came the fitted, short-sleeved tunic in the same green-and-gold floral print that bordered the leaf-green skirt. A pair of white sandals, a white cardigan for chilly airliner cabins, my tortoise shell ring, and Island Girl was ready to take flight.

Almost. The finishing touch: masses of shell *ulas* — long necklaces typically bestowed on travelers. Mrs. Ieti's class had given them to me when they'd learned I was going away, along with a handmade booklet of their drawings, inscribed with carefully printed notes: *Dear Nancy Sanders, I just want to thank you for all the things* . . . *Dear Nancy, It's very good to have a teacher like you* . . . *Dear Nancy Sanders, I do not want you to leave. I will miss you very much* . . . *I love you very much* . . . *Come back in Samoa.* I must have had at least ten pounds of shells around my neck, but there was no way I was going anywhere without the children's gifts.

The layover in Hawaii was brief, but walking through the terminal I felt welcome — and not because some enterprising photographer's ti-leaf-clad assistant threw a lei around my neck. This time things were different. On our previous visit, en route to Samoa, I'd assumed all the brown-skinned people I saw were Hawaiian, but now I could pick Samoans out of the crowd — more by gestalt than definable differences — and because of the way I was dressed, the Samoans recognized me as a compatriot, albeit one forced to travel with some strange *palagi* couple. In every corridor, I was met with eyebrow flashes and friendly greetings of "*Malō!*" By the time our L.A. flight was announced, I was radiating island energy like a tin roof.

Some of that glow may have been a residual buzz. Marnie, Eric, and another schoolmate, Brad, had also been on the flight from Samoa to Honolulu, and once the other passengers settled in to sleep, we four flocked to an empty row near the back of the plane, where we spent the rest of the night drinking ginger ale mixed with scotch from little bottles that Brad swiped from the galley when the stewardess wasn't looking.

On the Honolulu-to-L.A. flight, though, my friends were no longer with me, and as the buzz and the warmth of companionship wore off, the jet engines' drone became a fitting accompaniment to the dullness that overtook me. Each passing minute corresponded to miles traveled, and as the minutes added up, I felt ever more disconnected from my island world, with its consonance of crowing roosters, biscuit-tin drums, rippling laughter, and raucous shouts, and the pervasive scent of those little white flowers: frangipani. My mother tried to cheer me up with stacks of magazines in plastic binders. I laid them on my lap, stared out at the clouds, and wept through the whole flight.

When we landed in L.A. and made our way through the terminal to catch our connection, I scanned the throngs of fellow travelers, looking for brown skin, broad noses, and colorful clothing. I saw one or two possible Polynesians but failed to make eye contact, and instead of eyebrow flashes and friendly *Malōs*, my Samoan dress elicited only curious stares.

I'm back in the States now—I'm excited, right? I tried to remember what I'd missed while I was away, the things I'd dreamed of doing and seeing and hearing and tasting when I returned. Department stores. Bobbie Brooks outfits. Yardley Slicker lip gloss. Radio stations that played teenage music all day. Sonic tater tots. Driving. The Tri Chis. *Danny.* But each trickle of anticipation was swamped by a wave of strangeness— a sense of being out of place in an environment that once had felt familiar.

But this is L.A., after all. Oklahoma will feel different. I'll be home.

I consoled myself with that thought on the LAX-to-OKC flight, and by the time we touched down, a seed of expectancy swelled into excitement. The wait for other passengers to open overhead bins, gather belongings, and move down the aisle and through the jetway seemed longer than the six-thousand-mile journey, but finally we emerged into the terminal, and I caught sight of my cousins Mary, Martha, and Debbie, waiting with Aunt Wanda and Uncle Bruce.

We four girls had been stair-step playmates in childhood: Mary was three years older than Martha, who was two years older than me; I was two years older than Debbie. That, and the unusual nature of our relatedness, had made us especially close. We were first cousins *and* second cousins, due to the small-town circumstance of my father's sister Wanda marrying my mother's cousin Bruce. It was all perfectly legal — not one of those hillbilly cousin-to-cousin deals — but eyebrows always arched when we tried to explain the connection to friends, so we'd learned to keep our double kinship to ourselves.

It was close to 10 p.m. when we arrived, but Wanda and my cousins were dressed, made up, and coiffed as if it were noon and they were on their way to lunch at Val Gene's Cafeteria in Penn Square — all in coordinated slacks and tops, with hair teased, smoothed, and sprayed into immobile bubbles. How enviable their perfection. And for me, how unattainable. No matter how hard I tried to copy their hairstyles and fashions, I always felt rumpled and just short of the mark.

Martha hugged me, then stepped back and eyed me up and down.

"You look so pretty," she said. "Is that some kind of Samoan costume?"

"It's a Samoan *dress*," I told her. "It's called a *puletasi*."

"Pool-a-*what*-ee?" Martha waited for me to repeat the word, but I was distracted. Her word — costume — had spiraled me back in time to another night with these same cousins.

It was Saturday of Halloween weekend, and while Mary, Martha, and I were almost too old to trick-or-treat, for Debbie's sake we dressed up to make the rounds. Technically, we were a day early — Halloween fell on Sunday that year, but because Monday was a school day we were convinced Saturday was the proper night to go begging for candy. We spent most of the afternoon and early evening preparing outfits and applying makeup. Martha went as the Queen of Hearts, wearing poster-sized playing cards like a sandwich board, along with a sparkly crown and circles of rouge on her cheeks. Debbie wore a black satin cat costume and drawn-on whiskers. Mary dressed as a flapper, and I was a gypsy in a purple taffeta skirt and peasant blouse, heavy makeup, and strands of beads and gold coins. For once, I felt every bit as glamorous as my cousins. As we set off around the block I took the lead.

"Let's go to Mrs. Lane's house first—she always makes caramel apples and popcorn balls." We rang the doorbell at the brown-shingled bungalow, and after a minute the porch light flicked on and the door opened, a crack at first and then wide to reveal a sixtyish woman with a pinched expression.

"Trick or treat!" we chimed, as if the neighbor lady only needed reminding of the purpose of our mission to produce some spectacular goodie.

"Halloween's tomorrow, girls," she said, not very charitably. "I've got nothing to give you but an old onion. You want that?"

We shook our heads and retreated. Still believing we were in the right, we hit the next house. No one came to the door. On around the block we went, picking up an occasional handout, but more frequently, reproofs.

Defeated and chagrined, we finally slunk home. I felt so foolish in my gypsy garb and makeup I vowed never again to venture out of the house in fancy dress.

Now, standing beside my cousins in my *puletasi* in Will Rogers International Airport, I felt every bit as ridiculous, all dressed up in a costume when it wasn't even Halloween.

"You don't sound like *you*."

That was the first thing Cindi said when I called her from Aunt Opal's house in Stillwater the next afternoon.

"You talk so fast. And you've got some kind of accent."

"No, *you* have." After nine months away, Cindi's drawl sounded as alien to me as my Californian-Samoan-pidgin patois must have sounded to her, but within a few minutes we were speaking the same language: boys, clothes, pop music, school.

"Why are we talking on the phone?" I finally said. "I have to *see* you!" I borrowed the red Mustang convertible my father had rented for our stay and drove across town to Cindi's house, past the high school, Griff's Burger Bar, and the Sonic; past the Leachman Theatre, with its Art Deco murals, marble floors, and plush seats; down a leafy side street that took me by the junior high, where Danny and I once exchanged love notes in a classroom that smelled of disinfectant and oiled wood. Memories came at me like fat grasshoppers thwacking against the windshield, each one transporting me completely to its own place and time, supplying all the associated sounds, smells, and sensations before being bumped by another recollection. Once, this was my world—my whole world. Now, sweet as it was to recall, it all seemed so . . . small. So far removed from what I'd come to think of as my life.

Cindi was waiting outside when I pulled into her driveway, her frosted blond hair parted in the middle and hanging straight, a gilt frame for her dark eyes and prominent cheekbones. She slid into the bucket seat as if our separation had been minutes, not months.

"First order of business: tater tots." I turned the car around and headed back across town. The day was typical of Oklahoma in midsummer: a sky the color of infinity, with clouds that started out like dandelion fluff and gathered into pillowy heaps. The sign on the bank read 86°—about the same as it would have been in Samoa—but the feel of the heat was altogether different, a blazing, baking warmth that penetrated down to the level of atomic structure. Not an unpleasant feeling; in fact I preferred it to air conditioning's artificial chill, and as we drove along with the top down and the sun frying our bare arms, with the radio dialed to 1520 KOMA-AM (*KO-ma in Okla-HO-ma*) and the Beatles singing "Paperback Writer," my estrangement began to soften like overheated asphalt.

The Sonic drive-in had two wings of parking spaces that stretched out on either side of a boxy hut where carhops picked up orders of burgers, footlong Coneys, Frito-chili pies, cherry limeades, and those delectable little nuggets of potatoey crunch. Everyone—at least everyone who mattered—knew the protocol for selecting a parking spot. The north wing of slots was the "cool side," with the two spaces at the very end understood to be the coolest. That wing was where you parked when you wanted to see and be seen, and you knew you were cool enough for everyone else to *want* to see you. The south wing was for losers and kids who suffered the humiliation of coming to the Sonic with their parents.

Even those who had legitimate claim to the cool side had conventions to follow: while it was fine for girls—in carloads or in pairs—to park there during the day and on weeknights, doing that on Friday or Saturday night was an advertisement of one's datelessness. And except for the most popular senior guys, no one ever, I mean *ever*, parked at the Sonic alone.

It was just after noon on a Friday when Cindi and I reached the drive-in, so parking and ordering was admissible. As usual, I ordered a lime Dr. Pepper to complement my tater tots—as perfect a pairing as Merlot and filet mignon. Cindi opted for Frito-chili pie and a chocolate Coke. We sipped and smacked for a few minutes, then Cindi asked how it felt to be back.

"Good, kind of. I mean it's great seeing you, and I can't wait to see everyone else, and I love all the stores and the radio stations and being able to drive again. But I sort of feel—" I let the sentence trail off and was grateful the radio filled the silence. How to explain that here in my old hometown, where foods and faces were familiar, where I knew the language and the rules, I felt more like an outsider than I had at that first *fiafia* in Aoloau?

"Probably just a little culture shock." Cindi jabbed a plastic fork into her chili pie. "You just got back, after all. Before you know it, it'll be like you never left."

I dipped my last tater tot in ketchup but bit off only half. "Yeah," I said, "I guess."

Back at my aunt's house, a note sat atop my suitcase: *Danny called. Will pick you up at 7.* With the prospect of seeing him again, my uneasiness at being *home*, yet not *at home*, dissolved.

Dinner almost made me forget all about taro and breadfruit. Aunt Opal had cooked up a feast of fried steak with country gravy, mashed potatoes, okra dredged in cornmeal and fried popcorn-crisp, sliced tomatoes, and pole beans simmered with bacon, all served with tall tumblers of iced tea. For dessert, peach cobbler. I hated to pass that up, but it was getting late and I wanted to look my best for my date with Danny. Opal said she'd save me a piece and make sure there was some ice cream left, too.

I hurried upstairs and changed into the stretch denim shorts and red-and-white striped top I'd worn the last time Danny and I were together. That was a year before, when he'd come up from Alabama to spend a month in Stillwater, leaving a couple of weeks before my family took off for Samoa. That month had been the kind of summer dream I'd read about in teen-girl magazines: a suntanned swirl of dances, drive-in movies, and kissing, lots of kissing. Now Danny was back in town, and I was ready to relive the rapture.

The doorbell rang. I bolted, but Aunt Opal beat me to it. By the time I got to the door, Danny was already in the foyer, and Opal was offering him iced tea. He politely declined, and my aunt ducked back into the family room, leaving us alone and first-date awkward.

Then Danny smiled, and that inanimate, disembodied face from the frame on my dresser lived and breathed again. I catalogued his features. Eyes, a color not quite blue but not gray — like the sky on a day that can't make up its mind. A nose that sloped out and then hooked under at the last minute, perfectly shaped for tracing with a fingertip. A smile that occupied half his face and listed to the left when tentative or twisted with sarcasm. Sun-streaked hair that grazed his right eyebrow and ventured over the tops of his ears.

Feature by feature, this was the same Danny I'd bid goodbye a year earlier. And yet, not. Before, we'd been the same diminutive size, a pair of pixies and almost as innocent. Now he was taller, more handsome than cute, with a serious tinge to his barely familiar voice. A boy emerging into manhood. A man impatient with a boy's preoccupations. The Danny-not-Danny differences threw me off. I had changed, of course, I knew that. Why had I not expected he would, too?

After the requisite small talk with my parents, we drove off in Danny's car, a Panama Beige VW Beetle with black racing stripes that ran from front bumper, across hood, top, and back, to rear. I'd been with him when he applied the stretchy, vinyl tape, lining up the stripes laser-straight and pressing out the bubbles. The Beetle had transported us to all the scenes of the past summer's pleasures — to Crystal Plunge for Teen Night dances, to the swinging bridge at Couch Park for hand-in-hand strolls, to a dead-end country road where we'd found privacy to talk and test the limits of our nascent libidos.

That's where we ended up this night. Danny's hands had grown surer in our year apart, his lips more assertive, and I responded with fervor fueled by the tang of memory and the titillation of the unfamiliar.

The next night found us there again, after a day spent entirely in each other's company. Danny was leaving the following morning, due back in Montgomery at his summer job, and as he switched off the engine, satisfying physical urges seemed less pressing than saying everything we still needed to say before parting again.

For probably the hundredth time that weekend, we professed our love. Then Danny said, "You're still gonna wait for me, aren't you?"

I ran my hand over the ID bracelet I'd given him two Christmases ago, fingering the links like rosary beads.

"I want to."

"Well then, do." His voice cracked, and I felt a swell of affection for the boy he'd been and hadn't quite left behind. "Just tell me you'll still be my girl when you come back next year."

I touched the tip of his nose, took my hand away and laid it in my lap.

"See, that's the thing. I'm starting to think I don't want to come back when my parents do. I think I want to stay in Samoa. To *live* in Samoa."

Saying those words felt like gulping air after flailing underwater. In a rush of run-on sentences, I confided to Danny how out of place I'd felt since coming back to the States, how much more at home I'd come to feel in Samoa. I rambled on about *aiga* and *fa'a Samoa* and houses with no walls. I told him about Fibber and Peki, Daisy and Eti, Tui and his second-grade schoolmates, the plucky scouts Sylvia and I led on hikes over the mountains—all the characters who populated my new world. I complained about conflicts with my parents, and about *palagis* who didn't understand the superiority of the Samoan people and their ways. With each confession my emotion escalated until I was teary and blubbering.

"It's the island we always dreamed about, Danny, only it's way, way better because it's *real*." The vehemence in my voice startled even me.

I pulled away and searched Danny's face for the familiar smile of acknowledgement and acceptance. The left corner of his mouth twitched.

I waited for him to say something. He reached into the glove box, took out a cigarette, lit it, and sat there smoking (a new habit) and staring through the windshield at the rutted, moonlit road, overhung with pecan trees. I stared at him and wished I had something to do with my hands, besides twist them on my lap.

"What are you thinking?" I asked when I couldn't stand another silent second. My fingers played at the cut-off sleeve of his sweatshirt. I wanted to touch his face again, to extract an answer with a kiss, but I knew how hollow I'd feel if that didn't soften his stoniness.

With cigarette half-smoked, he turned to me, eyes more slate than sky.

"What am I thinking?" He started the Beetle's engine, let out the clutch and took off down the road, raising his voice to be heard over the motor's thrash and rattle. "I'm thinking you've lost your mind."

After Danny left, I started thinking he might be right. Something *was* wrong with me. I wasn't the girl who'd left Stillwater nine months before, and maybe the stranger I'd become was just plain strange. Was good old, normal Nancy still in there somewhere? Could I change back into her, at least for this visit?

Over the next week, I tried, I really did, to imitate my old self as I immersed myself in Stillwater social life. There were shopping trips, sunbaths and sleepovers with girlfriend after girlfriend, miniature golf games with cousins, and Teen Night at Crystal Plunge, where I danced every dance with a string of heart-throb boys. I drove through the university campus and tried to revive my enthusiasm for college classes and sorority rush—interests that seemed faraway and foreign to me now. I went to a Tri Chi meeting and rode around with Cindi afterward, honking and waving and cutting up.

My diary recorded the remoteness I really felt: *I don't want to live in the States again ever! Ugh . . . I'm so homesick . . . Samoa is the only place for me.*

I thought I'd feel better when I spent the night with one girl who'd been a friend since first grade and always made me laugh. After she filled me in on her crushes, I pulled out the pack of pictures I'd been daydreaming over every night of the trip. I showed her snapshots of house parties and afternoons at the beach, scenes of mountains and lava shores, post-hurricane shots of barren hillsides and broken palm trees, and my prizes: a group shot of Mrs. Ieti's class and a close-up of Tui, grinning gap-toothed. After a dozen or so pictures, she grew bored.

"The kids are cute," she said, "but I don't know what you see in those Samoan guys. They look like a bunch of greasers. And everything looks so *primitive*."

No fun, I wrote in my diary the next day. *I cried almost the whole night.*

At the Moonlight Drive-In Theatre another night, I ran into a frequent Sonic-cruising companion. I was so excited to see her I grabbed her hands as I'd learned to do when talking to Samoan girls. She squeezed back, but when I kept holding on she gave me a strange look.

"Um . . . you can let go now. Any time, lezzie." Her laughter had edges like broken glass.

I let go and tried to explain about the hand-in-hand strolls I often took with Daisy or Eti, meeting other pairs of girls who were similarly intertwined.

She took a step back. "Yeah," she said, "well, that kind of thing won't fly in Stillwater, sweetie. Sorry." Later I saw her huddled with a group of girls who kept glancing over their shoulders at me. *Just can't connect,* I wrote before bed. *I feel like I'm going to crack up.* Before moving to Samoa, I'd worried that I'd feel isolated there, but here I was in my own hometown, feeling more cut off on this vast continent than I ever had on the tiny island of Tutuila.

My last day in Stillwater, Cindi and longtime friends Sarah, Michelle, and Marla came to Aunt Opal's house to say goodbye.

We walked to the end of the block, where a cul-de-sac overlooked Boomer Lake, a reservoir of red-brown water with a playground and picnic shelters. It was Sunday afternoon, the day before Independence Day, and families were unpacking picnic lunches and spreading out red-white-and-blue tablecloths. My friends bubbled with plans for a picnic at another lake the next day.

"I wish you could come, too," Michelle said. "I can't believe you're leaving again so soon."

Cindi made a mock-pouty face. "And *I* can't believe you won't be here for senior year. Are you sure you want to go back? Maybe your parents would let you stay here with your cousins. Then we could all graduate together."

The other girls bobbed their heads.

Fingering the tortoise shell band that had taken the place of my Tri Chi ring, I looked at the red lake and pictured Pago Bay, looked at the families with their picnic spreads and thought of afternoons at Larsen's beach, felt the sun beating on my face and wished for a trade wind.

"It's all right," I told my friends. "I'll be home again before you know it."

I suppose they didn't realize I wasn't talking about Stillwater.

Chapter 26 — Return to Paradise

Amuia le masina, e alu ma sau.
(Blessed is the moon; it goes, but comes back again.)
— Samoan proverb

Tom got the full report on the trip before anyone else, because he was the first person I saw the morning after our return — he'd moved in with my family before we'd left for the States. Except when he was on duty at the satellite tracking station, he slept on a daybed in a corner of our living room and spent waking hours playing his guitar and serving as my sounding board.

"It was weird, Tom, really weird," I told him over toasted bread from Jessop's bakery. Spreading margarine out to the crusts, I detailed the disconnection with Danny and my girlfriends and the unexpected strangeness of the place that once defined down-home comfort. "Thank goodness we didn't have to *stay* there. I just wish I could forget we ever went."

Tom tried for a sympathetic look, but his eyes eased into the Liberace slant. "You need a distraction — I'll show you my latest project."

He pulled me to the corner where his record albums and clothes were organized in crates. Reaching into a crevice between folded shirts, he pulled out something furry, yet oddly rigid.

"What on earth . . . ?" I took a step back as he held it out to me. Chasing toads was one thing, but he couldn't expect me to cozy up to a petrified . . . *whatever it was.*

Tom was in hysterics. "Relax—it's not dead. Well, it is, but it's stuffed. I'm teaching myself taxidermy." He told me he'd been trapping the mice that skittered around the house at night and honing his craft on their sad little corpses.

"Mmm. I see." I stared at the lifeless fur slab in his hand. This was supposed to cheer me up? The mouse was stretched out straight, front legs up by its ears as if playing Superman. Its tiny feet were curled, claw-like; cotton stuffing showed through holes where bright eyes had been. "No offense, but it's not very lifelike."

Tom snatched the mouse away. "Give me a break, I'm just getting started. I haven't learned naturalistic posing yet."

"What else have you got?" I ran my index finger along the spines of his albums. "Any new records? New shoes? *Anything?*"

Tom laid down the mouse and sifted through papers stacked atop one crate. "Okay, so you're not impressed with taxidermy. What about . . ." he extracted a slip of paper that looked like an airline ticket and waved it in front of my face. ". . . a trip to Apia?"

"Are you kidding?" I lunged for the ticket, but he pulled it away and held it over his head. "I'd go there in a minute if my parents would let me."

Apia was the capital of Western Samoa, and Western Samoa was, according to the tour books, the place to go to see the *real* Samoa, meaning one unspoiled by American influences. Not that Western Samoa had been walled off from the rest of the world for its whole history. Its two major islands and eight islets had been under foreign rule—first Germany's, then New Zealand's—from 1900 until 1962, when the nation won its independence. But most of Western Samoa had resisted cultural contamination more than its American-governed cousin to the east, perhaps due more to geography than geopolitics: Western Samoa's eleven hundred square miles were undoubtedly harder to infiltrate than American Samoa's seventy-six.

I was eager to experience the pristine beauty of its countryside and outlying villages, to get a closer look at traditional Samoan life and absorb more of its lessons. It also didn't hurt that Western Samoa boasted a capital city with a rocking nightlife.

I'd visited Western Samoa's main island, Upolu, over spring break with my parents. While we'd had a pleasant time strolling through Apia's markets and trekking up a mountain to Robert Louis Stevenson's home and final resting place at Vailima, I'd spent a good bit of the trip consumed with envy of Wendy and Kathi, whose parents had let them travel to Apia unchaperoned. The two girls were staying at the same hotel we were, and every evening I watched them head off to nightclubs with a rotating cast of good-looking Samoan boys as I sat in the lobby with my parents, reading or making conversation with an officious, old German woman who was vacationing on the island.

Tom brought the ticket down to eye level and fluttered it like a fan. "What if I could make that trip happen?"

"Then we'd be friends for life," I swore, "and I'd get you invited to every party on the island."

He promised to talk to my parents, but when I heard the details of his upcoming excursion I was dubious. He and a tracking station buddy planned to fly over the following week and spend five days and four nights sightseeing and hitting Apia's notorious bars: RSA, the Polynesian Club, and Hula Town.

Right. As if my parents were going to let me fly off to another island with two older guys on a drinking spree. I was not holding my breath. Yet over the next couple of days, Tom worked some kind of magic on my mother and father, and quicker than you could say, *These people are not my parents,* I had my own airline ticket and a reservation at the legendary Aggie Grey's Hotel (along with lots of ground rules).

~ ~ ~

The flight to Western Samoa being just over eighty miles, we flew in a small prop plane, not a jetliner. We'd just settled into our seats when Agnes Chan, a Polynesian Airlines flight attendant I'd seen around town, stopped in the aisle beside me and said something in Samoan. I turned toward my seatmate, a heavy-set woman in a purple *puletasi*, thinking the comment or question was intended for her. Agnes touched my shoulder and repeated herself, speaking directly to me.

I shrugged. "I don't know what you're saying. My Samoan's not that good."

Agnes scrunched her eyebrows. "You're not Samoan?"

I shook my head.

"Not even *afakasi*?"

"Nope."

"Huh. I thought you were. Well, fasten your seat belt."

I wanted to ask Agnes what made her mistake me for an authentic islander, but before I had a chance she was hustling down the aisle to secure the doors and strap herself in for takeoff, so I spent the flight speculating. Was it my suntanned skin, dark hair, and tortoise-shell jewelry? Or had some signet of belonging been imprinted on my being?

A short time later, the plane touched down on what passed for a landing strip—a grassy expanse where coconut trees had been cleared away—and I felt transported to the Samoa that Tutuila had been before the current campaign of "improvements."

Tom hailed a taxi. The three of us loaded our bags into the trunk and set off on the fifteen-mile drive through coconut groves and garden-like villages with traditional *fales* and stately stucco churches. Children flocked to the roadside and waved as we passed. One little boy with a grin like Tui's held out a hibiscus blossom. I wanted to stop the car and scoop him into my arms. We drove on, but I kept visualizing myself back in that village, surrounded by children, loved and in love.

Soon, we reached Aggie Grey's iconic South Seas inn, a two-story, white-frame building with shuttered windows. Aggie's was the sort of place where in the movies, you'd see the roguish leading man — say, Gary Cooper — hunched over the bar, submerging regret in swirls of scotch and barking, "Rosie! More of the same!" In fact, Gary Cooper *had* stayed there, along with the rest of the cast and crew of "Return to Paradise," when the film was shot in Western Samoa in the 1950s.

That wasn't the hotel's only claim to fame. Its proprietress, for whom the place was named, was rumored to have inspired the character Bloody Mary in James Michener's *Tales of the South Pacific*. But instead of the feisty souvenir dealer that Juanita Hall portrayed in the stage and screen versions of *South Pacific*, the real Aggie — at least by the time I met her — reminded me more of my grandmother. Not twinkly Grandma Dunn, who served up hugs with biscuits and gravy, but my father's mother Nellie, a no-nonsense woman who sold foundation garments in a women's wear shop and clerked in a drugstore that smelled of pipe tobacco and Campho-Phenique. And because my parents had notified Mrs. Grey of my visit and asked her to watch out for me, I was as wary of Aggie as I was of the austere Nellie and determined to evade her surveillance.

When my parents and I had stayed at Aggie's in April, we'd been assigned to a modern, motel-like wing out back. This time I had a corner room on the original hotel's second floor — a quintessential tropical bedchamber with a mosquito-netted four-poster and louvered doors that opened onto a balcony overlooking the sweeping blue arc of Apia harbor. I had to share a toilet and shower down the hall, but the room had a washbasin in the corner for freshening up and a small table where, every morning of our stay, a bellboy would set a pot of breakfast tea and a china cup.

I'd never had my own hotel room, always shared with my parents. Now, each minor act of independence — opening the door with my very own key, unpacking and arranging my clothes in my very own closet and dresser, stepping out onto my very own balcony—triggered a tiny, rippling thrill. Here I was, the consummate solo traveler exploring the world on her own, unfazed by the unfamiliar, glorying in the experience.

As soon as we'd checked in and unpacked, I was ready to go exploring, but Tom and his friend Jay were tired from tracking satellites all night. They retired to their rooms for naps, and I reluctantly followed suit. When the boys finally got moving again, it was early evening and time for our first foray into Apia nightlife. I suggested Hula Town, having heard stories from Wendy and Kathi about long nights of dancing and romance punctuated by the occasional drama of a fistfight.

The nightclub, like my room at Aggie's, could have been lifted straight from the set of a South Seas movie: multicolored lanterns on the patio, a grass-roofed bar, a dim interior with slants of dusk's last light slipping through gaps in the shutters. We took a table in an out-of-the way corner, and Tom ordered beers all around. No one asked for my ID. This really *was* going to be a different kind of vacation. Tom was no fuddy-duddy stand-in parent; he was treating me like the grown-up I felt myself to be.

In contrast to the tepid, watery stuff I'd forced down at Suzi's, the brew our waitress brought had a bready taste and a carbonated zing that made the top of my head feel like it was floating several inches above the rest of me. I liked it! The boys and I nursed our beers and waited for the excitement to begin. But the place we'd expected to be rollicking remained largely empty and quiet except for a radio playing Samoan music. Even the hibiscus blossom behind the barmaid's ear looked listless.

"When do things get lively here?" Tom asked when the waitress brought a second round.

"You come back Friday," she said. "Live band. You have good time then."

When we returned to Aggie's, Tom and Jay called it a night, but I was still keyed up and over-rested from the afternoon nap.

I wandered into the only part of the hotel where I saw any activity: the bar. Had it been a murky, smoke-clouded saloon, I wouldn't have had the nerve to venture in alone, but the open-air lounge on the hotel's lower level was bright and welcoming, with clusters of cushioned chairs around low tables, and the bartender—I remembered her from the previous visit—was a motherly Samoan woman named Nana.

I ordered a Coke and took a seat near the bar, not noticing a group of men in the corner until one spoke to me: "What's a little girl like you doing all alone in a big hotel like this?"

I turned toward the voice. A man I guessed to be in his thirties smiled with a brilliance I'd seen only in touched-up toothpaste ads. He had olive skin and black, wavy hair, but his features looked neither Samoan nor *palagi*.

Flattered at the attention of an older man, I smiled back. "I'm not exactly alone," I told him. "I'm here with friends."

The man rotated in his chair like a radar dish, scanning the room and settling his eyes back on me. "So, where are they?"

I shredded the edge of the soggy cocktail napkin beneath my drink. "Sleeping. They sleep a lot."

He stood and walked toward me. I noticed wide shoulders beneath his island-print shirt. I also noticed Nana keeping her eyes trained on my table like she expected it to burst into flames that she'd have to rush over and extinguish.

"Mind if I join you?"

I said I didn't. He told me his name was John and that he was Maori—an indigenous New Zealander. He said he was part of a diving team working off a New Zealand ship that was in port.

A Maori diver, trying to pick me up? I was sure Wendy and Kathi hadn't had any encounters equal to this one.

John raised a hand to get Nana's attention—as if he needed to—and called out, "Another scotch and whatever this young lady is drinking." Then turning back to me: "After we finish our drinks we can walk down to the harbor and I'll show you the ship."

That sounded fun. And risky. My parents would have a fit if they knew I was even talking to this guy, much less thinking of leaving the hotel with him. But Wendy and Kathy had gone on dates when they were here, so why shouldn't I, the dauntless traveler living it up on holiday? I gave John the slanty, shady look I'd perfected with Dick and picked a little more at the napkin, trying to decide what to say. Before any words came to me, Nana emerged from behind the bar, scowling.

"This young lady needs to get to bed," she said.

John gave her the same smile he'd used to initiate our exchange, one I'd begun to suspect he'd cultivated over the years for just such situations.

"Oh, I'll make sure she gets to bed," he said. The men at the other table laughed, rough laughs that sounded like rasping machinery, and John turned and winked at them.

Was I supposed to laugh, too, or was the joke on me? All of a sudden I didn't know how to act. But Nana did. She slammed John's drink on the table so hard I thought the highball glass would shatter. Then she picked up my empty glass with one hand, and with the other swept me out of my seat—not exactly yanking, but employing a grip so firm I knew there was no arguing with it.

I made an exasperated face for John's benefit, but honestly, I wanted to give that woman a hug.

The next morning Tom rented a car, and we drove through mile after mile of unspoiled scenery, marveling at sugary beaches and mountaintop views of the island's vastness. Such purity. I daydreamed about living in such a setting, with Samoans who weren't so swept up in Americanization. Would their *fa'a Samoa* grace and generosity rub off on me, displacing my *palagi* ways? As I took in the sights, I felt less like a tourist than a prospector, collecting gems to stash in the pockets of my imagination.

By afternoon it was naptime again—for Tom and Jay, at least. "Will you be okay on your own for a couple of hours?" Tom asked before heading off for his siesta.

I assured him I'd be fine—I'd brought a book to read, and I'd see him at dinner. As soon as he and Jay disappeared into their rooms, I set off to explore Apia on my own, familiar enough with its layout by then to be confident I could find my way back.

Apia had more of a real downtown than Fagatogo or Pago Pago, with white stucco buildings facing the harbor, a maze of back streets begging to be investigated, and constant traffic directed by police wearing military-style, khaki shirts and caps, matching *lavalavas,* black leather sandals, and white gloves. One cop stood on a traffic island in front of Apia's famous landmark: a spire-topped, stucco clock tower in the heart of town. I circled the tower and wandered over to the open-air market to examine jewel-toned fish, piles of taro, and banana bunches as big as upside-down Christmas trees. An old woman with saddle-leather skin beckoned to me, and when I approached, handed me a glass of milky liquid she'd poured from a coconut. I took it and drank without stopping to think about germs or the dangers of accepting things from strangers, simply wanting to taste whatever was offered.

The coconut juice and the whole scene gave me the heady feeling of being immersed in adventure: a sharpness of sensation, a newfound boldness, an awareness of myself as not a mere observer but a fully involved participant in the world around me.

That feeling carried over into evening, when the hotel hosted the weekly *fiafia,* with its block-long buffet of roast pig, breadfruit, taro, *palusami,* and other traditional treats, including the cake-like steamed concoction known as Samoan pudding—a gooey dish I'd detested ever since I accidentally stepped barefoot into a basket of it at a Rec Hall dance. On the previous visit with my parents, I had daintily picked at the *fiafia* fare with a knife and fork, but this night, I dug in with my hands, Samoan style, savoring the smoky-sweet-sticky-squishy combination of flavors and textures.

"You cannot believe how much better food tastes this way," I told Tom, who poked a tentative fork into pinkish pig flesh. "I'm eating everything with my hands from now on."

Skirting the pork, he speared a gray chunk of boiled taro. "I can't wait to see *that* at your parents' next dinner party."

From behind the buffet came clattering and clapping, the sounds of sticks on hollowed wood and hands on bare chests, beating out cadences that accelerated into frenzied rattling. Dancers emerged and put on a floor show, performing the slap dance, in which young men rhythmically smacked their open palms and inner arms against their chests and thighs, and the gasp-inducing knife and fire dances.

Then the music turned more melodic, with guitars lacing in and out. Half a dozen women in *puletasis* emerged, moving in that Locomotion-like *step-step-step-HOP* dance I'd first seen at the *fiafia* in Toni's village. Unsuspecting hotel guests were about to be enlisted to join in a *sivasiva* free-for-all. I knew this from seeing similar floor shows at the new hotel on Tutuila. Usually I shifted in my seat and tried to make myself invisible when the dancers got to this part of the program. This time I didn't even wait to be pulled from the crowd, I leapt onto the lawn and fell in step with the sideways, toe-to-toe, heel-to-heel shuffle. I kept dancing as long as the music continued, outlasting several contingents of red-faced tourists and earning smiles from Aggie Grey, who swayed in her own *sivasiva* style on the sidelines. When I finally stumbled, sweat-soaked, back to my seat, Nana was waiting there, her face creased chin to forehead in benevolence.

"How'd you like to go to a real Samoan dance?" she asked. "I've got the rest of the night off, and there's a big party in my village. I'll take you there."

"I'd love that!" I said, not bothering to consult Tom, who'd returned to the buffet for more Samoan pudding. When he'd finished eating and was ready to hit the night spots again, I begged off.

"You guys go ahead, I'm pooped out from all the dancing." I slumped in my chair and dabbed my forehead, quite convincingly, I thought. "I'll just hang out here with Nana for a while and call it a night."

The minute the boys crawled into a taxi and took off for the evening, I found Nana and chirped, "Ready!"

What I remember most about the drive that followed is darkness and disorientation. Once we left Apia, I had no idea where we were or which direction we were headed. Unlike Tutuila, with its solitary, coastal highway, Upolu had back roads — and a serious shortage of streetlights. It was the first time in my life I experienced that *I-could-die-out-here-and-nobody-would-know-what-became-of-me* feeling, but instead of fidgeting with my ring or picking at my cuticles, I sank into my seat, surrendered to the strangeness, and waited to see where we would end up.

Finally I saw twinkling in the darkness, and as we drew closer, a festive scene that reminded me of the midway at the Payne County Fair. Strings of bare light bulbs stretched from *fale* to *fale*, and people of all ages milled around on the *malae*. The only village dances I'd been to on Tutuila had been school- or church-sponsored affairs for teenagers, but here the whole village had turned out, and once the music started, no one stayed on the sidelines.

I danced as heartily as I had at the hotel, but now, instead of being on display with a bunch of self-conscious *palagis*, I was part of a laughing, whooping mass of exuberance, our faces aglow from the overhead lights and the conviviality. All around me, people were talking in Samoan, and though my vocabulary was still too limited for me to know what they were saying, the now-familiar sound of those cascades of vowels, mingling with the plinkity-plinkity guitar melodies of the *sivasiva*, made me forget I was the only *palagi* in town. This was Samoan village life the way I'd longed to experience it, and in a funny way, being part of it felt like a homecoming. Not returning to a place I'd once lived, but coming to a home I'd been trying to find.

When our legs ached too much to dance any more, Nana took me to her sister's *fale*, where we sat cross-legged on pandanus mats and drank tea with sweet biscuits. The two women conversed in Samoan, but Nana interpreted every exchange so as not to exclude me. From time to time, teenage boys strolled by the *fale*, and flirtatious looks were exchanged, but Nana shooed the boys away with tirades she refused to translate. I didn't mind. I was content to sip my tea, watch the dancers move from shadow to light, light to shadow, and reflect on this place where adventures came sheathed in safety, and acceptance was as easy as joining in the dance.

Long after midnight, Nana took me back to Aggie's and walked me to my room. I started to open the door but stopped and turned to her.

"This has been the best day of my life, Nana," I told her. "I mean my *whole life*." Then I gave her the hug she'd earned the night before.

Moments before Tom took the picture of me standing beside the waterfall in my *lavalava*, we'd been watching caramel-skinned boys ski barefoot down the cataract's face. They started from a height as tall as the rooftop of a two-story house and slid, standing straight up, down the nearly vertical drop into a rocky pool. One by one, they slid and splashed and clambered back up the cliff to do it again, giggling and yelling "Chahoo!" — that odd whoop I'd heard other islanders make, a cross between a cowboy's holler and a sneeze.

As I watched the boys, Tom was watching me. "You seem so at ease," he said. "Like you belong here."

Tom didn't seem at ease, didn't look like he belonged in this scene that Gauguin could have painted. He was still dressed like a college boy in khakis and those ridiculous leather loafers. It had been his idea to come to Papase'ea Sliding Rock the morning after my visit to Nana's village, but as we hiked down the forest trail from the road, sweat collected in the furrows of his forehead, and he complained that his feet hurt. After taking a few shots with the fancy camera he'd lugged from the car, he'd said he wanted to go back to town for a nap.

"I want to stay here," I said. "Not *here*, by this waterfall, but here in Samoa." I pronounced it SAH-moa, the way the Samoans did.

"For how long?"

I sat down on a lava rock the size of an ottoman and ran my fingers over its spongy surface. "I don't know. Forever?"

Another round of whoops and splashes came from the waterfall. I turned toward the sounds and smiled, thoughts of the Stillwater trip, college plans, and marriage to Danny far from my mind. Thoughts of villages, laughing children, *sivasiva* dances, and *umu*-baked *palusami* so much more vivid and appealing.

"That look on your face right now," Tom said, "that look you get when you're in a place like this, around these people— it's so rare." He bent over, slipped a heel out of his loafer, and rubbed a blister. Then straightening, he wiped his forehead with the back of his hand.

"I could see you living here," he said. "I really could. Not me. Not a lot of people, but you, yes."

Chapter 27 — Like a Woman

Talanoa atu, 'ae le talanoa manu.
(The bonitos swim about thoughtlessly, but the seagulls are on the alert.)
— Samoan proverb meaning "Woe to the incautious."

I waited all the next morning for Tom's naptime to roll around. When post-lunch torpor finally took him down, I wandered into the hotel gift shop to visit La'e, a young woman who worked there and had promised to take me shopping. With her beehive hairdo, big-sister chumminess, and urbanity, La'e reminded me of Daisy and Eti. I felt right at home under her wing. As she finished waiting on customers, I poked around the shop, admiring carved tikis and bowls, shell necklaces, and leis made from sheer, loopy ribbons of some woody fiber. Like everything in the shop, the leis were infused with a camphory smell that reminded me of the drugstore where my grandmother had worked. But without the pipe tobacco notes, the scent was much more agreeable. I *had* to have one of those leis; Wendy and Kathi had come back from their Apia trip wearing them, and I'd coveted them ever since. I bought two.

La'e left a coworker in charge, and we walked along Beach Road toward the business district. The scene shimmered: the aqua harbor; the sky a shade paler, with a fluff of clouds at the horizon like pompons stitched to the hem of a skirt; the whitewashed buildings clustered along the shoreline. At intervals, the outstretched canopies of flame trees interrupted the expansive vista and offered momentary shade.

"First we'll go to some shops, then I'll take you to see the *fa'afafines*," La'e said.

I tried to mirror her cosmopolitan air. "Oh, I've seen *fa'afafines*," I informed her. "There's one in my school, and Apia is crawling with them."

Fa'afafine means "like a woman," and that was an apt description of my schoolmate Vena, with his plucked eyebrows, shaved legs, and formfitting *lavalavas*. Apt, but not disparaging: in Samoa, there was no shame in being a girly guy. Daisy and Eti had told me that in the old days, families with a surplus of sons and not enough daughters to keep up with the women's work would pick out a boy to be raised as a girl. Nowadays, though, *fa'afafines* were more likely to be truly transgender. The ones I'd seen around American Samoa displayed only subtle signs of femininity like Vena, but here in Apia, *fa'afafines* looked like drag queens in their miniskirts, stiletto heels, blue eye shadow, and peroxided bouffants.

La'e laughed, a musical ripple. "Of course you've seen *fa'afafines*. Who hasn't? What I mean is, I'll take you to see the *fa'afafine dressmakers*, and we'll have them make you a *holomuu*."

"But I'm leaving tomorrow night. Won't I need to be here for fittings?" I thought back to tedious sessions in my mother's sewing nook, standing like a statue as she tucked and pinned; flinching when a straight pin grazed a sensitive spot. My mother was a whiz of a seamstress, but even she needed days to turn out a creation that fit just right.

"They'll have it done by the end of the day. You can wear it to Hula Town tonight, and the boys will be lining up to dance with you." La'e poked a playful elbow into my ribs. I giggled and poked her back.

After we'd hit all the shops on Apia's main drag and bought each other gifts—an azure scarf for me, a tortoise shell bangle for her—La'e led me down a dusty side street, and the sharp colors of Beach Road drained away. We came to a long, pavilion-like building with screening above wooden half-walls that needed painting. Inside, sewing machines hummed like swarms of industrious insects. A *fa'afafine* with a towering coiffure wolf-whistled through the screen. I stared at the ground and pretended not to hear, but La'e released another trickle of laughter and shouted back, "Lookin' good today, honey."

We climbed a couple of steps and entered through the open door. La'e spoke to the *fa'afafine* in Samoan, and the two of them steered me to a wide table where bolts of flowered fabric were stacked like logs on a woodpile.

"Take your pick, sweetie," the *fa'afafine* directed. "Personally, I'd go with orange."

I fingered the cotton fabric. It was silkier than the stiff yard goods I'd bought in Fagatogo's shops.

"This one has a beautiful drape." The *fa'afafine* ran a tapered finger along a bolt of orange-and-white floral print — giant, stylized flowers splashed across a tangerine field — and I noticed that his (or her) fingernails were longer and better cared for than mine. I trailed my hand behind the *fa'afafine*'s; the fabric flowed like cool liquid beneath my fingers, and I imagined how it would feel encircling my shoulders, sheathing my hips, grazing my thighs. Other colors caught my eye — turquoise, coral, parrot green — but the orange-and-white pulled me back.

"Okay, that's the one," I said. "Now what — do I pick out a pattern?" That was the usual order of events when my mother and I shopped at Frye's fabric store in Stillwater.

"Pattern?" The *fa'afafine* took a step back and clutched her hands over her chest. "*Pattern?* No, no, dear! We'll just measure you up and you can be on your way." She grabbed a tape measure and looped it around my chest, then slid it down to my waist and hips, calling out the measurements to another *fa'afafine*, who scribbled them on a notepad.

"That's it, dear," she said. "Five pounds cash please. We'll deliver the dress to your hotel before dinner."

I counted out five, one-pound notes. Was I making a mistake? The thought flicked across my mind, and I held back for a beat before handing over the money. But no, I assured myself, La'e wouldn't let me get swindled. *Would she?*

We passed the rest of the afternoon like longtime girlfriends. La'e took me to a cousin's house on the outskirts of Apia, a *palagi*-style ranch with jalousie windows and family portraits hung curiously close to the ceiling. Over lukewarm lemonade, we swapped confidences about boyfriends. All the while, I kept thinking about that cash I'd left with the *fa'afafines*, hoping I wouldn't come home empty handed and have to explain to my parents where the money had gone.

When I returned to the hotel after five, I shot straight to the front desk. Before I could ask, the clerk handed me a parcel wrapped in brown paper. I squeezed it to my chest and hurried up to my room, trying to temper my excitement with the very real prospect that the dress wouldn't fit and I'd feel like a fool for wasting my money.

Slipping out of my shift, I pulled the *holomuu* over my head and zipped up the side. The fit was beyond belief. The bell-shaped sleeves hung perfectly from my shoulders; the bodice accentuated my waist and even made me look like I had boobs; the skirt skimmed my hips before flaring out and spilling down to the floor. Nothing my mother made me had ever fit like this. This was a *woman's* dress.

When I met Tom and Jay for dinner in the hotel's dining room, their eyes widened.

"My gosh," Tom said, "I've never seen you look so . . . va-va-voom-ish. I'd better bring my boxing gloves to Hula Town tonight. I'll have to fight off the other guys to get a dance with you."

Sure enough, young men queued up to ask for dances that evening. It was Friday night, and true to the barmaid's word, Hula Town came alive with the squeals of electric guitars and the thrum of wriggling bodies and romantic promise. During a break in the music, I sank into a chair beside Tom and took mental snapshots of the scene: the colored lanterns like holiday festoons, the bustle and blur around the tiki bar, the throngs of handsome boys.

Wendy and Kathi had nothing on this worldly woman.

On our last day in Apia, I had a few loose ends to tie up. First, I asked Tom to take a picture of me with Aggie Grey. The hotel proprietress and I had scarcely exchanged two words, but I wanted to create the illusion, for my parents' benefit, that I'd been under her watchful eye throughout the hotel stay.

Aggie graciously consented when Tom made the request. He posed us—Aggie in her *puletasi*, me in my flowered shift— across the street from the hotel, beside a flame tree, with Apia harbor in the background. In the snapshot, we're both smiling but our posture is a tip-off to our actual level of intimacy: we're at least a foot apart, and Aggie's arms are clasped behind her back, while mine dangle, impassive, at my sides. My parents probably didn't think the poses unusual when I later showed them the picture. I'm sure they had similar ones of my grandmother Nellie and me.

After the photo session, I headed downtown to pick up a few more souvenirs I'd been eyeing. Then one last stop for something else that had caught my eye. When I'd gone out exploring that first day, I'd passed a tennis court where a stunning Samoan boy in tennis whites was practicing. We'd exchanged glances—well, he glanced, I shamelessly ogled—but then I'd hurried on, embarrassed. I knew he probably wouldn't be there again, but what was the harm in checking?

When I got within a block of the tennis court, I saw a white blur and instantly knew it was the same boy. I picked up my pace, the flapping soles of my flip-flops impatient on the pavement. I found a spot under a tree across the street from the court where I could watch without being too conspicuous and, after sitting there a few minutes, had the bristling sense that I wasn't alone. I turned to look over my shoulder. A Samoan girl about my age stood behind me. She wore a short shift like mine,

and her hair was bobbed, not braided or piled into a bun the
way most Samoan girls wore theirs. She wasn't pretty, but her
face had a scampish appeal.

She nodded toward the tennis boy. "Nice. You wanna meet
him?"

Something inside my rib cage fluttered like riffled paper.
"You know him?"

The girl sat down beside me, closer than I expected. "His
name is Randall. He's my cousin." She yelled across the street,
"Eh! Randall!" and the boy turned and raised his racquet. Then
to me again: "You and me, we go for a walk. You meet him
when we get back."

As we walked together back toward the heart of town, the
girl, who told me her name was Ati, wanted to know all about
me — what I was doing in Apia, where I was staying and for how
long. I answered her questions and tried to ask her about herself,
but she always steered the subject back to me, the way my
mother had told me good conversationalists did.

When we returned from our walk, the tennis court was
empty. Ati saw my face fall and threw an arm around my
shoulder.

"No matter. I take you to party tonight. Randall will be
there."

I told Ati I needed to get back to the hotel to pack for my
late-night flight to Tutuila. She offered to help, and on the walk
to Aggie's nattered on about the party and all the good-looking
boys who would be there. By the time we reached the hotel she
was getting on my nerves, and I really wanted some solitude.
Then I thought about the night in Nana's village and the
conversation with Tom at the waterfall. If I was serious about
staying in Samoa and living among the Samoans, I'd have to
adjust to their ways, intrusive as they sometimes seemed.

Up in my room, Ati nosed around, picking up and
examining every item on the dresser as I opened my suitcase and
started packing dresses and separates. When I came to the

fa'afafine dress, Ati lost interest in my accessories and rushed across the room to run her fingers over the smooth cotton.

"Can I put it on?"

I hesitated. I could be generous with my friends, but sharing clothes with anyone but my mother was where I usually drew the line. What's more, Ati's shape was nothing like mine; she was stocky and looked like she still had a band of baby fat around her middle. I envisioned splitting seams.

"Well . . . okay. But be careful. It's new."

"From the *fa'afafines?*" she asked.

I nodded and watched her operate the zipper like she was ripping open a Christmas present. She tugged the dress on and, to my astonishment, fit into it and didn't look half bad. Then, from downstairs came the rat-a-tatting of a stick on wood. One of the kitchen helpers was playing the fish-shaped drum that summoned guests to dinner.

"I've gotta go now," I told Ati. "Come back after dinner, and we'll go to the party."

Ati sat down on the bed and began folding one of my blouses.

"I wait for you. I finish packing while you eat."

Tempting. The sooner the packing was done, the more time we'd have at the party. *Why not?* I thanked Ati and told her I wouldn't be long.

Dinner was Samoan lobster — more like a giant crayfish than the Maine lobster I'd eaten on a few special occasions, but tasty. When I excused myself before finishing mine, Tom gave me a sideways look.

"Are you sick or something? You never leave food on your plate. And we haven't even had dessert — I hear it's coconut ice cream."

"Yeah, I know," I said, "but I still have to pack, and I want some time to write in my diary before we leave for the airport." Amazingly, Tom hadn't caught onto any of my secret excursions, so I figured I could pull off one more.

"You and that diary." Tom waggled his head from side to side. "I don't know what you could possibly have to write about all the time."

I smiled, backed away from the table, dashed upstairs and burst into my room. Most of my clothes were still heaped on the bed. Ati was gone and so was the *fa'afafine* dress. I yanked out the drawer where I'd left my wallet. Still there — *thank God.* I snapped open the bill compartment. Empty.

Dizzy and sweating, I sank onto the bed, stung as much by the shame of my gullibility as by the betrayal. My thoughts scattered and spun; I tried to funnel them into some logical sequence. *What to do? What to do?* Admitting to Tom that I'd been duped by one of my newfound Samoan friends would give lie to the Rousseauesque scene at the waterfall. And what could he do anyway? If we reported the theft to the hotel, police might be called in, and that would surely get back to my parents. There was only one person I could tell about this.

Nana was mixing a screwdriver when I slipped into the lounge.

"I have to talk to you," I stage-whispered. Then remembering she was working, added, "when you have a minute," and sat at the bar tapping my thumbnail against my tortoise-shell ring.

My face must have communicated urgency. Nana delivered the drink and hustled back to the bar, her broad behind laboring to keep up with her shoulders.

"What's wrong?"

I told her about the missing dress and money and the girl I was sure had taken them.

"Who is this girl?" The folds of concern on Nana's face sharpened into a fierce expression.

"She said her name was Ati."

Nana made a sound like spitting.

"*Ptuh!* Ati! Ati is a bad girl. Very bad girl." On the bar, a candle flickered in a red glass hurricane lamp; its reflections blazed in Nana's eyes.

"You stay here," she ordered and then disappeared around a corner. A few minutes later she was back with several of the hotel's waiters and kitchen workers, burly young men whose eyes burned with the same fire as hers.

We piled into someone's car—I didn't notice who'd been left in charge of the bar, and maybe Nana didn't either—and took off on a wild chase worthy of an action movie. As we careened through Apia's darkened streets, Nana and the other passengers shouted to the driver in Samoan and pointed in different directions. Every so often the car lurched to a stop in front of a house or a hall where a party was in progress, and the sounds of music and laughter punctured the gravity of our mission. Then Nana, henchmen in tow, marched inside to search for the larcenous Ati as I waited in the car, playing with my ring, slipping it off, putting it back on, taking it off again, until at one stop I dropped it onto the back seat floor.

I reached down and felt around, but my fingers found nothing but filth and grit.

No! Not this. Not my ring, too. The thought of losing that *and* the dress *and* my money made my insides squish like Samoan pudding. I dropped to the floor and crawled around in the dark, groping and grinding grit into my knees and cursing my carelessness until finally, almost out of reach beneath the front seat, I felt the ring's smooth contours. Hands shaking, I slipped it back on and left it alone for the rest of the night.

After half a dozen or so unsuccessful raids, I reminded Nana I had a plane to catch and suggested it might be time to give up. Going home broke and dress-less would be bad, but not as bad as missing the flight and not making it home at all. How would I ever explain that to my parents? Plus, Tom had no idea where I was. He'd be out of his mind if I didn't show up in time to leave for the airport, and my parents would be furious with him for losing track of me. This was awful and getting worse. And it was all my fault.

But my pleas to speed up the search or call it off altogether went unheeded. By now, the quest was no longer about me and my concerns; it had taken on a larger significance to everyone else in the car.

Finally, with maybe twenty minutes to spare before I absolutely had to be back at the hotel, we hit one more hall. When Nana and her posse didn't emerge after a quick sweep, I knew they'd closed in on their quarry. Now we were getting somewhere. Maybe I'd get my dress and money back, but more important at this point, maybe this ordeal would soon be over.

Through the open car windows came shouts and the commotion of chairs being pushed aside. Someone opened the hall's front door to come outside and I caught a glimpse of Nana and the men in a tight circle around a cowed figure. More minutes passed. Then the gang burst through the door, waving the *fa'afafine* dress like a banner. Later I would wonder what they'd left Ati wearing, but at that moment the thought didn't cross my mind.

The money was gone, and that still stung. A fifteen-dollar lesson learned the hard way. But I had my glorious dress, Ati had been brought to justice, I would make it to the airport in time, and with any luck, Tom and my parents would never know about this caper.

On the flight back to Tutuila, I slumped in my seat and closed my eyes but didn't sleep. My mind was busy replaying scenes of the past five days—the shopping, the village dance, the waterfall, the flirtations, the betrayal—and processing the conflicting emotions that accompanied them. Painful as it was, I had to admit that no matter how bold, how *womanly*, I believed myself to be, I still was largely unprepared to function on my own in a world where calamity was the flipside of adventure. What troubled me more than my wobbly self-image, though, was the speck of tarnish corrupting the shining stereotype I'd been constructing over the past ten months. Samoans, I now realized, could be as humanly flawed as their *palagi* counterparts. For all the Nanas and La'es and Daisys and Etis, there might always be, lurking on a shadowed side street, an Ati with fifteen pilfered dollars in her pocket.

Ptuh! Ati! Hateful, hateful girl. I despised her for ruining my perfect adventure and hated her even more for spoiling my illusions. I thought of Nana and her gang circled around Ati and hoped they'd scared and shamed her. Maybe even slapped her for good measure. Yeah. That'd serve her right.

I brooded on bitter thoughts until I'd exhausted my inventory—and myself. Then, lulled by the plane's drone, I burrowed into my seat and let my mind sail away from Apia and back to Tutuila. A memory floated by, trailing a feeling that drifted down to my heart and ballooned there, filling it up. It was the feeling that came over me as I walked around the island the morning after the hurricane, seeing palm trees stripped and splintered and hills denuded. And with that feeling came this thought: If I could love Samoa with its ugliness exposed, surely I could be as generous with its people.

Chapter 28 — Arrivals and Departures

Aua ne'i galo Afi'a i lona vao.
(Let not Afi'a be forgotten in his forest.)
— Samoan proverb interpreted as "Remember those left behind."

The scrap of aqua paper, cut into the shape of a soda bottle, looked cheerfully intriguing stuck in the screen door, but when Val pulled it out and read it, she grimaced.

"Another *tofa* party."

I read over her shoulder to see whose farewell it was this time. The honoree was Kathi and Bev's brother Chris, the latest in a string of schoolmates going back to the States for college or because their parents' contracts were up.

"I'm just glad *you're* not leaving," I told her. "Otherwise it might be just me and Mr. Hieronymus at school this year."

Val tucked the invitation into the pocket of her shift and opened the door. "You think I'd leave you here to have all the fun? It's bad enough you went on that little spree in Western Samoa without me."

I didn't want to dwell on that escapade, so I tried distracting Val with a fashion dilemma. "What'll we wear?" With so many going-away parties lately, we'd already worn all our best outfits. I trailed her into her room and pushed a pillow aside to wallow into my usual spot on the bed.

Val opened her closet door and stared inside like a hungry person surveying a barren refrigerator. She shut the door with thudding resignation, then flopped down beside me. We tallied up who was left on the island — we could practically do it on one hand. Us. Marnie. Joyce. Sylvia. Ed. Pili, for now, but he had a scholarship to some college in Missouri and soon would be gone. Daisy and several other Samoan kids were headed for a community college in Colorado. Thank goodness I had another year before I'd face pressure from my parents to return to the States. I hadn't divulged my desire to stay in Samoa, but they'd picked up the vibes and already were offering to send me back "for a visit, *after college.*"

"Maybe we'll get some new kids that we like." It felt funny saying that. It hadn't been even a year since I was the new kid. Now it would be my turn to watch Fibber stroll up to some other, fresh-from-the-States girl at the tennis court, and for me to befriend her as Marnie and Val had befriended me in those first, sweet-strange days on Tutuila.

From outside came the crescendo and diminuendo of a blaring radio from a passing car. I heard it and wondered why I had. Slivers of music, laughter, and shouting had become such familiar background noise that I barely noticed them anymore. I was habituated to the rhythms and refrains of life in Samoa, yet even when I failed to notice the details, I still savored the overall marvelousness. The steadiness of my summer routine grounded me as well. With Mrs. Ieti's help, I had lined up jobs tutoring children from her class in reading. Now, purpose, as well as passion, fed my connection to the place.

"Hey," Val said, "Mom was talking to Barb Harold's mom at Kneubuhl's, and she said Barb's coming back this week." She made the comment offhandedly, unaware of the bedroom graffiti and its hold on me.

A wave of dizziness rippled through my head. Consciously or unconsciously, I'd been remaking myself in Barb's image—or at least the image I'd concocted from what little I knew of her— for the past ten months. Now I'd find out how I stacked up against her in real life.

At home that evening, I rooted through fabric I'd gotten for my birthday until I found a Polynesian print in shades of green and brown with touches of metallic gold. Then I pulled out a pattern I'd been saving for my next sewing project. There was a good chance Barb would be at Chris's party. I wanted to look every bit the *Palagi* Princess for the meetup.

I carried everything into the dining room, spread the fabric on the table and laid out pattern pieces. The canvas curtains were open, and music from the floor show at the hotel around the bend mingled with ocean smells and wafted in as one synesthetic sensory infusion. Just as I started pinning pattern tissue to fabric, the wind picked up and whipped at the curtains. One gust lifted a pattern piece from the table and took it on a fluttery tour of the room. I chased the piece to a corner and brought it back to the table. No sooner had I smoothed it into place than another draft snatched one of its companions and transported it like a magic carpet into the living room. I toted it back, anchored it with a box of straight pins, and pulled the curtains shut. I returned to my pinning, but spastic breezes burst in through gaps in the curtains and ripped at the pattern edges.

Damn damn goddamn wind. I-hate-you-I-hate-you-I-hate-you!

My curses had no effect, and I had no more patience. I gathered fabric, patterns, and pins into a giant wad and stalked to my room, my only consolation the wisdom of having claimed a bedroom with solid walls on all four sides.

My room was arranged like a sitting room, with two daybeds in an L-configuration at one end and a low, wooden table in front of them. My photo album, bound in brown leatherette and thick as a major metropolitan telephone directory, sat on the table.

Settling onto one bed, I picked up the album, opened the cover and smoothed the Mylar overlay on the first page, where a five-by-seven color print showed me standing on a balcony in Waikiki, wearing that silly striped-and-dotted travel dress and a frangipani lei. Other pages, filled with photos I'd shot with my Kodak Instamatic or had printed from my father's slides, showcased views of Centipede Row and Pago Harbor from the cable car and scores of scenes from dances, beach parties, and ordinary afternoon walks, all populated with people who had defined my island experience as much as frangipani and Fanta but now were gone: Dick, Wendy, Wayne, Suzi, Karl, Eric, Carlson, Kathi, Barry and Bev, the Baker girls. It was the reverse of those poltergeist pictures where someone takes a photo of an empty room and sees a ghost when the film is developed. These ghosts had been there in the flesh when I took the pictures, but now had disappeared from all the settings where the photos were shot.

Page by page, my melancholy deepened until I came to a snapshot that changed my mood as abruptly as that infuriating wind. Taken at a lively party, it was a close-up shot of Suzi and a Samoan friend Maika, with Suzi's brother Karl inserting his head between theirs to crash the picture. Just seeing the angle of his jawline and the impertinence of his expression made my face burn.

It wasn't only his face that provoked me. Just before school had let out for summer, at the very party where I'd taken that picture, Karl had developed an unexpected and intense interest in me. For the next ten days he'd kept up the pursuit, paying me visits at all times of day and night. I was flattered and, frankly, floored. Though even more caustic than his sister Suzi, Karl wasn't bad looking, and he was one of the brainiest among us, headed for Harvard the following fall. If this genius was interested enough in me to spend hours at my house—not just making out when my parents were asleep, but talking about smart stuff—I must have something going for me.

Then one afternoon, with no preface to soften the blow, he casually informed me that he'd "made a mistake" in getting involved with me.

"I don't really like you," he said with no expression. Then turning a fire hose on the bridge he'd just set ablaze, he added a postscript: "But I might get lonely sometimes, so if I do, will you still be around?"

The steadiness of my voice surprised me as much as the words I heard myself speak: "You know what, Karl? I don't like you either. I'm not sure I ever have." I wasn't retaliating, I was being truthful. He offered no smart-alecky retort, just a dispassionate "Okay" before he walked away.

I felt victorious about my assertive comeback until the last day of school, when I passed around my autograph book. That night, sitting on my bed, I leafed through page after pastel page of reminiscences, gibes about chemistry homework, and exhortations to keep in touch, until I ended up at a butter-yellow page with writing on the diagonal and Karl's signature in the bottom right corner.

My feleni, it began. "My friend." I didn't think I cared what he'd written, but apparently I did. The salutation triggered a flutter.

Next time I have a beer I'll make a toast to you and your beautiful eyes. Was he being sincere or ironic? It was impossible to intuit his tone, so I read on.

I'll remember you for a long time (but eventually I'll forget you), and, oops, I almost forgot, I'll remember your sweet, effeminate father, too.

When I reached the end of that sentence, my face fluoresced, and my head pulsed. I forced myself to read the page again, quietly closed the cover, carried the book to the dresser, and buried it beneath my underwear.

I knew as well as anyone that my father's penchant for domestic arts was unconventional, but to think that exhibiting his true nature would open him up to ridicule made me feel ripped and gaping myself. It was then I decided once and for all I had no use for the Karls of this world, whose coolness disguises a cruel core.

Thinking back to that day as I sat in the same spot on my bed looking at Karl's picture, it struck me that living in a place where the cast of characters rotated in and out with tidal regularity was not entirely a bad thing.

~ ~ ~

I hadn't resurrected the sewing project by party time, so I wore a dress I'd brought from the States and kept in reserve for pull-out-all-the-stops occasions: a sleeveless, hot pink, A-line mini with buttons down the front and orange ruffles running from scoop neck to hemline on either side of the buttons. I wondered how the dress would compare to Barb's ensemble. It was hard to envision how she'd look, since I hadn't met her or seen a photograph, but I'd always pictured her as long-haired and persistently smiley like Toni, the girl from the *fiafia* village. Perky in her *puletasis*. Shapely in her *holomuus*. Fetching in her floral shifts.

The party hostess was Fatima, who belonged to a group of girls that called themselves The *Mo'os* (The Geckos)—Samoa's answer to the Tri Chis. When Val, Tom, and I walked into Fatima's house on a Fagatogo backstreet, I felt for a moment like I was new to the island again. So few of the old, familiar faces. But then as I scanned the room, I picked out Fibber, Peki, Li'i, Daisy, Eti, Tau, and Poloka, along with a high-spirited mass of *Mo'o* girls.

The band was playing—swells of surf music and a roomful of bouncing bodies. Coconut oil hung in the air like olfactory fog. Fatima, a smiling beacon, motioned us in and gave us hugs.

"I'm so glad you came," she said. As if anyone ever stayed home from a party. "Barb Harold is coming, too, you know." She said the name as one word: Barbharold. Everyone said it that way, a syntactical peculiarity that added import.

"I know." My voice came out like a squeak. It didn't matter. Fatima, distracted by the entrance of another guest, was no longer paying attention to me.

"Oh, look! Here's Barbharold now!"

I turned toward the door and searched the crowd for a Toni look-alike. All I saw was a round-faced girl with bobbed hair and a comfortably pillowed shape. I tried to merge the real-life Barbharold into the image I'd been carrying around all these months, but the fit was as if she'd tried to squeeze into my party dress, buttons popping all the way down the front.

Barb made her way over to where we stood, and after receiving Fatima's hugs and *I'm-so-glad-you-came*, introduced herself.

"I wasn't sure I'd still know anyone here," she said. "Things change so fast."

"Don't I know it," I said, as in my mind a goddess packed up and left, and an ordinary girl — just like me — moved in.

My father was making scrambled eggs. His articulate fingers, tipped with clean, flat nails, cracked the shells on the edge of a metal mixing bowl — he always used the same one — and slid in yolks and whites with a twisting motion that probably was unnecessary but added flair. He added a splash of cream and shakes of salt and pepper before whisking the eggs to a sunshiny froth. On the stove, bacon grease shimmered and popped in a skillet. My father turned down the heat with one hand and poured the eggs into the pan with the other. Then, wielding a spatula as if he'd studied at Le Cordon Bleu instead of Oklahoma University College of Medicine, he played at the firming edges of the eggs, letting the uncooked liquid run underneath until the whole thing was uniformly done to moist-but-not-runny perfection. I had eaten scrambled eggs all across America and never tasted any like my father's. Whether it was technique or the specific proportions he used, his always came out with a slight sweetness that counteracted the eggy overtones I objected to in other cooks' attempts.

He delivered my eggs alongside toast he'd brushed with melted butter and cut on the diagonal. Jam, as always, was served in a small porcelain dish, not straight from the jar.

I smiled the kind of smile I used to lavish upon him before we came to Samoa, before we came to odds. Lately, I'd been overlooking my father's failings and irritating quirks, guarding his feelings with ferocity reignited by Karl's entry in my autograph book and everything I'd absorbed about *aiga* loyalty.

"You never told me about that party at the muu-muu girl's house." He sat down at the table to watch me eat. Always an early riser, he'd had his own breakfast hours before and was letting my mother sleep in this Saturday morning.

"Not muu-muu, Daddy, *mo'o*. Like gecko." I fed him tidbits of party gossip, which was easier now that Dick was gone and I didn't have to watch what I said.

When we were both satiated, we got up from the table and started clearing away dishes. The phone rang, and my father's forehead corrugated in concern.

"Who'd be calling this early on a Saturday morning? I don't have any patients about to deliver." The furrows tightened into knife pleats of irritation. "They'll wake your mother."

He strode to the rotary phone and lifted the receiver midway through the second ring. I half-listened as I finished clearing the table and ran water in the sink. Probably a nurse needing guidance.

"What? Oh, no . . . Oh, no . . . I'm so sorry . . . When? . . . Where are you now? . . . We'll be right there."

After the second *Oh no*, I came out of the kitchen, damp dish towel slung across my shoulder, and saw my father's face turn the color of dust.

When he hung up, he pressed his hand to his forehead as if he'd been hit with a crushing headache. "Dr. Puckett," he said. "Died in his sleep. Go wake your mother and get dressed."

I took a step toward the bedrooms, but the air jelled around me, and my mind congealed. *Val's father is dead.* That one thought stuck in my consciousness and swelled like a sore, forcing out all others. When I tried to consider what it meant and what might happen next, I couldn't move beyond the singular fact. *Val's father. Dead.*

~ ~ ~

Val sat at the kitchen table where we'd talked, prickly with newness, my first day on the island. Now, her eyes haloed red and desolate, her face streaked, she was unrecognizable as the ballsy girl I'd met that afternoon. I smoothed a wayward curl off her forehead. It sprang back at me. I put both arms around her.

"Oh, Val." I had no idea what else to say. My parents, more practiced in comforting the grieving, talked in low tones to Mrs. Puckett in the living room. I strained to overhear, but picked up only a word now and then: *ambulance . . . heart failure . . . funeral.*

In disconnected phrases, Val filled in the details. Her mother had awakened her early that morning, just in time for Val to see the ambulance pull away. Not long after, Mrs. Puckett was on the phone, checking on departing flights.

"She wants to get us all out of here as soon as possible, back to Kalamazoo, where things will be more normal."

What would normal be like without a father? I didn't ask.

Val fiddled with a spoon that lay on the placemat before her. I noticed the wart on her finger, the one she now made no attempt to hide. I went to the refrigerator and slid out two bottles of orange Fanta. In so many ways, the moment was identical to so many others over the past eleven months. In so many ways, it was nothing like any moment we'd ever lived before.

With all the departures of friends and the knowledge that our time on the island was limited, we'd thought we had a handle on impermanence. But whenever the ground had shifted before, we'd always had our parents—and each other—to anchor us. Now it was clear that even anchors sometimes slipped their moorings.

Chapter 29 — Samoan Sickness

Mo'omo'o, Mo'omo'o 'oe
Tu mai ā tu mai 'oe
Oso i le fi, oso i le vao māoa
Oleā ou velosia 'oe

Mo'omo'o, Mo'omo'o
Show yourself, show yourself
Flee to the cordyline tree, flee to the deep forest
Before you are impaled on my spear
— Samoan healing incantation

Val and I sat at a table by the hotel pool, same as always. Only not. The topic of discussion: not parties, but pathologies.

"What *is* sprue, anyway?"

Val had just told me that was the disease that precipitated her father's death. Sprue—something vaguely botanical about the term, something nineteenth-century sounding, too softly benign to be fatal, unlike the clinically consonanted *tuberculosis* or *cancer*.

Val picked at a breadfruit chip as if it were a fleck of lint instead of something edible. "I can't tell you the medical details—Mom could—it's some kind of wasting disease. You eat, but your body can't take in what it needs. At least that's how it was explained to me." She told me her father had contracted an intestinal infection on a visit to Korea—for a World Health Organization conference, ironically enough—and afterward developed sprue.

"I did notice he was getting thinner," I said. My parents had commented on it, speculating that hospital politics and clashing cultures were taking a toll on Dr. Puckett's health. Worried the same might happen to my father, I'd become as alert to his physical state as I was to his emotions, sensitive to pallors now, as well as psychic pain. I fretted about my mother's health, too. Though the move to Penicillin Row had invigorated her, she still had days when her energy flagged, and she couldn't put on weight no matter how much she ate.

"Down to a hundred pounds by the time he diagnosed himself," Val said. "Mom wanted him to go back to the States, but he thought he could treat it."

A hundred pounds. That was what my mother weighed. The thought of my own father withering down to my mother's size was heartsickening. My nose tingled and felt cotton-stuffed—a sensation that usually preceded tears. I glanced at Val. Her eyes were dry, but there was a tremor in the hand that toyed with her food.

"Can we not talk about this anymore?" Val pushed her plate away as if it were attached to the subject matter.

What else was there to talk about? Conversation about the future seemed pointless; she was leaving the next day. We'd promised to write and make every effort to get together back in the States, but by now we both knew how hard it was for intimacy to survive separation, how easy for substitutes to take center stage.

We sat and stared into the distance until a vivid blur appeared in my peripheral vision. I turned to see Iakopu, the tenacious tour operator, in a blue-and-white flowered shirt and a red-and-yellow *lavalava*, standing between our chairs, ukulele clasped behind his back in a respectful parade rest position. Somber-faced, he bowed in Val's direction.

"My condolences."

Val forced a smile. "Thank you, Iakopu. That's very kind of you."

Touched by his tender gesture, I smiled, too.

Iakopu's eyebrows shot upward, almost merging with his hairline. "Maybe you girls would like to go on a picnic?"

Val shook her head, "Not today, Iakopu." After he'd walked away, she began to laugh. Val's laugh was one of her contradictions. From a girl so bold, you'd expect uninhibited howls, but her laughter was muted, almost pantomime. First her face would crinkle into an expression like the "comedy" half of those comedy/tragedy masks—eyes slitted, forehead wrinkled, lips exaggeratedly upturned. Then she'd duck her head and press one palm against her chest, sinking through the shoulders, as if bowed by the hilarity. Finally, she'd begin to shake, and only then would the softest chuckling escape her lips.

"Gee, Val," I teased. "Maybe you should've gone with him just this once. Now you'll have to spend the rest of your life wondering what you missed."

Val laughed harder. She shook and shut her eyes and threw back her head and laughed more audibly than I could remember her laughing before, and every so often sighed and started over again with the kind of laughter that escapes the grasp of whatever prompted it, rising and floating and pulling out like magicians' scarves every emotion that's been compressed inside. She laughed and laughed and laughed so hard that by the end her eyes brimmed over. Those tears, I didn't try to wipe away.

Samoans recognize two kinds of health problems: *ma'i palagi* (white people's sicknesses—brought to Samoa by outsiders and best treated with Western medicine) and *ma'i Samoa* (Samoan sicknesses—physical and psychological disorders indigenous to the islands and best treated by traditional Samoan healers known as *fofō*). Among the *ma'i Samoa* are ailments stemming from the pain and stress of separation or rifts in relationships. After Val left, with a tearful airport scene to top all previous *tofas*, I knew firsthand how losing a friend could cause real suffering. My malaise was as wearying as any flu, and if I'd known where to find a *fofō*, I'd have shown up at her *fale o'o* asking for herbs or incantations. Instead, I practiced the only healing art I knew: applying pen to paper.

My letters to Val, each written over the course of several days, ran on for twenty pages or more and were illustrated with Ug cartoons, never as funny or cleverly drawn as hers, but the best I could do in my sick-hearted state.

A week after she left, my father, passing through the hallway on his way to the kitchen, caught me staring, tongue extended, into the bathroom mirror.

"That's not another monkey you're making faces at, you know," he teased. He'd been extra jokey since Val left, trying to prod me out of my funk.

"Vewy funny." I talked with my tongue out so I could point to the shiny, pinkish spot on its right side. "Wook."

My father took my head in his hands and tilted it this way and that until the light was right. "What'd you do—bite it?"

"I think I burned it on boiled taro, but that was a week ago. It still stings when I get toothpaste on it." With tongue retracted, my articulation improved, but I still lisped.

My father swung open the medicine chest door, reached behind the deodorant and took out a small, brown bottle. "Put some of this merthiolate on it, but try not to swallow any. If it doesn't get better in a couple of days, we'll take another look."

I unscrewed the cap, pulled out the glass rod attached to it, and dabbed the glowing orange liquid onto the side of my tongue. The burn and metallic taste assured me it would do the trick.

In the kitchen, my mother was making sandwiches on Jessop's bread. I told her not to make me one, and I opened a cupboard and slid cans around, searching for soup.

"But I thought you loved wahoo." The look on her face, halfway between befuddled and wounded, was the one she got whenever my tastes inexplicably shifted and I rejected something she was sure I'd enjoy.

"I do. It's just this canker sore — or blister or whatever it is — on my tongue. It hurts to eat anything crisp like that crust."

"Sore tongue, huh?" My mother lost the pained look and turned playful. "Been telling fibs?"

Pretending to be absorbed in searching through canned goods, I didn't answer.

My mother moved closer, near enough for me to catch the honeysuckle scent of her White Shoulders cologne. "I had a dream about you last night."

Uh-oh. Her so-called dreams were always cause for alarm. They usually involved me committing some transgression — one that, uncannily, I actually *had* recently committed behind my parents' backs. Whether my mother was psychic or just wise to my ways and using made-up dreams to confront me without actual confrontation, the effect was the same: it rattled me all to hell.

"I dreamed you came home from that party the other night on the back of Peki's motorbike instead of with Tom, like you were supposed to."

I burrowed deeper into the pantry. "Huh." In fact, I had been spending time with Peki lately and had accepted a few furtive rides on the bike (and kisses at the end of those rides). But how could my mother know that? Tom wouldn't rat on me, and with Mrs. Puckett gone, the parental intelligence network was seriously compromised. I almost believed my mother really did have telepathic visions. Living in Samoa made it easy to accept such an explanation, with all those legends about *aitu* — busybody spirits that inserted themselves into people's lives. Maybe one of them had taken over for Mrs. Puckett.

"Weird dream, Mother," I said. I could avoid confrontation, too.

~ ~ ~

I found myself thinking a lot about *aitu* and other Samoan beliefs over the next few days, as the canker sore continued to bedevil me. Was I somehow responsible for its lingering? I remembered what my father had told me about the Samoan view of health: that it depended on balance among the social, natural, and supernatural aspects of your life. If you were sick, you needed to identify what was out of balance and take action — appeasing a specific *aitu* or apologizing to someone you'd offended — to restore harmony.

I had no idea how to identify, much less assuage, an *aitu*, but I did believe an apology was in order. I took out my airmail stationery and in contrite, blue-black longhand, composed a letter to Aggie Grey, the Apia innkeeper. I started by expressing my appreciation for her hospitality during my recent stay and complimenting her hotel's cuisine and service. Then I told her how much I regretted my poor judgment and apologized for involving Nana and the other hotel staffers in the Ati mess. I addressed and sealed the envelope, walked it to the post office in Fagatogo, and prayed that Mrs. Grey never would respond. I hadn't told my parents about the dress debacle — or most of my other Apia adventures — and so far my mother hadn't intuited anything about them. The last thing I wanted was to have to explain a letter from Aggie accepting my apologies.

The letter healed my troubled soul, but it did nothing for my tongue. That evening I asked my father to take another look. This time there were no jokes about monkeys in the mirror.

"I don't like the looks of this," he said. "You'd better come to the clinic tomorrow."

The prospect didn't faze me. With a live-in doctor, I was used to finger-sticks, swabs, and X-rays for complaints that always ended up being something minor. A sprained elbow instead of a broken arm; a persistent cough that wasn't pneumonia after all.

"What do you think it could be?" I asked, more out of curiosity than concern.

The soft lines in my father's face stiffened into a look that made my gut contort. "Well . . . the only thing I know of that looks like this is syphilis."

Syphilis. I was too stunned, and too uncertain of the means of transmission, to protest, so I just stood there twisting my ring around my sweaty finger and saying nothing, which turned my father's face sterner.

"Be ready when I leave for work tomorrow. We'll run some tests first thing in the morning."

In my room that night, I tried to remember what little I knew about venereal diseases and how you could catch them. Toilet seats, no. Kissing? I didn't think so. It had to be through sex, and that let me out. If not exactly untouched, I was still as virginal as when I'd arrived on the island. But what if this strange affliction wasn't VD? What if it was some *ma'i Samoa* that I'd caught from kissing Peki? Or from angering an *aitu* who didn't like *palagi* girls messing around with Samoan boys? Or simply from causing conflict in my family? Could my father's tests reveal that kind of sickness?

Chapter 30 — My Samoan Chief

No matter how small and steep this little rock in the Pacific might prove, I was prepared to stick by it for life.
— Fay G. Calkins, *My Samoan Chief*

For the next week, I tried to put the sore spot out of my mind — except at mealtimes, when its presence was painfully obvious. I lived on scrambled eggs and boiled taro and otherwise carried on as usual. My test results would be coming soon from a medical lab in Hawaii; no point in worrying in the meantime, right?

Okay, I did worry. What if it *was* syphilis? How could I ever convince my parents there was no way I'd caught it by the usual route? But then, what if it wasn't syphilis? What the hell was it — some strange new form of mango rash? I kept thinking about *ma'i Samoa*, and the more I thought, the more the idea of being stricken with some exotic tropical disease, scary as that was, took on a tragically romantic appeal. I could see myself languishing in a tent of mosquito netting, chestnut hair attractively splayed on my pillow. Friends filling my room with frangipani and spikes of red ginger, me afloat in viscous fragrance as my parents spoon-fed me coconut ice cream. (No, chocolate — gallons of it.) And then, a miraculous cure, perhaps from some *fofō* in the shadowed depths of jungle. I'd be restored to perfect health and made an honorary *taupou*, worthy of fine-mat robe and fancy headdress.

When I wasn't indulging in suffering-heroine fantasies or helping out at home, I occupied myself with *sivasiva* dancing lessons, tutoring sessions, long walks, and writing in my journal—not just brief, factual entries in my Every Day Diary, but longer, more reflective passages in a kraft-covered notebook imprinted on the front with three palm trees and the words *American Samoa Exercise Book* in midnight blue. With Val gone, I'd become my own confidant. In myself, I found a friend who had infinite patience with my foibles, took my side on every issue, and applauded my wisdom and wit.

One topic I explored in depth with myself was exactly how to extend my stay in Samoa beyond the thirteen months remaining in my father's contract. Without a college degree I couldn't get a teaching job, but I believed I could support myself by adding a few more kids to my tutoring roster.

But where would I live? Only U.S. employees could stay in government quarters, so I'd have to rent a room or insinuate myself into a village. Or join the Peace Corps—I'd read that the agency was establishing a program in Western Samoa. I wrote for information and even showed it to my parents, who weren't opposed to the idea—*after college.* My dad, after all, had answered a call to help out in Samoa. How could he deny me the opportunity?

There was another option: I could marry into an *aiga* and have an instant home and family. I even had a likely candidate in Peki, who visited regularly now, perhaps because he knew I needed cheering up after Val's departure, but also because our new home on the bay was tailor-made for a timid visitor. Instead of knocking on the front door and standing anxious and exposed on the front stoop, he could slip up to my open bedroom window and tap the screen or make little snuffling animal noises until I noticed his presence.

One morning, as I sat on the bed writing in my journal, I heard music and recognized the signature slides and vibratos of the Vampires. It was too early in the day for a dance at the Turtle, and the sound didn't advance and recede like spillover from a passing car; it seemed to be right outside my window. I pulled the curtain open. Nothing there. I craned for a better view. Peki and Poloka were crouched beneath the sill, a portable tape player between them.

"We thought you'd like a wake-up concert." Peki stood up, and the scent of his coconut-oiled hair drifted into my room with his nervous giggle.

Poloka smoothed his madras shirt and poked the machine's off button. "We're going downtown. Want to come?"

I'd run out of thoughts to obsessively examine in my notebook, so I told the boys I'd be right out. By the time I got outside, Poloka was astride his motorbike, headed in a different direction, tape machine hazardously clenched under one arm.

"I just remembered I have to go slice bread at the store," he said, nodding in the direction of his family's bakery. The lopsided curl of his lip was a tip-off to the boys' ploy. "You two go ahead," he called over his shoulder as he rode away. "Have fun."

Peki and I waved to Poloka and set off along the path to Fagatogo, Peki's broad feet leaving Sasquatch prints beside my size five-and-a-half narrows. I no longer felt self-conscious walking around the island, but with Peki beside me I felt even more like a local and less like an uninvited guest.

"I've been sad since Val left, Peki."

He nodded, sympathy visible in the crimp between his eyebrows. "Maybe it's time for Mike to come back."

Months before, I'd given Peki the gray kitten when it was clear he was more attached to Mike than I was. Until Mike got too big, Peki had carried him around on the motorbike, zipped inside his jacket with just a furry head poking out at chest level. The bike's whizzing and whirring didn't unnerve the animal at all, which I took as further evidence that Peki was the better cat parent.

"No," I told him. "Mike belongs with you, at home — wherever that is."

Peki's frown lines deepened, and he waved an arm in a sweeping arc. "I told you. On the mountain." All these months

I'd known him, and this was as much as I'd ever gotten out of him about where he lived. His home life and family were as unknown to me as the far side of the island, undeveloped and accessible only by mountain footpaths.

At the end of Centipede Row, we passed the warehouse where Peki worked after school. I'd seen him leaning, arms crossed, against the frame of the open door at break time, but I had no idea what went on inside. Whenever I asked him what he did there, the answer was the same: "Work." This time, I didn't bother asking.

The asphalt parking lot at Nia Marie's general store was sticky and the air filled with tarry fumes. Young men in *lavalavas* lounged against parked cars, old women sat cross-legged beneath the broad tin roof that shaded the building's side entrance, and shoppers streamed in and out of the open doorway. We *smuck-smuck-smucked* our way across the lot, through the door and into the cool and dim interior.

Peki spoke to the clerk in Samoan, pointing at a box on a shelf behind the counter. She retrieved it and set it in front of him.

Amazing how easy it was to be waited on when you weren't *palagi*.

Peki paid, and as we walked back outside, he opened the box, extracted a fistful of gingersnaps, and held them out to me. I took one and bit down, then winced and put my hand to my mouth.

"Ow!"

Peki looked at the cookies and then at me, his eyebrows in a twist that mixed alarm and perplexity so comically I burst out laughing and almost spit half-chewed cookie at him.

"It's nothing!" I assured him. "I forgot about my sore tongue. Probably burned it on boiled taro. Should've let it cool longer."

"Don't be in such a hurry." Peki shook a scolding finger but smiled, all at once more handsome than he'd looked in recent memory.

In my bedroom that night, I took out the brown notebook and my fountain pen, along with Skrip ink cartridges I'd bought at a stationery store in Stillwater and carefully rationed. Jet Black, Blue Black, Green, and Peacock Blue. Before beginning to write, I reread a long entry I'd written on graduation day, when I'd volunteered to usher with several friends from the Samoan section of Samoana High, kids I'd met through National Honor Society.

June 18, 1966

I was over at the auditorium by 8:00 wearing my usher's uniform and ribbon, and the bow Palesitina had given me. I was so glad to see that Misiuaita, Fasega and Jack were working there. I stood at the door, across from Misi, handing out programs. All that time we were joking and teasing each other and everyone else. After a very long time the seniors started to march in. The first one I knew was Peki. He smiled at me and squeezed my hand. Each one that I knew took my hand as he passed and I stood there smiling and loving them all.

When they all took their seats I went and sat on the table in back with Jeannette, Clement, Mike, Helen, Misi, Fasega and Jack. We all kept playing and laughing. Whenever something was said in Samoan, whether by the speaker on stage or just in conversation, Jack would say, "Do you understand?" If I didn't, which was almost always the case, he would translate it all for me.

Then the program started and the seniors chanted the Lord's Prayer. I had never heard it that way before, and it was beautiful. After many speeches and music, it was time for the presentation of diplomas. As I watched Peki, Eric, Gus, Li'i, Pili and Fibber walking across the stage I cried. Then the seniors sang that beautiful Samoan hymn once more, and when they had finished the seniors marched out. The parents all started pushing to get out and present their children with ulas. Fasega pushed me right into the crowd and there I was, being shoved against walls and laughing at Fasega, who couldn't get out himself. I squeezed back to the table to pick up a program to keep always.

I went outside and stood at the door for a few minutes, looking at all the happy people. Then I walked out in the rain to look for Peki and the others. First I found Li'i. We shook hands and kissed each other on the cheek. I went on, shaking hands and giving congratulations. Finally I went back inside and saw Peki standing in the middle of the room, surrounded by his family and friends. He was the one I wanted to see.

It was true. Even when keeping his distance, Peki always had his eye on me, and even when chasing after other boys, I still felt real affection for him. He was one constant in the ever-shifting tableaux of my life. Shelter from the rain. Breathing space in the surging crowd. Good feelings, all right, but did they amount to love?

I turned to a blank page in the journal, loaded a Blue Black cartridge into my pen and began exploring my thoughts.

I realize that emotion has a lot to do with love, but more than emotion must be involved. For two people to really be in love, they must know each other so well that one knows what the other will say or will think before it happens. This must all come automatically — without either really realizing that it happens. The two must always be best friends with each other; sharing everything until it really seems like they were always together.

I laid down the pen and thought about all the boys I had loved or thought I had. Danny and I had once had that kind of connection. With Dick it was hard to say. Every time we started getting close, some drama erupted, and whatever bridges we'd begun to build were buried in the ash and lava of crisis. With Peki there were no upheavals; his devotion was unwavering, and though I'd never felt wildly in love with him, he'd always been my friend and sometimes more. But what did we really share? Laughs. Kisses. Cookies.

I went to my dresser and pulled out a paperback I'd stashed under clothes, along with Margaret Mead's *Coming of Age in Samoa*. I'd bought the book at a Fagatogo bookstore and pored over it as much as Mead's opus. The cover illustration showed a bare-chested Samoan man against a stylized background suggestive of a pandanus mat. The man's raven hair was swept back from his forehead into crests and troughs like ocean swells in moonlight. Black eyes, bright as burning candlenuts, peered out beneath caterpillar eyebrows, and his nose, a broad triangle, was centered above perfectly-shaped lips. The book's title, *My Samoan Chief*, was printed in red above the man's left ear, and the author's name, Fay G. Calkins, floated alongside his left shoulder.

I stared at the cover for a long time before thumbing through the book, the story of an American woman who met and married a Samoan in the States and came to live with him in the islands. The jacket copy made reference to the "totally new and charming, if at times frustrating and confusing" way of life Fay Calkins encountered in Samoa. I could relate to that, but it was the book's cover, not its words, that held my attention.

The man in the picture was handsome in a classic Polynesian way, but I found myself wondering what made Fay willing to follow him to his jungle village and whether she found happiness there. My connection to Samoa—and to my own Samoan suitor—was deepening by the day. But while I could easily see myself staying longer than the two-year stint my father had signed up for, could I imagine myself doing it as a wife, boiling taro and birthing babies in some palm-thatched hut or tin-roofed shack?

I set the book aside, picked up my pen, laid it down, thought some more, picked it up again and wrote in deliberate, backhand script:

Language barrier would prevent me from ever knowing a Samoan well enough to know all of his mind. Because of the difference in our backgrounds I could never feel that he had always been a part of my life.

The argument was persuasive, though even as I wrote it I wondered who I was trying to persuade. Was I expressing what I really felt, or making excuses for holding back from the unfamiliar? After all, if I stayed here for good, I'd learn the language and ways, just as Peki would pick up mine. Yet no matter how much I talked it over with myself, the answers seemed as out of reach as details about Peki's personal life.

It was all so uncertain. The only thing I knew for sure: one way or another, I was staying in Samoa.

Chapter 31 — Last Dance

O le latalata a alafau.
(Although the eye is close by the cheek, it cannot see the cheek.)
— Samoan proverb meaning a person may be close to a thing he strives for and yet not reach it.

A flurry of red blossoms drifted down from the cable car overhead. One fell at my feet; I picked it up and stuck it behind my ear.

"What do you think?" I asked Marnie. "Does it make me look more Samoan?"

Preoccupied with smoothing the waves in her bangs, she gave me a sideways *why-are-you-asking-me-this* look. Then to humor me, she shrugged and said, "I guess."

The *Mariposa* was in port again, and we'd come to the dock to tour the ship. Almost a week had passed since the tests on my tongue, and I needed distractions to keep me from wondering when the results would come back from Hawaii. But while Marnie was good company, she didn't know how to improvise hilarity the way Val did. No playing pranks on tourists while posing as Samoans today (and really, that was okay; it wouldn't have been the same). Besides, I'd adopted a kinder attitude toward visitors lately, offering to show them around when they looked lost and, when they asked, sharing tidbits about life in Samoa. Reaching out to strangers made me feel like an ambassador for my island home, more like a true member of the community than I'd ever felt pretending to be Samoan.

I pulled the flower from behind my ear and looked around for some other way to amuse myself. At end of the dock, I spotted a young *palagi* man I'd never seen before, turning in slow circles and craning to gawk at mountains, cable car, and flower shower, as a punch-drunk grin stretched across his face.

I jerked a thumb toward him. "Who's that guy?"

Marnie wasted no time sliding into official greeter mode. "I don't know — let's find out!"

We scurried over and introduced ourselves to the young man, who looked to be in his early twenties. He told us he was Sal, from Elmont, New York, traveling alone, not on some sweeping tour of the South Pacific, but interested only in spending time in Samoa.

I was flabbergasted. No one in the States seemed to know — or care — about the island territory, and he'd made a special trip here? I looked him up and down, taking in his flowered shirt, khaki pants, and flip-flops, then leaned closer to study his face like a rare specimen.

"How'd you even know about this place?"

Sal told us he'd seen a troupe of Samoan dancers performing in the Polynesia Pavilion at the New York World's Fair the previous summer and was so entranced with the performance he'd returned to see the show again — and again, and again — and eventually made friends with the dancers.

"I've been saving up ever since to come here and visit them." Sunlight struck his face in a way that made him look like he had light bulbs behind his cheeks. Or maybe the shine really was coming from inside. I'd never met anyone so instantly enthralled with Samoa. I had to get to know this guy.

After Marnie wandered off to shop in Fagatogo, Sal and I spent most of the afternoon sitting on a palm-shaded bench behind the Jorgensens' old house on Centipede Row — both of us admiring the plush mountains, the hunter green water, and the swaying, flower-spraying cable car — and talking with a passion that seemed ours alone about the place, the people, and our heartfelt connections to it all. When I had to leave for my dance lesson, we agreed to meet the next afternoon at the hotel, where the World's Fair troupe would be performing.

The next afternoon Sal was waiting in the snack bar as the dance troupe's musicians milled around, preparing to perform. A crowd of tourists had gathered, but we managed to find a table near the front. Like Sal, I'd seen the troupe's routine plenty of times—they often performed at the hotel—but each time, the clatter of drums, the swish of grass skirts, and the flash of knives and fire batons brought my own internal rhythms more in tune with the island's.

At the program's end, the musicians eased into a gentle *sivasiva*, and dancers pulled guests onto the floor. Sal and I exchanged split-second glances before springing from our seats and gliding across the pavement in the alternately knock-kneed, bow-legged shuffle of the dance. Sal was surprisingly good, and when, still moving in pace with the beat, I lowered myself toward the ground, he mimicked the move without tottering.

I thought back to that first *fiafia* in Aoloau, when I'd envied Toni for knowing the dance. Now I knew the steps, too.

We danced until the music ended and the dancers and tourists drifted away. Then we sat on a lava wall with a view of the harbor's mouth and picked up the thread of the previous afternoon's conversation. Sal told me he planned to stay in Samoa as long as he possibly could. I told him I did too and confided my own schemes: Peace Corps, tutoring, marriage to Peki.

"I really think I'd *die* if I had to leave," I declared.

Sal nodded—a single, slow nod—and pulled from his shirt pocket several folded sheets of onionskin paper.

"I wrote this on the plane coming down here." His slender fingers peeled the paper open. "I wouldn't let most people read it, but I have a feeling you'll understand."

I took the paper from him and read the three-page poem he'd printed in blue ballpoint. It was bad, sappy verse, but I didn't know it at the time, and it wouldn't have mattered if I had. Its lines about "greenness on blueness sea, white and whiteness sand," and "never ending passion and fondness" for the people and the paradise where his soul washed to shore expressed all my own overwrought emotions.

I told him it was the most beautiful thing I'd ever read and asked if he'd make a copy for me. He said he'd do it that night and give it to me when we met up again the next day.

I could have *sivasiva*ed all the way home, buoyed by my new friendship with someone who saw Samoa the way I did and who didn't think it was crazy to want to spend a lifetime — or at least a few more years — here.

Still smiling as I opened the front door, I stifled my joy and made what I thought was an appropriately sober face when I saw my parents' troubled expressions.

"What's wrong?" I hoped another doctor hadn't died. I looked past my parents and searched the living room for Tom, hoping he'd waggle his eyebrows to telegraph what was going on or reassure me with the Liberace crinkle. He was nowhere to be seen.

My mother put an arm around me but turned her face away. My father took both my hands in his. "We got your test results."

My mind shifted into high gear, racing through scenarios as I tried to read the medical report from my parents' faces.

It can't be syphilis — they wouldn't be acting this nice if it was. So that's good, right? But why do they look so upset?

"The pathologist in Hawaii called me long-distance to make sure I hadn't mislabeled the sample," my father continued. "He said, 'This is not something we see in a seventeen-year-old girl.' I told him I was sorry to say that I was sure it was the right sample; I took it myself from my own daughter." At that, my father teared up, but the only emotion I felt was impatience. This was no time for one of his anecdotal lead-ins.

"So what is it?"

Pulling himself together into the composed physician, my father delivered the diagnosis: "Carcinoma," he said. "Cancer."

I should have been knocked senseless, but my first reaction was relief that instead of a shameful social disease I had something dramatic that would elicit sympathy and leniency from my parents. A brain tumor would've been better—more suffering heroine potential. Tongue cancer didn't sound nearly as impressive and, in fact, was downright gross. Still, I'd work with it. I didn't know enough about cancer to realize the odds weren't in my favor. I only knew that my mother had had it and was still alive, so I imagined I'd have some sort of treatment, be tired for awhile and then get back to life as usual.

I couldn't figure out what to say, so I said nothing as I continued to study my parents' faces. Once again, I was causing them pain—not through anything intentional, but perhaps through some thoughtless act or oversight that triggered a *ma'i Samoa* that turned into cancer. I was supposed to protect my parents from disappointment, sadness, and stress. How could I do that now?

"Don't worry, honey." My mother stroked my hair the way she had the night of the fire. "We'll get you the best care we can find, no matter where we have to go."

That was when it sank in that our lives were going to change considerably more than I'd thought. And then came the news that crushed me more than any diagnosis could have.

"We've already made arrangements," my father said, thinking he was reassuring me. "Tom's gone to the airport to pick up our tickets. We're leaving for Oklahoma Sunday night; you'll be back home soon."

It was already Thursday. Another year on the island wouldn't have been enough, but now I had just three more days. My recurring dream was reality: my time in Samoa was too quickly slipping away.

"But we'll come back here as soon as I'm better, right?"

My father's eyes told me he wasn't going to make promises he couldn't keep.

"Someday we'll send you back to visit," he said. "But no, we won't be coming back to live."

Chapter 32 — Tofa

Ua fa'ala'au tu i vanu
(Like a tree standing near a precipice)
— Samoan proverb interpreted as "The future is unknown."

I've heard people say that when something disastrous happens, life changes in the blink of an eye. It's true, fate is redirected in a matter of milliseconds. But the sinking in, the conscious course correction—that's a more gradual, layered process.

The next three mornings I awoke as always, with sunlight filtering through my curtains and slowly returning color to my bedspread and wall hangings. Minutes passed before I remembered my diagnosis and looming departure. When reality eventually broke through, I tried to push it away and burrow back into my den of ignorance, but truth, insistent as the sun, forced me into full awareness.

When it did, I jumped out of bed, only because if I lay there any longer I'd think too much about how far away Val was and how much I needed her zaniness to distract me.

Other friends tried, but how could they know what to say to a girl with cancer? They faltered and fumbled and hung their heads and made me feel as bad for them as for myself. Even Peki made himself scarce, as if afraid he'd catch my *ma'i palagi*. If my sweet, accepting Samoa friends were this uneasy with my illness, how would it play in Stillwater, where I already felt like a misfit?

It was worse when someone tried too hard to lighten the mood, like when Marnie blithely remarked, "I guess we should call you Cancy now, huh?" I laughed it off instead of burying my head in a sofa pillow like I wanted to. I'd been struggling for the past eleven months to define myself; was a disease now going to hijack my identity? Not if I could help it. I'd stood up to my parents, to Suzi, and to anyone else who tried to tell me who or what I was. I'd be damned if I'd let cancer pigeonhole me.

Especially not *tongue* cancer. A disease no one but raspy old men got. There was absolutely no glamour to be eked out of that—not the disease, and certainly not the afflicted body part. A breast was sexy, a brain was essential, but a *tongue*—really kind of disgusting when you looked at it closely, which I'd been forced to do lately. Yuck.

In a way, it was good we were leaving so soon. With my days now a schizoid scramble of life-as-usual and frantic, last-chance bustle, I had little time to dwell on distress or anything else. I showed up for my tutoring jobs, got a haircut, guzzled milkshakes with Tom at the hotel, declined another picnic invitation from Iakopu, and raced around the island handing out invitations to my thrown-together *tofa* party and snapping pictures of everything I hadn't yet documented.

With my Kodak Instamatic, I shot landmarks like *Fatu* and *Futi*, the "flower pots" that jutted out of the ocean just offshore. Tall as two- and three-story buildings, the massive black lava outcrops topped with vegetation looked like oversized planters spilling with greenery. For centuries, those mute sentinels had watched islanders and temporary inhabitants come and go. Had they taken note of me?

Farther down the coast, I tried to capture the backlit glow of that particular patch of ocean that dazzled me so on the drive to Aoloau for our first *fiafia*. How little I'd known then! How much I knew now—not just about customs and dance steps, but about resilience and survival. As I clicked away at a sunset over an expanse of ocean, I thought about Wayne staying afloat, whistling in the waves. When I photographed *fales* in the picture-book village of Pava'ia'i, I remembered Samoans rebuilding and rebounding after the hurricane. Even my shots of our old apartment building, the airport, and the palm-lined sidewalk behind Centipede Row dredged up memories of strength and grace in the face of adversity: friends helping out after the fire, Val and her mother pulling themselves together and taking care of business after Dr. Puckett died.

The survival lessons of the past year were everywhere, and as I made my rounds, everything seemed amplified: the shouts and snatches of music louder, the shades of sky and sea deeper, the fragrance of frangipani headier, as if every sound, color, and scent were striving to imprint itself on my consciousness.

I communed with my mountain muses, viewed through a scrim of tears. *Malosi* had taught me not to ask *why me, why now*, but still I raged and mourned. Cancer was tearing me away from these mountains, from children's hugs and crayoned sketches, from palm trees, bay breezes, swooning guitars, and swaying rhythms. From all I had loved and all I had imagined. Cancer was stealing my dream.

The last pictures in my Samoa album are from the night of my farewell. There's me, pre-party, in the same *lavalava* I wore by the waterfall at Papase'ea Sliding Rock, wearing a wistful expression as I stand beside the Vampires' drum set in my living room. And later that evening, me in the *fa'afafine* dress, framed by brown faces; me in the kitchen with my parents, whose smiles look forced; me dancing with Bill Bigfoot (in crewcut and muscle shirt, not Mohawk and kimono), who kept telling me, "Sure gonna miss you, little girl." There's Marnie laughing with a boy she thought she loved; there's Fibber with his arm flung around his cousin Gus's shoulder, and Maika and Bill Bigfoot making strong-man muscles. There's a close-up of Sal in a turquoise aloha shirt, his features washed out from the flash. There's Pili and Poloka clowning around on a break between sets. The Mo'o girls teasing a pack of boys. Eti beaming, but looking half-complete without her sidekick Daisy. Peki, dear Peki, huddled with a bunch of other boys on the daybed in the corner.

Thirty-one photographs, not so very different from the other party pictures in my album. Not so very different from the snapshots of any *palagi* girl whose stay on the island was brief.

There was nothing much to see through the double-paned window. Runway lights and a glimmer from the terminal. Mountains and sea lost to night's blackness. Everything receding, growing smaller.

The lightlessness reminded me of the night I rode with Nana to her village, over highways whose mileposts and landmarks were invisible to me. This night, on a jet bound for Honolulu, I was again unsure of what lay ahead, yet inexplicably free of fear.

Settling into my seat, I reflected on all that had transpired since this *palagi* girl burst from the sky and landed on the island that now was disappearing from view. In the span of eleven months, I had witnessed the perfect beauty of a frangipani blossom and found beauty in imperfection. I had observed human beings—*palagi* and Samoan—at their finest and most flawed. I had sought transformation, expecting to find it in grand experiences, and found it instead in small moments: sitting by a waterfall, dancing in a village, sharing love and laughter and friendship. I had yearned for a challenge that would redefine me, and imagined setting off with a rucksack filled with topo maps and hardtack, or sailing away with a change of clothes, a bilge pump and emergency flares. Instead, I was bound for a very different kind of challenge, equipped with memories and a spirit imbued with *malosi*.

EPILOGUE

*M*alosi served me well: I survived. Not just the five years my prognosis predicted, but long enough to look back and reflect fifty years later. In the years between, I've navigated the alien world of illness and its aftermath, faced down surgeries and scars, learned the language of recurrence and metastasis, suffered losses, pondered impermanence, and tried to do it all with as much grace as I could muster.

Those first months back in Oklahoma were a jumble of ups and downs. Still jet-lagged from traveling six thousand miles, I was hustled off to an Oklahoma City hospital for more tests and biopsies—all negative. My doctors wore puzzled looks and talked about a possible mistake in the earlier results from Honolulu. My hopes rose. If I wasn't sick after all, we could still turn around and get back to Samoa for my senior year.

Further tests turned up spots that *were* cancer. No return ticket to Samoa for me.

There was alarming—and mercifully brief—talk of surgery to remove my jawbone and half my tongue. When I refused to consider any such thing, my parents backed me up and found specialists in Colorado who would see me for monthly check-ups and take a wait-and-watch approach, allowing me to start school in Stillwater. I packed away my *puletasi*, cruised the Sonic with Tri Chi friends, and broke the habit of reaching for girlfriends' hands when walking together. From every outward appearance, I'd made a smooth transition back into stateside life.

My diary entries told a different story: "I hate it here," I wrote night after night. "I want to go home to Samoa." After I'd cried myself to sleep, that recurring dream—the one of being back in Samoa, but not for long—still haunted me.

In time, my mood and health stabilized. My mother's health, however, deteriorated. Two years after our return, her cancer slipped back and stealthily spread. By the time her back pain led to its discovery, the disease was too advanced to be deterred. Under my father's and brother's care, she held on for more than a year, exhibiting her own brand of *malosi*. When she died, shortly after my twenty-first birthday, I wondered if I would ever again find anyone or anything to hold on to.

I anguished, too, for my father. Knowing how he'd suffered through my mother's illness and death, I worried he'd be destroyed if I took sick again.

Years passed: long stretches of perfect health punctuated by recurrences, surgeries, and more aggressive treatments. Cancer, it seemed, would always be part of my life. Lucky for me, so would Samoa. The dream, yes, and the memories and the lessons learned, but also the friendships.

Close as my mates and I felt during that extraordinary year, we never expected any *forever* from our friendships. Yet the bonds forged in that islet of time have lasted longer than parts of our lives that seemed so much more durable back then. When I page through my old photo album, I see faces of friends with whom I'm still in touch: Val, Wendy, Barry and Bev (married to each other now), and others. Over the years we've shared connection and dispensed comfort through crises more excruciating than we were capable of imagining in youth.

Other faces are ghosts. Marnie, Daisy, Suzi, Toni, and so many more left us too soon. And yet they are friendly ghosts whose pictures remind me that it's worth forming attachments, even if pieces of you crumble away each time one breaks.

I lost track of some friends. Lee sailed away, but I learned about the rest of his voyage and his life after that adventure from two books he wrote: *Dove* and *Home Is the Sailor*. Other friends I reconnected with when, finally, I returned to Samoa twenty years after my hasty departure. That trip is a story for another time. Suffice to say that thanks to a helpful Samoan postmaster (who remembered my family and also happened to be Pili's aunt) and the hospitality of Pili, Abe, and others, I enjoyed a homecoming sweeter than any in my dreams. Nearly forty years old at the time, I tracked down Fibber at his job in Tafuna and instantly felt the kinship we'd shared in our teens when he lived on the hillside behind my apartment. He told me Peki was married and living in California, news that made me glad for Peki, but wistful about the likelihood of ever seeing him again.

One evening I accompanied Pili to a club where his band (no longer the Vampires, but a new band with the same island sway) was playing. During a break, he introduced me to a young man whose name I recognized. The strapping fellow who shook my hand was little Tui, all grown up. I told him I still had the *fale* he'd drawn for me twenty years before. His grin, just as before, lit me up inside.

My return to Samoa drained the bitter from my bittersweet memories and reminded me that as much as we think we have a grasp on one place at any given point in time, things shift, and we can't hold on. Yet if we allow ourselves to experience it fully, love it as much as we're capable of loving, mourn its loss as deeply as we're capable of mourning, we'll carry its essence with us and be sustained in other times of change and loss.

We all inhabit islands of impermanence, all try to find our ways in this strange territory of life as human beings. Sometimes we howl into the wind; sometimes we cower from the storm's fury; sometimes we pursue false idols; sometimes, in our carelessness, we set things ablaze. But when we listen to the music around us and summon our strength, we can all find the rhythm and dance.

We can all find our *fa'a Samoa*.

ACKNOWLEDGEMENTS

Ua le sula fala o 'Ie'ie.
('Ie'ie's mats were not acknowledged.)
— Samoan expression of joy for such abundance that one hasn't enough strength to adequately express thanks

An enormous *fa'afetai tele lava* to everyone who helped me turn a mishmash of memories into this book.

Lynn Price, I want to shower you with hibiscus blossoms from the cable car high above Pago Bay. Some wondrous alignment of stars brought us together at the Pacific Northwest Writer's Association conference to give *Mango Rash* the perfect home at Behler Publications. Your enthusiasm for this book has meant the world.

Sister Scribes Cristina Trapani Scott, Cyan James, Cathy Stocker, Laura Bailey, and Elizabeth Solsberg were the midwives who so skillfully assisted with the birth of the manuscript and nurtured it as it grew. Brilliant suggestions, support, and occasional baked goods from members of the Artworks Second Monday Writers Group and the Fremont Area District Library Writers Group were much appreciated as well. Special thanks to Artworks writers Susan Stec, Thea Heying, Christopher Rizzo, Chris Wyman, Magen Gombosh, Millie Gillies, Sally Kane, Wendy Nystrom, and the late Mikki Garrels.

Reading chapters aloud at the River Stop Writers Salon provided a different perspective on my words and listeners' reactions to them. *Alofa* to salon leader Sandra Bernard for the opportunity and to Tonya and Eldon Howe, Jonathan Riedel, and everyone else who showed up to listen and read.

Early encouragement from Jerry Dennis and Richard McCann at Bear River Writers' Conference gave me the courage to attempt a book-length project. Workshops led by Anne-Marie Oomen at Interlochen Center for the Arts and Ludington Center for the Arts, Dinty W. Moore at Far Field Retreat for Writers, Bob Comenole at the University of Michigan, Elizabeth Stolarek and Phillip Sterling at Three Ponds Farm, and Ray Gonzalez and Joyce Maynard at the Tucson Festival of Books Literary Awards Masters Workshops helped me hone individual chapters. Andrew Foster, Emily Everett, and Judith Sara Gelt also offered masterful advice on specific chapters. Arielle Eckstut and David Henry Sterry of The Book Doctors gave incisive guidance on the book proposal and cheered me on as I careened down the publication path. I festoon you all with *ulas*.

I'd like to throw a *fiafia* for all who read the full manuscript. Assessments and edits by Robert Root, Phillip Sterling, and Brooke Warner were invaluable and kept me moving forward. Beta readers Katherine Girod Myers, Kitty Kole, Susie Moise, Rebecca Howey, Sally Kane, Janet Glaser, Valerie Roberts, Wendy Badgley, Barry and Beverly Read, Pili Legalley, and the late Utu Abe Malae further fine-tuned the work-in-progress. I'm grateful to Abe, too, for promptly and patiently answering all my questions about Samoan customs, idioms, and other details. (Also for helping me pass chemistry all those years ago.) Bert and Mary Tarrant, Richard Whitaker, and Barbara and Isidore AhKuoi, our eleventh-hour connections have been a delight. Oh, the memories, eh? (And thank you, Bert and Mary, for clearing up the mystery of where Peki lived.)

This book never would have come about if Cindi Schroeder McDonald had not saved the letters I wrote from Samoa. All the Frito chili pie and tater tots in the world would not be enough to thank you, Cindi, for that and for more than fifty years of faithful friendship.

To Val and Wendy I present the finest of my fine mats and a truckload of *pisupo*. Without you, Samoa undoubtedly would have been interesting, but it wouldn't have been nearly as much fun. I can't imagine that year—and the years since—without the wisdom and humor you both possess and the gift of your friendships.

Emily, I wish I could buy you your very own island as a show of gratitude and love for that thing you did—and for everything else you do and are.

Namaste and *fa'afetai* to the Monday morning yoginis and the Wander Women for helping me keep my balance and stay on the path while working on this project. Let's all join in and dance the *sivasiva*!

Ray: I could fill another whole book with tributes to you. Your inquisitive spirit and creativity inspire me every day. Your love, encouragement, and genuine interest in my endeavors make every success sweeter and every disappointment more bearable. Plus, though I've never seen you in a *lavalava*, I have no doubt you would rock the look. Thank you, too, for making me the aromatherapy pen that soothed my pre-publication jitters. And for saying, "You really should go to that Pacific Northwest Writer's Association conference in Seattle. Maybe you'll win the contest and get a book deal." Never let me doubt your wisdom.

GLOSSARY

afakasi -	a Samoan person with some European ancestry
aiga -	family
aitu -	ghost
alofa -	love
fa'afafine -	literally, "in the manner of a woman." A person whose birth gender is male but who is raised as a woman, and identifies with neither, both, or a combination of male and female genders. *Fa'afafine* is a recognized gender identity in traditional Samoan society and an integral part of Samoan culture.
fa'afetai –	thank you
fa'a Samoa -	literally, "the Samoan way." The traditional way of life in the Samoan culture.
fale -	house
feleni -	friend
fiafia -	literally, "happy." A Samoan celebration, often a feast with music and dancing.
fofō -	traditional healer
holomuu -	(Hawaiian) a fitted, ankle-length dress
lava -	enough
lavalava -	a rectangular piece of cloth worn as a wrap-around sarong or loincloth
ma'i palagi -	diseases brought to Samoa by outsiders and best treated with Western medicine
ma'i Samoa -	literally "spirit sickness." Physical and psychological disorders indigenous to the islands and best treated by traditional Samoan healers (*fofō*).
malae -	village green
malō -	good. Used as an informal greeting.

malosi -	strength
manuia -	Cheers! Good health!
matai -	chief; person holding a Samoan title
moetotolo -	literally, "sleep-crawling." Rape
mo'o -	gecko
palagi -	white-skinned person; foreigner
palolo -	a polychaete worm (*Palola viridis*), the reproductive portion of which is considered a delicacy in Samoa.
palusami -	coconut cream baked in taro leaves
paopao -	outrigger canoe
pisupo -	corned beef
puletasi -	traditional Samoan two-piece dress with a fitted top and an ankle-length, wrap-around skirt
sami -	sea
sivasiva -	traditional Samoan dance
tama -	boy
taupou -	a ceremonial hostess selected from the young girls of a village, elevated to a high rank, and charged with the formal reception and entertainment of visitors.
teine -	girl
tofa -	goodbye
ua sa -	forbidden
ula -	necklace or garland. *Ulas* are worn for festive occasions and given to arriving or departing guests.
uma -	finished, completed
umu -	traditional Samoan oven